Vague Language Explored

Also by Joan Cutting

PRAGMATICS AND DISCOURSE
ANALYSING THE LANGUAGE OF DISCOURSE COMMUNITIES
THE GRAMMAR OF SPOKEN ENGLISH AND EAP TEACHING (*editor*)

Vague Language Explored

Edited by

Joan Cutting

palgrave
macmillan

First published 2007 by
PALGRAVE MACMILLAN
Houndmills, Basingstoke, Hampshire RG21 6XS and
175 Fifth Avenue, New York, N.Y. 10010
Companies and representatives throughout the world

PALGRAVE MACMILLAN is the global academic imprint of the Palgrave
Macmillan division of St. Martin's Press, LLC and of Palgrave Macmillan Ltd.
Macmillan® is a registered trademark in the United States, United Kingdom
and other countries. Palgrave is a registered trademark in the European
Union and other countries.

ISBN-13: 978-1-4039-8817-1
ISBN-10: 1-4039-8817-X

This book is printed on paper suitable for recycling and made from fully
managed and sustained forest sources.

A catalogue record for this book is available from the British Library.

Library of Congress Cataloging-in-Publication Data
Vague language explored / edited by Joan Cutting.
    p.   cm.
    Includes bibliographical references and index.
    ISBN 1-4039-8817-X (cloth)
    1. Ambiguity. 2. Grammar, Comparative and general.   3. Semantics.
    I. Cutting, Joan.
    P299.A46V34 2007
    401'.43—dc22   2006047264

10   9   8   7   6   5   4   3   2   1
16 15 14 13 12 11 10 09 08 07

Printed and bound in Great Britain by
Antony Rowe Ltd, Chippenham and Eastbourne

Contents

List of Tables

List of Figures

Acknowledgements

I would like to thank very much all the contributors to this volume for their readiness to collaborate, constant enthusiasm and meticulousness: Svenja Adolphs, Sarah Atkins and Kevin Harvey, University of Nottingham; Winnie Cheng, Hong Kong Polytechnic University; Guy Cook, Open University; Janet Cotterill, Cardiff University; Almut Koester, University of Birmingham; Michael McCarthy, Anne O'Keeffe and Jane Evison, University of Nottingham; Tim Rowland, University of Cambridge; Agnes Terraschke and Janet Holmes, Victoria University of Wellington; Hugh Trappes-Lomax, University of Edinburgh; and Martin Warren, Hong Kong Polytechnic University.

I offer very many thanks too to the Moray House School of Education, the University of Edinburgh, especially to colleagues in the TESOL academic and administrative team, for supporting me. Thank you to friends and family for talking through the meaning of language, and bearing with me while I brought this volume together.

JOAN CUTTING

Notes on the Contributors

Svenja Adolphs is a lecturer in applied linguistics at the University of Nottingham. Her research interests are in the area of spoken corpus analysis and pragmatics, particularly in relation to different contexts including professional communication. She is currently working on the development of multimodal corpus resources to aid the analysis of the interaction between verbal and visual elements in conversation.

Sarah Atkins is a postgraduate student of applied linguistics at the University of Nottingham. Her research interests are in sociolinguistics, particularly in the field of healthcare communication, and metaphor. She is part of the Health Language Research Group (HLRG), an interdisciplinary forum for research into language use in healthcare settings.

Winnie Cheng is a professor in the Department of English of the Hong Kong Polytechnic University (PhD applied English linguistics). Her current areas of research include corpus linguistics, conversation analysis, discourse analysis, pragmatics, discourse intonation, intercultural communication in professional contexts, and online education. She is the author of *Intercultural Conversation*. Her articles on spoken discourse and intercultural communication, mainly co-authored with Martin Warren and based on analyses of the Hong Kong Corpus of Spoken English, have appeared in several international journals, including *Applied Linguistics, International Journal of Corpus Linguistics, Journal of Pragmatics, Pragmatics, English World-Wide, International Computer Archive of Modern English (ICAME) Journal, System, Anglistica, Semiotica* and *Language & Intercultural Communication*.

Guy Cook is professor of language and education at the Open University in England. He has published extensively on discourse analysis, literary stylistics, and applied linguistics. His most recent work is on the discourse of food politics. His books are *Discourse, Discourse and Literature, Language Play, Language Learning, The Discourse of Advertising, Applied Linguistics* and *Genetically Modified Language*. He is co-editor of the journal *Applied Linguistics*.

Janet Cotterill is a senior lecturer in language and communication and director of studies of the MA in forensic linguistics at Cardiff University. Janet is co-editor of the *International Journal of Speech, Language and the Law*. She has worked in the UK, France, Egypt and Japan. Her current research includes a joint project looking at the experiences of vulnerable adults in police interview contexts, and a major research project which analyses the training of solicitors in effective lawyer–client communication skills. She is preparing a co-authored monograph entitled *Courtroom Corpora*, an edited collection on *The Language of Sex Crimes* (Palgrave, 2006) and, in collaboration with Malcolm Coulthard, *Introducing Forensic Linguistics*.

Joan Cutting is senior lecturer in TESOL in the University of Edinburgh. She has taught EFL/TESOL/applied linguistics in Cuba, China and Russia. She has published articles on vague language, the spoken codes of academic discourse communities, the English of conferences, the English of airport ground staff, TEFL teacher training, and the needs of Chinese international students in the UK, in journals such as *Applied Linguistics* and *Journal of Pragmatics*. She is editor of *The Grammar of Spoken English and EAP Teaching*, and author of *Analysing the Language of Discourse Communities* and *Pragmatics and Discourse*.

Jane Evison is a university teacher in TESOL at the School of Education and also a tutor in applied linguistics and English language teaching at the School of English Studies at the University of Nottingham, UK. She is a research assistant at the Center for Advanced Language Proficiency Education and Research at Pennsylvania State University and a member of the Inter-Varietal Applied Corpus Studies (IVACS) Research Centre. Her research interests are corpus-based and centre on the grammar and lexis of spoken discourse, interaction in spoken academic discourse and the use of corpora in language teaching.

Kevin Harvey is a postgraduate research student and member of the Health Language Research Group at the University of Nottingham. He is currently researching in the area of adolescent health language. His research interests are in health communication, with an emphasis on non-physician–patient interaction.

Janet Holmes is professor of linguistics at Victoria University of Wellington, where she teaches a variety of sociolinguistics courses. She is director of the Language in the Workplace Project. Her publications include *An Introduction to Sociolinguistics, Women, Men and Politeness, Gendered Speech in Social Context*, the *Handbook of Language and Gender* and *Power and Politeness in the Workplace*.

Almut Koester is lecturer in English language in the Department of English, University of Birmingham. She has a PhD in applied linguistics from the University of Nottingham, and is author of *The Language of Work* and *Investigating Workplace Discourse: Approaches to Analysing Spoken Interactions at Work*, published by Routledge. She is interested in the analysis of spoken workplace discourse.

Michael McCarthy is emeritus professor of applied linguistics, University of Nottingham, UK, adjunct professor of applied linguistics, Pennsylvania State University, USA, and adjunct professor of applied linguistics, University of Limerick, Ireland. He is author/co-author/ editor of more than 30 books and more than 70 academic papers. From 1994 to 1998 he was co-editor of *Applied Linguistics*. He is co-director (with Ronald Carter) of the 5-million word CANCODE spoken English corpus project, and the 1-million word CANBEC spoken business English corpus. He has lectured on language and language teaching in 37 countries and has been actively involved in ELT for 40 years.

Anne O'Keeffe is a lecturer in applied linguistics at the Department of English Language and Literature, Mary Immaculate College (MIC), University of Limerick, Ireland. She is director of the Inter-Varietal Applied Corpus Studies (IVACS) Research Centre and coordinator of the learner support unit. Her research centres on corpus linguistics and the grammar of spoken English, particularly its description and pedagogy, and its application in the study of language in the media. She is co-director of the 1-million word Limerick Corpus of Irish English (LCIE), and has also been responsible for the LI-BEL corpus of academic English in cooperation with Queen's University Belfast.

Tim Rowland is a senior lecturer in mathematics education at the University of Cambridge. His research and publication has addressed various topics in his field, notably mathematics and classroom language, proof, creativity and the knowledge bases of mathematics teaching. He retains an active interest in doing and teaching mathematics. His initiation in the study of linguistics, and vague language in particular, arose in the research reported in his book *The Pragmatics of Mathematics Education*. Tim has acted as consultant in mathematics education to a number of educational publishers and agencies, and broadcast on national radio on topical issues in mathematics education.

Agnes Terraschke completed her undergraduate studies at Aberdeen University and is currently enrolled in a PhD programme at Victoria University of Wellington, New Zealand. Her thesis explores the use of pragmatic devices by German non-native speakers of English.

Hugh Trappes-Lomax has worked as a teacher in Kenya, Tanzania and Scotland. At present he is deputy director at the Institute for Applied Language Studies in the University of Edinburgh. He teaches courses in discourse analysis, language description, how and why English is changing and, occasionally, English for academic purposes. He is interested in most aspects of how languages are or might be described for language teaching (and other applied) purposes. He is author of a thesaurus-like dictionary for learners – the *Oxford Learner's Wordfinder Dictionary* – and has co-edited volumes on *Theory in Language Teacher Education* (with Ian McGrath) and *Language in Language Teacher Education* (with Gibson Ferguson).

Martin Warren is a professor in the Department of English of the Hong Kong Polytechnic University. He currently teaches and conducts research in the areas of corpus linguistics, discourse analysis, intercultural communication and pragmatics. He has published a number of articles with Winnie Cheng based largely on their analyses of the Hong Kong Corpus of Spoken English, which they have jointly compiled.

Part I
Introduction

1
Introduction to *Vague Language Explored*

Joan Cutting

Exploring vague language

Aim of the volume

The danger of being known as someone who is fascinated by vague language is that you run the risk of friends and colleagues using it just to humour you. Thus a University of Edinburgh colleague once ended an email to me, 'See you whenever it is, if not before,' and another, also from the university, engaged me in this email exchange:

> Colleague: So do you know about the charity ceilidh at St Brides Centre Saturday week then?
> Me: On 4th yeah – are you going?
> Colleague: I'm certainly thinking about it. I'm inclined to. How's that for being wishy-washy?

What this demonstrates to me is that there is more than one perception and definition of vague language (VL), and that it can have an informal, socially cohesive function.

VL is a central feature of daily language in use, both spoken and written. But what is it exactly and why is it used? What is the use of studying it and what is still unknown? Do language students need to learn it? *Vague Language Explored* is a collection of chapters about VL in context. Gathering descriptions from a variety of specialisms, it examines the function of VL in a range of social contexts. It then suggests applications of findings and directions that VL research could take next.

The volume contains a wide range of approaches, taken from the fields of pragmatics, corpus linguistics, genre analysis, language and power, interactional sociolinguistics, cross-cultural sociolinguistics and the psychology of language. This should make it relevant to students and scholars in areas of linguistics, English language studies, modern foreign languages, communications studies, media studies, philosophy, psychology and psycholinguistics, as well as to those that believe in cooperation and cross-fertilization among specialisms. It is hoped that the volume will appeal to experienced researchers seeking a new direction, as well as being an inspiration to new researchers.

Because of its emphasis on applications, the volume should be of interest to students, teachers and scholars in the fields of education, teaching English to speakers of other languages (TESOL), teaching English as a foreign language (TEFL), English for academic purposes (EAP) and English for specific purposes (ESP). It is hoped, too, that *Vague Language Explored* may serve as a resource for designers and writers of English-language coursebooks, thus satisfying the need for materials that train language learners to participate in casual conversations and understand VL. Some chapters may also be of interest to people in media, medicine and law.

The contributors to the volume come from several countries and cover a range of English varieties and other languages. Some are based in the UK (Birmingham, Cambridge, Cardiff, Edinburgh, Milton Keynes and Nottingham), others are in Hong Kong, Ireland and New Zealand. As far as Englishes are concerned, varieties discussed are British English, Irish English, North American English and New Zealand English. Other languages investigated are Cantonese and German.

History of vague language

In order to provide a theoretical background to the chapters in this book, I offer a brief history of studies of VL. First, I must differentiate between the terms 'VL' and 'implicitness'. Studies of VL look at language that is inherently and intentionally imprecise, describing lexical and grammatical surface features themselves that may refer either to specific entities or to nothing in particular. Studies of implicitness mention whole bodies of underlying meaning, and language dependent on the context, based on unspoken assumptions and unstated meaning. Implicitness can be expressed with VL and other language features; VL can express implicit meaning but it can be taken at its face value.

Most of the studies in the 1960s, 1970s and 1980s were of the 'implicitness' variety; theorists were aware of the social dimension but they were not interested in examining the language itself in any great detail. Garfinkel (1967, p. 3) talked of 'unstated understandings', and

Bernstein (1971) included context-dependent sentences in his list of the features of the restricted code. Goffman (1963) examined the way that social and interpersonal contexts 'provide presuppositions for the decoding of meaning' (Schiffrin 1994, p. 105). Grice (1975) saw implicitness as conversational implicature, in which speakers flout the maxims of the 'cooperative principle' (quantity, quality, manner and relevance), assuming that the hearer understands the implied meaning. Note that whereas conventional implicature is the logical relationship between two utterances where the truth of one suggests the truth of the other, conversational implicature is the indirect, unstated meaning of an utterance, additional to what is said. Gumperz (1982, p. 131) realized that members of social groups use implicitness: 'exclusive interaction with individuals of similar background leads to reliance on unverbalized and context-bound presuppositions in communication'.

A few of the 1970s and 1980s studies did mention VL, but they did so briefly, as part of an overall description of language. Lakoff (1972) pointed out that in phrases such as 'sort of' there is a meaning that 'implicitly involves fuzziness'. Crystal and Davy (1975, pp. 111–12) mentioned 'vague collectives' ('bags of'), 'number approximations' ('about 30') and 'dummy nouns' ('thing', 'stuff') and acknowledged that 'lack of precision is one of the most important features of the vocabulary of informal conversation'.

In the 1990s, researchers came to see VL as a central aspect of the communicative competence of the native speaker of English. In her seminal book *Vague Language* (1994), Channell says that 'Any social group sharing interests and knowledge employs non-specificity in talking abut their shared interest' (p. 193). She affirms that an expression or word is vague if (a) it can be contrasted with another word or expression which appears to render the same proposition, if (b) it is purposely and unabashedly vague or if (c) the meaning arises from intrinsic uncertainty. Her analysis of vague expressions shows that 'their meanings are themselves vague', that 'speakers share knowledge of how to understand them' and that 'it is apparently impossible to describe their meanings independently of consideration of context and inference' (pp. 196–8). She lists 'vague additives' ('around ten'), 'vague implicature' such as approximators and vague quantifiers ('15,000 died'), 'vague placeholders' ('thingy' and 'whatsisname'), and 'tags' ('or something', 'and things' and 'and so on').

Since Channell, VL has been recognized as 'a pervasive property of texts, and a property of considerable social importance' (Fairclough 2003, p. 55) and 'an important feature of interpersonal meaning / . . . /

especially common in everyday conversation' (Carter and McCarthy 2006, p. 202). They claim (Carter and McCarthy 1997, pp. 16–19) that:

> General words / . . . / are widely used in spoken discourse / . . . / general words *thing* and *stuff* are among the most frequent words in spoken English / . . . / Vague expressions are more extensive in all language use than is commonly thought and they are especially prevalent in spoken discourse / . . . / In most informal contexts most speakers prefer to convey information which is softened in some way by vague language.

At the end of the twentieth century, VL was finding its way into grammar books. The *Longman Grammar of Spoken and Written English* (Biber *et al.* 1999, p. 265) touched on it briefly under the headings of other features, explaining that approximators convey imprecision, that hedges such as 'like' can indicate imprecision of word choice, and that in generic reference the noun 'refers to a whole class rather than to an individual person or thing', the latter being superordinates, in my model. By 2006, VL had a section of several pages to itself in the *Cambridge Grammar of English* (Carter and McCarthy 2006, pp. 202–5). There it is seen as a separate, though closely related, category from 'approximations'. VL is described as words or phrases 'which deliberately refer to people and things in a non-specific, imprecise way' (ibid. p. 928), such as 'stuff', 'like', 'or anything', 'or whatever', and 'sort of'. Approximations as described as vague expressions used with numbers and quantities, as in '<u>around</u> six', 'five minutes <u>or so</u>', 'seven-<u>ish</u>', and 'loads and loads'. The present volume considers both these categories as VL.

Vague language in this volume

VL has been described in many forums and publications, but this volume is the first to bring together various descriptions under one title. Although each chapter gives a definition of what the writer understands as VL, this debate is, in fact, not central to our volume. We are not hoping to reach a consensus.

The contributors in *Vague Language Explored* look at intentional vagueness, which occurs by choice. Some contributors examine vague expressions referring to people and things, and others focus on those referring to numbers and quantities, but most look at them all together, under the heading of VL. All the contributors, with the exception of Cook, look at spoken VL. Some take a mainly quantitative approach, the others a mainly qualitative one.

Most of the chapters have a bottom-up approach, starting with the lexis and grammar, and going to the interactional macro level of implication. Their categories are not identical and there is a certain amount of overlap. Some focus exclusively on general extenders: witness Terraschke and Holmes ('and things like that') and Evison, McCarthy and O'Keeffe ('and all the rest of it'). Others examine general extenders along with a series of other VL features. Cotterill looks at approximators ('some sort of', 'this, that and the other') and 'etcetera' additives or tags ('and everything', 'something like that'). Adolphs considers the vagueness of 'exemplar followed by a tag' ('gasping for breath or anything?'), 'kind of', 'like' and 'a bit'. Koester points to vague nouns ('things') general extenders and approximators ('about 40'). Cheng examines a wide range of markers, quite different from others in the volume: 'VL by scalar implicature' ('more', 'lot'), 'VL by choice of vague words or phrases' ('something', 'things') and 'vague additives to numbers' ('about'). Warren looks not at VL itself but at the meaning of VL combined with discourse intonation patterns, some of which add to the vagueness.

A few chapters have a top-down approach, starting with the wider picture. Cook sees VL as ambiguity and uncertainty of truth, as indeterminacy and imprecision; he looks at the vagueness of language in general. Rowland starts from an analysis of uncertainty and looks for linguistic realizations of it, such as hedges ('I think', 'maybe') and approximators ('around', 'fairly'). Trappes-Lomax sees VL as one means of addressing issues of face: a tool for expressing politeness while protecting self. Cutting looks at in-group markers in general, focusing on different degrees of vagueness that surface and deep structures can be used to express: metonymical proper nouns, superordinate nouns, and general nouns and verbs, non-anaphoric demonstrative pronouns and adverbs, non-anaphoric third-person personal pronouns, vague clauses, clausal ellipsis and humorous conversational implicature.

Social function of vague language

History of social function

This volume focuses on VL that is intentionally vague, but of course, not all VL use is intentional. Sometimes speakers are tired or in too much of a hurry to find the right word. Sometimes they do not process words properly or as they would wish. It can also be the case that there are emotional reasons for non-processing. Let us turn now to the social history of intentional VL.

In the 1970s and 1980s, although theorists were aware of the social dimension, studies of the social context of VL were relatively rare. Crystal and Davy (1975, pp. 111–12) noted that 'the use of lexical vagueness is undoubtedly a main sign of social and personal relaxation'. Brown and Levinson (1987), describing positive politeness strategies, mention ellipsis and in-jokes among their in-group identity markers, used to claim common ground. Tannen (1984, p. 31) lists ellipsis, indirectness, implicature and unstated meanings as interpersonal involvement signals of 'high involvement style'. She claims, 'the more work / . . . / hearers do to supply meaning, the deeper their understanding and the greater their sense of involvement with both text and author' (1989, p. 23).

Since the mid-1990s, linguists have looked in greater detail at the social usage of VL. Channell (1994) examines the micro-functions: she suggests that general nouns can be used to avoid being offensive, derogatory or pretentious, deliberately withhold information, avoid showing uncertainty or a lexical gap, and protect oneself or somebody/something else. Others talk of the function in more general terms, but they nearly all point to VL as a marker of social cohesion. McCarthy (1998, pp. 108–18) says that VL makes 'an important contribution to naturalness and the informal, convergent tenor of everyday talk'. Carter (1998) sees VL as a social leveller: it 'puts the speakers on an immediately casual and equal footing with their interlocutors'. Carter and McCarthy (2006, p. 202) state:

> Vague language softens expressions so that they do not appear too direct or unduly authoritative or assertive. It is also a strong indication of an assumed shared knowledge and can mark in-group membership: the referents of vague language can be assumed to be known by the listener.

Cutting (2000, 2001, 2002) finds that discourse communities use VL to assert in-group membership and show solidarity, as well as to exclude outsiders.

Critical discourse analysis takes quite a different position, seeing implicitness as a social divider. Although Fairclough (2003, p. 55) claims that 'All forms of fellowship, community and solidarity depend upon meanings which are shared and can be taken as given', he makes the point that written or spoken texts with power can carry implicit assumptions that they impose upon the reader or listener by making them bring the same assumptions into the process of interpretation (Fairclough 1989). Wodak (1996, p. 2) examines the effect of speakers in a position of power using implicit language. She explains that confusion can result when there are 'gaps between distinct and insufficiently coincident cognitive worlds', since these can separate 'insiders from outsiders, members of institutions from clients of those institutions, and elites from the normal citizen uninitiated in the arcana of bureaucratic language and life'.

In the field of second-language acquisition, Roberts (2003, p. 117) follows on with the view that heavily context-dependent language is associated with the assertion of power. She makes the point that contextualization cues call up backgound knowledge which relates to social relations, rights, obligations and ideologies. This, she says (ibid. p. 118), is a problem for second-language acquisition of minority-language-speakers:

> Knowing how to use and interpret a particular cue means at least for that interactional moment that you are a 'belonger'. And in contrast, the failure to pick up on a cue not only creates misunderstanding but sets the minority linguistic speaker apart. She is not in that interactional moment an emergent member of the same communicative community. As a result, small interactive differences can contribute to large social consequences.

Social function in this volume

The most distinctive feature of the volume is that it focuses on the function of VL *in context*. The contributors examine the reasons for using VL and the result of using it.

The contributors entertain readers with a wide range of social contexts, participants, genres and purposes. They describe bosses mitigating orders in office meetings, staff hedging gossip in the corridor, and health professionals mitigating directives and softening potentially distressing subjects so as not to alarm patients. They show mathematics students indicating their uncertainty in problem-solving activities, witnesses covering up memory-loss and untruths in the courtroom, and paper-presenters saving their faces at conferences. They describe pop-song writers leaving themselves open to interpretation, food and tobacco public relations websites showing how caring and sharing the companies are, and callers to radio phone-ins implying that their views are everybody's. They show German and New Zealand students getting close, and British and Canadian students claiming in-group membership. They encounter Hong Kong Chinese and native-speakers of English indicating how vague they mean to be through intonation. They reveal British people in casual conversation, giving little importance to the referent, to be friendly or critical.

Applications and further research in vague language

Need for applications to TEFL

Second-language teaching research and methodology books in 1970s and 1980s did not discuss VL in depth, but since the mid 1990s applied linguists have realized the need to apply the findings from studies on vagueness to TEFL. Channell (1994) says that VL 'merits specific attention in the description of English, as well as in the teaching programmes of learners of English and their teachers.' Jordan (1997, pp. 240–3) recommends that EAP teachers make their students aware of vague written language so that they can write using hedges such as modals expressing possibility, probability adverbs and approximators, and so that they can understand and speak using colloquialisms such as 'thingy' and 'whatsisname'. Carter (2006) advocates the teaching of ellipsis, and of vague word clusters ('and all the rest of it', 'and all that sort of thing' 'and things like that') because they occur as frequently as individual words.

However, as Eggins and Slade (1997, p. 8) say, 'there is still a paucity of adequate materials for teaching casual conversation to learners of English as a second or foreign language'. Carter (1998, pp. 43–56) goes further: 'Several English language coursebooks do not exhibit many examples of vague language, even though it is always pragmatically highly significant, and nearly always enables polite and non-threatening interaction.'

Applications and further research in this volume

The second most distinctive feature of this volume is that it puts emphasis on applications of findings about VL. These applications are in the fields of L1 performance in schools, second-language acquisition (SLA), TEFL, EAP, forensic linguistics, clinical pragmatics, counselling and law. The most obvious application out of all of these is TEFL; questions asked include 'What should learners of English as a foreign language be taught to use?' and 'What should learners be taught to understand but not use, and why?'

The volume brings together the research of the theorists and the needs of the practitioners. Most of the contributors feel that their findings will inform those involved in the teaching of and material design for EFL, ESP and EAP. Some have even higher aspirations: one hopes to improve teacher awareness and sensitivity, another wants to contribute to transparent conduct of public affairs, and another wishes to improve relations between speakers of different languages.

Each chapter of the volume concludes with a suggestion as to where future research should go next. Some contributors suggest that the study of VL described here be taken further, others recommend an investigation of types of VL other than the ones covered here and others still point to new contexts for VL analysis.

Map of the volume

To enable navigation around this volume, I provide a map with a brief synopsis of each chapter. Three of the chapters (Cheng, Cutting and Trappes-Lomax) are reformulated and updated versions of papers presented in a colloquium entitled 'Vague Language' at the annual conference of the British Association for Applied Linguistics 2003, in the University of Leeds. Each contributor has participated in the writing of their synopsis.

Vagueness and genre

In Chapter 2, ' "This We Have Done": The Vagueness of Poetry and Public Relations', Cook points out that many of the world's most acclaimed literary 'masterpieces' are also those whose meaning is most contested, and that a variety of approaches to literature consider indeterminacy to be a literary virtue. Literary criticism and stylistics have catalogued formal devices which encode and ensure such ambiguity, making the text capable of yielding an apparent infinity of valid possible interpretations. Cook notes that in recent years corporate web pages have adopted many of these formal literary features.

Cook's chapter explores the contrast between the use of such devices in a Bob Dylan song and in a corpus of public-relations discourse on food and tobacco websites. It illustrates the formal devices which realize literary indeterminacy, and documents the presence of such features in public-relations prose. It discusses why the vagueness of meaning in these two contexts has such different effects, and what the implications of this are both for an understanding of literature and for the transparent conduct of public affairs.

In Chapter 3, ' "About Twelve Thousand or So": Vagueness in North American and UK Offices', Koester investigates conversations across a variety of office environments and shows that VL occurs regularly in work-related interactions. She analyses conversations from organizations recorded in North America and the UK, focusing on vague nouns, ('things', 'bit'), vague categories ('and stuff', 'something like that'), and vague approximators ('about', 'or so'). She finds three types of genre: (a) collaborative, where all participants contribute equally, for example decision-making or discussions, (b) unidirectional, where one speaker plays a dominant role, for example instructing or briefing, and (c) non-transactional, 'off-task' conversations, as in office gossip or small-talk. She finds that VL occurs more frequently in unidirectional genres and suggests that the risk of performing face-threatening acts is higher here, and that VL is therefore used as a hedging device.

In Chapter 4, 'Caught Between Professional Requirements and Interpersonal Needs: Vague Language in Healthcare Contexts', Adolphs, Atkins and Harvey note that in a number of healthcare contexts, a tension exists between the communicative aim of minimizing impositions and the institutional requirement for clear and concise information. Health professionals are required to explain illness and disease to their patients in an understandable and direct way and are discouraged from using any VL (Sontag 1991). Yet, research shows that VL is pervasive in health communication contexts and plays an important part in the negotiation of advice and thus in affirming patient choice (Adolphs *et al.* 2004).

This chapter examines examples of VL in a sample of the Nottingham Health Communication Corpus (NHCC), a 1-million-word corpus comprising of a variety of contexts and groups of health professionals and patients. Adolphs Atkins and Harvey focus on the relationship between types of VL and institutional requirements that relate to two distinct healthcare contexts: NHS Direct phone-ins and hospital–chaplain interaction. The results show that different levels of vagueness may serve different contextual requirements.

Rowland's Chapter 5, ' "Well Maybe Not Exactly, but It's Around Fifty Basically?": Vague Language in Mathematics Classrooms', reminds us that mathematics is typically characterized as a precise and exact discipline, and that for students there are intrinsic and extrinsic penalties associated with 'wrong' or even hesitant responses to questioning. Rowland makes the point that uncertainty is a valid response to a mathematical challenge, and that such a cognitive state is to be expected when students are asked to make predictions and generalizations in enquiry-based, problem-solving activities. In such circumstances, in the social setting of the classroom, uncertainty must be recognized, and handled with care and sensitivity. Rowland analyses transcripts of talk in mathematics classrooms from primary school to university undergraduate, focusing on 'hedges' such as 'about', 'maybe' and 'I think', and teachers' linguistic strategies associated with 'politeness' (Brown and Levinson 1987) such as use of indirect speech acts.

Cotterill's Chapter 6, ' "I Think He Was Kind of Shouting or Something": Uses and Abuses of Vagueness in the British Courtroom', points out that the law represents a professional and social context characterized by a search for precision and directness, and that, in contrast, the language of witnesses and defendants at trial is typified by imprecision, doubt and vagueness. Eyewitnesses may be uncertain of what they have observed, memories may by decayed by the passage of time, and defendants may produce vague responses in an attempt to be evasive or deceptive.

This chapter draws on a 1-million-word corpus of witness examinations and cross-examinations taken from trials held in the late 1990s in the UK, and studies the semantics, pragmatics and discursive characteristics of vague responses given by witnesses to lawyers' questions in the courtroom setting. It analyses the ways in which vagueness is handled by the legal system and explores the degrees of tolerance to VL in courtroom interaction. The chapter suggests that, whereas vagueness has traditionally been seen as a negative phenomenon in the legal setting, it may be considered common and necessary in witness examination and cross-examination.

Psychology of vagueness

In Chapter 7, Trappes-Lomax looks at 'Vague Language as a Means of Self-Protective Avoidance: Tension Management in Conference Talks'. He argues that speakers and writers use strategies to minimize risks, and specifically to avoid interpersonal trouble (threats to the face of the addressee), interactional trouble (misunderstandings, misalignments), and personal trouble (threats to the face of the addressor). He notes that work on politeness, tact and hedging has focused little on strategies to avoid personal trouble, or self-protective behaviour in the biologist's sense of 'behaviour that tends to protect an animal by minimizing its exposure to hazard' (Allaby 1999).

Trappes-Lomax asks what kind of hazards we expose ourselves to in speaking and writing, and by what linguistic means we attempt to minimize these. He analyses the hazards faced by presenters at medical conferences, and the kinds of VL speakers employ to protect themselves.

Chapter 8, ' "Looking Out for Love and All the Rest of It": Vague Category Markers as Shared Social Space', by Evison, McCarthy and O'Keeffe, describes the connection between VL reference domains (what the categories refer to), the level of shared knowledge (social group, national or global) and the speaker relationship. The contributors hold that, in order to use VL successfully, speakers must negotiate expectations about what their co-participants know within social space (Vygotsky 1978), and that the shared knowledge required in order to interpret vague categories has a common core of socio-culturally ratified 'understandings'. Vague category markers are a tool for creating short-cuts when referring to sets, prototypes and projected and negotiable categories, as in 'everybody's looking out for love <u>and all the rest of it</u>', 'university courses <u>and that sort of thing</u>' and 'I've got to wash my hair <u>and everything</u>'. This chapter uses the British English CANCODE corpus and the Irish English LCIE corpus to explore VL in contexts where the participants have different degrees of shared knowledge and intimacy, notably casual conversations, spoken academic data, and calls to a radio phone-in show.

Cross-cultural vagueness

Chapter 9, 'The Use of Vague Language Across Spoken Genres in an Intercultural Hong Kong Corpus', by Cheng, uses the 2-million-word Hong Kong Corpus of Spoken English (HKCSE) of the English Department of the Hong Kong Polytechnic University. The HKCSE is made up of naturally occurring conversations, academic discourses, business discourses and public discourses, involving Hong Kong Chinese and native-speakers of English. The use of VL is examined in an intercultural context.

It is found that the major determinant of the forms of VL (word combinations containing 'very', 'more', 'some', 'much' 'many', 'quite', 'most', 'lot', 'few', 'bit', 'something', 'things', 'kind of' and 'about') and the frequencies with which they occur is related more to the genre than to whether the speaker is Hong Kong Chinese or a native-speaker of English. For example, this study suggests that when conversations are compared with public discourses, the forms of VL employed for similar functions are often different and the overall VL frequency is higher for conversations than for public speeches. The findings are compared with the forms of VL extracted from a database of EFL textbooks, and the implications are discussed in relation to the teaching of VL.

In Chapter 10, '{ / [Oh] Not a < ^ Lot > }: Discourse Intonation and Vague Language', Warren examines VL and the communicative role of the discourse intonation choices (Brazil 1997) in the HKCSE (see Cheng above). He reminds us that VL is particularly associated with spoken language (Carter and McCarthy 1997), and that discourse intonation system is an important resource to contribute to context-specific meaning. Discourse intonation consists of a set of choices (tone, prominence, key and termination) not formulated with reference to grammar and without fixed attitudinal meanings. Warren's study examines five manifestations of the role of intonation in adding situation-specific meaning to a speaker's use of VL: vague tagging ('or something'), alternative 'or' ('hot-dog or hamburger?'), approximate use of numerals ('two or three'), pre-modification of vague determiners ('quite a lot of money'), and repeated vague forms. The interplay between VL and discourse intonation is discussed and exemplified with reference to the specific social contexts, in combination with the local context within the discourse itself.

In Chapter 11, ' "Und Tralala": Vagueness and General Extenders in German and New Zealand English', Terraschke and Holmes explore the use of 'general extenders', pragmatic devices 'which serve referentially as expressions of vagueness, and interpersonally to build rapport, and which conform to a specifiable structural pattern', namely CONJUNCTION (PREMODIFIER) VAGUE NOUN (POSTMODIFIER). In English, examples are 'and stuff', 'and everything' and 'or something like that'. In German, they are '*und so was*' and '*oder so was*'.

The data is a corpus of informal dyadic interactions: between (a) native-speakers of New Zealand English, (b) native-speakers of German, and (c) native-speakers of New Zealand English and native-speakers of German. The study focuses on the English 'general extenders' used by Germans speaking English with native speakers of New Zealand English. It indicates that extenders serve politeness functions, their meaning based on an assumption of shared background knowledge (Brown and Levinson 1987; Overstreet 1999) and rapport management (Spencer-Oatey 2000), and examines the extent and principle areas of transfer of general extenders from German to English. The chapter stresses the need to increase awareness among learners of English as a Second Language (ESL) about the politeness functions of extenders, so to facilitate relations between native speakers of different languages.

Conclusion

In Chapter 12, ' "Doing More Stuff–Where's It Going?": Exploring Vague Language Further', Cutting describes her model of vague in-group code of academic discourse communities (2000): non-anaphoric demonstrative pronouns and adverbs, and third-person personal pronouns, metonymical proper nouns ('How's your Chomsky?'), superordinate and general nouns ('that thing') and general verbs ('I haven't <u>done</u> any Chomsky'), clausal ellipsis and conversational implicature. This VL is used mostly with a socially cohesive function as a high-involvement strategy for asserting in-groupness. She claims that formality, depth of relationship and social function affect VL use

(Cutting 1998). She describes various studies, some using CANCODE, on the influence of social factors, such as function, depth of relationship and gender.

She suggests that research be carried out on the relationship between VL and other social groups, and on VL in other languages. She advocates an exploration of whether VL is used mainly for social cohesion or as a tool to assert. She explores the applications, describing her study of the extent to which international students can be trained to appreciate when the cause of their lack of comprehension is because of their own linguistic or cultural gaps and when it is because of the VL (1999). Applications to clinical pragmatics and forensic linguistics are also considered.

Note

*/. . ./ is used througout to denote omissions from quoted text, as distinct from pauses in discourse, which are indicated by . . .

References

S. Adolphs, B. Brown, R. Carter, C. Crawford and O. Sahota, 'Applying Corpus Linguistics in a Health Care Context', *Journal of Applied Linguistics*, 1/1 (2004) 9–28.

M. Allaby, *Dictionary of Zoology* (Oxford University Press, 1999).

B. Bernstein, *Class, Codes and Control, Vol. 1* (London: Routledge & Kegan Paul, 1971).

D. Biber, S. Johansson, G. Leech, S. Conrad and E. Finegan, *Longman Grammar of Spoken and Written English* (London: Pearson Education, 1999).

D. Brazil, *The Communicative Role of Intonation in English* (Cambridge University Press, 1997).

P. Brown and S. Levinson, *Politeness: Some Universals in Language Use* (Cambridge University Press, 1987).

R. Carter, 'Orders of Reality: CANCODE, Communication, and CULTURE', *ELT Journal*, 52/1 (1998) 43–56.

R. Carter, 'Spoken Grammars, Written Grammars', unpublished talk given to the National Association for Teaching English and Community Languages to Adults (NATECLA), (Stevenson College Edinburgh, 22 April 2006).

R. Carter and M. McCarthy, *Exploring Spoken English* (Cambridge University Press, 1997).

R. Carter and M. McCarthy, *Cambridge Grammar of English: A Comprehensive Guide. Spoken and Written English Grammar and Usage* (Cambridge University Press, 2006).

J. Channell, *Vague Language* (Oxford University Press, 1994).

D. Crystal and D. Davy, *Advanced Conversational English* (London: Longman, 1975).

J. Cutting, 'The Function of Inexplicit Language in "CANCODE" Casual Conversations', unpublished paper in Sociolinguistics Symposium 12, University of London (1998).

J. Cutting, 'Vague Language and International Students Seminar of the British Association of Applied Linguistics', in *The Grammar of Spoken English and EAP Teaching* (University of Sunderland Press, 1999).

J. Cutting, *Analysing the Language of Discourse Communities* (Oxford: Elsevier Science, 2000).

J. Cutting, 'Speech Acts of the In-Group', *Journal of Pragmatics:* 33/8 (2001) 1207–33.

J. Cutting, 'The Function of Academic Discourse Community Code in Tutorials', unpublished paper in 35th BAAL Annual Meeting, University of Wales Cardiff (2002).

S. Eggins and D. Slade, *Analysing Casual Conversation* (London: Cassell, 1997).

N. Fairclough, *Language and Power* (Harlow: Longman, 1989).

N. Fairclough, *Analysing Discourse: Textual Analysis for Social Research* (Oxford: Routledge, 2003).

H. Garfinkel, *Studies in Ethnomethodology* (Englewood Cliffs, NJ: Prentice-Hall, 1967).

E. Goffman, *Behaviour in Public Places* (New York: Free Press, 1963).

H.P. Grice, 'Logic and Conversation'. In P. Cole and J. Morgan (eds), *Syntax and Semantics: Speech Acts 3* (New York: Academic Press, 1975).

J. Gumperz, *Discourse Strategies* (Cambridge University Press, 1982).

R.R. Jordan, *English for Academic Purposes: A Guide and Resource Book for Teachers* (Cambridge University Press, 1997).

G. Lakoff, 'Hedges: A Study in Meaning Criteria and the Logic of Fuzzy Concepts', *Proceedings of the Chicago Linguistic Society,* 8 (1972) 183–228.

M. McCarthy, *Spoken Language and Applied Linguistics* (Cambridge University Press, 1998).

M. Overstreet, *Whales, Candlelight, and Stuff Like That: General Extenders in English Discourse* (Oxford University Press, 1999).

C. Roberts, 'Language Acquisition or Language Socialisation in and Through Discourse? Towards a Redefinition of the Domain of SLA', in C. Candlin and N. Mercer, *English Language Teaching in its Social Context* (London: Routledge, 2003).

D. Schiffrin, *Approaches to Discourse* (Oxford: Blackwell, 1994).

S. Sontag, *Illness as Metaphor: AIDS and Its Metaphors* (London: Penguin, 1991).

H. Spencer-Oatey, 'Rapport Management: A Framework for Analysis', in *Culturally Speaking: Managing Rapport Through Talk Across Cultures* (London: Continuum, 2000).

D. Tannen, *Conversational Style: Analyzing Talk Among Friends* (New Jersey: Ablex, 1984).

D. Tannen, *Talking Voices* (Cambridge University Press, 1989).

L.S. Vygotsky, *Mind in Society* (Cambridge, MA: Harvard University Press, 1978).

R. Wodak, *Disorders of Discourse* (London: Longman, 1996).

Part II
Vagueness and Genre

2

'This We Have Done': The Vagueness of Poetry and Public Relations

Guy Cook

Introduction

This chapter compares VL in two very different discourses: poetry and public relations. To do this, it considers each one in broad terms, analysing both changing critical approaches to meaning in literary discourse in general, and the growing power and prominence of public relations. But to anchor this general discussion, it also homes in on a particular example, statements beginning with the structure 'FIRST PERSON PRONOUN + have + PAST PARTICIPLE', first in the Bob Dylan song *A Hard Rain's A-Gonna Fall* (which I treat as a poem) and second in a corpus of public-relations web pages by the world's largest food and tobacco companies. There is nothing inherently vague about this structure in itself. Indeed I have chosen it because of its apparent definiteness of reference to what has happened in the past. But its use in my two sources produces vague meanings, though with very different likely effects. The aim is to explore how and why this is, and its significance for the understanding and study of language use in the contemporary world.

Before turning to the quality of being 'vague' in poetry and public relations, however, it may be well (in order to rescue the concept itself from vagueness) to define this quality with reference to an antonym: being 'precise'. If we can define what we mean when we say that meaning is 'precise', then we may be able to say that vagueness is the absence of that quality. To this purpose, and to provide a yardstick against which to measure poetic and public-relations discourse when we come to them, I begin by considering a very different kind of language use: emergency procedures.

Emergency procedures

Emergency procedures are instructions about what to do in a crisis such as a fire, an emergency landing, the evacuation of a building, or someone suffering a heart attack, arterial bleeding and such (Lobianco 1999). Their aim is presumably to use language as precisely as possible. But what precisely do we mean by 'precise' in this context?

According to the much maligned conduit metaphor of communication (Reddy 1979), linguistic communication is a means of conducting thoughts and ideas from one mind into another, just as a conduit conducts water between locations. The current vogue is to dismiss this metaphor, as Reddy did, for its failure to take account of the active role of the receiver in constructing an interpretation of a message (for example Thorne 2000). Nevertheless, it remains true that the transmission of information is part of communication, sought after and substantially achieved, albeit only partially, and in some genres more than others. Consider for example the following emergency procedure, presented as typical by Lobianco (op. cit.) in her analysis of a corpus of 125 such texts.[1] This particular one is about what to do if somebody chokes.

Abdominal thrusts

NEVER use this on babies.

1. Stand or kneel behind the person. Put your arms around their abdomen.
2. Make a fist with one hand and grasp it with the other hand. Pull both hands towards you with a quick inward and upward thrust from the elbows to squeeze the upper abdomen. Pull hard enough to push the air out and dislodge the obstruction.
3. Repeat up to five times.

Here it seems reasonable to suppose that the main intention was to convey information known to the writer but not to all readers. Of course this simple characterization of the text is subject to many qualifications. Some of its linguistic choices may fail to achieve this objective, thus leading to an unintended vagueness. The second sentence of point 2 is a case in point, being linguistically and semantically complex and difficult to process. Technical terms such as 'upper abdomen' (though precise for those with medical training) and formal phrasing such as 'dislodge the obstruction' puzzled some of the readers in Lobianco's study, and may well have been motivated at least in part by a desire to impress and establish authority. In addition, understanding is, as always, dependent upon pre-existing world knowledge – in this case fairly basic and universal knowledge about the human body. Moreover, emergency texts can fulfil purposes other than giving instructions in an actual emergency: they may be used on training courses, or posted to indemnify an organization from prosecution. Nevertheless, despite all these caveats, it is very possible that some information is conveyed from one mind to another by this text – the fact that we should not use this technique on babies, for example.

The use of language here aspires to precision, where precision is defined as the choice of linguistic forms which facilitate the effective conveyance of non-linguistic information from one mind to another. And indeed such a text can be evaluated by its success or failure in this transfer.

Literary texts

Here then we have a genre which aims to avoid vagueness even if it sometimes fails. Other genres however do not necessarily share this aspiration, and consequently cannot be judged by the same criteria. They are vague for different reasons. Literary texts are a prime example.[2] Their tendency to lend themselves to different often contradictory interpretations is not a sign of failure. Indeed if it were then the literary cannon would need radical re-evaluation, for it is precisely those texts conventionally regarded as the greatest which also give rise to the most controversy and incompatible readings. Was Hamlet mad? Was Milton on God's side or, as William Blake claimed, 'of the Devil's party without knowing it'?[3] Part of the reason for the controversy is that, unlike the emergency text above, there is no extra-linguistic reality to convey. So it is not possible to assess the accuracy of an interpretation by the degree to which is corresponds to something else. Even if we treat the text as conveying information about a fictional world, we may still be unsure which of many competing voices within the text to believe. The text is all we have.

Yet in what can be called traditional 'literary scholarship' (Jefferson and Robey 1982, pp. 2–15), the task many literary critics set themselves has been to find the single true meaning of their chosen work, rather than to let it remain either multiple or unclear. Was the governess hallucinating when she saw ghosts in Henry James' (1995) novella *The Turn of the Screw*, or were the ghosts real? Alternatively, they may scour the literary work for an insight into the biography and character of the writer – for example, reading off facts about Alexander Pushkin from the character of the main character in his verse-novel *Eugene Onegin* (2003), whose life history shares certain features with his own. Inside the apparent surface message is assumed to be another hidden one. Critics of this persuasion are like the theologian who, faced with a cryptic scriptural passage, assumes the role of interpreter for the word of God. And like some religious exegesists, they can be dogmatic, narrow-minded and fundamentalist.

But this approach raises some curious questions, especially if we think back to the criteria for assessing emergency procedures. If there is a single true meaning, why was it not expressed more directly? Why dress it up or distract from it through literary mechanisms creating vagueness and ambiguity? Are the greatest writers after all not very good at expressing themselves, and therefore in need of paraphrase and explanation? Is there some kind of failure in the great works of literature to say what was meant?

Other critical approaches have bypassed these problems by abandoning a search for spurious precision, content to leave the meanings of a literary text both vague and various. The author and the world portrayed, whether fictional or autobiographical, melt into the background (Foucault 1969; Barthes 1977). Readers, each with a different reading, are brought to the fore. Reader-response theories, of various kinds, and to varying degrees, accept the validity of interpretations determined by the reader's varying identity, purposes and contexts, rather than the author (Tompkin 1980; Freund 1987). Certain types of text are seen as lending themselves to multiple interpretations. Bakhtin's frequently cited distinction between monologic and heteroglossic discourse, used in his analysis of literary works such as Dostoevsky's novels (Bakhtin 1984), portrays the latter as voicing many viewpoints simultaneously. The literary text has many voices, each contending with the other and capable of yielding radically different but valid interpretations.

In all of these views, despite differences between various schools of analysis, the implied virtue of the text is its capacity to yield many meanings, with possibilities increasing in proportion to the degree to which the writer is prepared to let go. If precision is the fixed quality of a single monologic truth (such as the correct procedure when somebody chokes) then we have no alternative but to say that literary texts are among the least precise. In this sense, the greater the vagueness, the greater the text.

Before we get carried away, however, it is worth adding three caveats to the sweeping statements with which I concluded the last paragraph. First, there is no reason to suppose that these revolutions in theories of textual meaning have actually changed the way people read literary works. We still interpret in particular ways as we go along, and indeed we may need to do this, if a literary text is to be meaningful for us. However well versed we may be in post-modern literary theories, we are still likely to argue the case (at least in a non-academic forum) for our own views of 'what it is about'. Indeed reader response theory is premissed on just such a view. Readers' interpretations are multiple taken as a whole, but that multiplicity is the sum of many unique interpretations. Second, literary works are still universally catalogued by author, suggesting a persistence of the view that they are to be understood by reference to a known individual, and that by reading them we come to understand that individual better. Last, to say the literary text yields many interpretations is not to say that it does not delimit the scope of possible interpretations. In the words of Widdowson (1992, p. 191), 'the meanings we read into texts are not independent of the texts themselves'. We may argue over whether *Paradise Lost* presents an orthodox Christian view of Satan, but we are less likely to say that the poem is comic.

We have then, in broad terms, two diametrically opposed views of literary discourse. In one it is the repository of a precise but hidden message, as though it were attempting, like our emergency procedures text, to communicate a single message, but somehow clumsily failing in the attempt, and therefore being in need of explication by a critic. In the other it has no single message, but is constructed to yield a variety of ever-changing interpretations whose truth, as they correspond to nothing outside the text, can never be finally resolved. The skill of the writer is in creating (whether intentionally or 'without knowing it') a text which will yield such multiple meanings. It is precisely this richness, and the consequent possibility of new readings always opening in front of us (as we reconsider, as our own experience changes, as we attend to new details, as we listen to the interpretations of others), which makes such texts so rewarding and so full.

A Hard Rain's A-Gonna Fall

Let us make these general points more precise by looking at a particular example: Bob Dylan's *A Hard Rain's A-Gonna Fall* (2004a, pp. 59–60). The literary standing of Dylan's lyrics is now widely recognized (for example Ricks 2003) and I shall treat it here as uncontroversial. Even for those of an opposite opinion the validity of the points made may still stand. I shall also treat the song as a poem. Further reasons for selecting this particular song will become evident when I turn to public-relations discourse below.

The first stanza is

Oh, where have you been, my blue-eyed son?
Oh, where have you been, my darling young one?

> I've stumbled on the side of twelve misty mountains,
> I've walked and I've crawled on six crooked highways,
> I've stepped in the middle of seven sad forests,
> I've been out in front of a dozen dead oceans,
> I've been ten thousand miles in the mouth of a graveyard,
> And it's a hard, and it's a hard, it's a hard, and it's a hard,
> And it's a hard rain's a-gonna fall.

This is anything but precise in the sense defined above. If Dylan's aim were to convey any exact information then he has failed. Given the success and popularity of this song then, precision cannot be the cause of its appeal. We are not told the identity of the two speakers, but only their relationship. The claimed experiences cannot be literally true and therefore must be interpreted metaphorically. Nor can we be sure who is speaking. We can relate these events either to events in the life of the young singer (he was only twenty-two when this song was released) and assume he is 'the blue-eyed son', or we can treat what is said as the voices of two characters, or, following a common way of relating to a first-person narrative, adopt it as a description of our own experiences (as either parent or son), but whichever we choose, there is no sure way of pairing up these metaphors with particular events.

This epic landscape of mountains and highways and forests is precise only in the most general terms, that it is difficult and ominous and the individual (whether singer or sung to) feels lost and threatened within it. But it is difficult to be more precise than that. Yet various features of this vague landscape are given with apparent precision, in exact numbers: twelve misty mountains, six crooked highways, seven sad forests, a dozen dead oceans, ten thousand miles. There is certainty too that worse is to come ('a hard rain') even if the precise nature of that rain is unclear too. When an interviewer tried to pin Dylan down on the meaning of this phrase, asking if he meant 'atomic rain', thus trying to limit the meaning of the song to the fears of nuclear war at the time it was written, he answered that no, he meant 'hard rain'.[4]

But it is all vague, despite being framed in apparently precise structures ('I have done X'). The limits of interpretation are set very wide. We might agree on some general points: that it is not a flippant or a light song, that it is apocalyptic and prophetic, broad in its description of life, about an individual's experiences and determination to deal with them. But if we try to make it any more precise, either as autobiography or political commentary, we can only interpret it as a catalogue of problems and threats. Which particular ones we make metaphorically equivalent to the oceans and forests and graveyards is up to us. We have almost *carte blanche*. Personally, I have always heard the 'dozen dead oceans' as a reference to environmental pollution. But in making such an interpretation I have no way of knowing whether these relate to Dylan's own correlations, if he makes any at all. The imagery is so vague as to lend itself to equally valid interpretations by people with political views quite contrary to my own. Right-wing evangelical Christians for example could see the deadness of the ocean as an image of godlessness. It is the very vagueness of these lyrics which is their strength, and very likely the source of their popularity and power. Their achievement is to avoid precise reference, and thus to lend themselves to a greater number of interpretations, notwithstanding the fact that many Dylan fans interpreted the song literally as a commitment by the author to political activism and later held him accountable for not having fulfilled his promise (Dylan 2004b, pp. 119–22).

There are many other features, typical of literary texts, which enhance this vagueness. There are indeterminate intertextual resonances, varying of course with the reader's knowledge. The song has a vague relation to other songs, especially the traditional ballad *Lord Randall* from which its opening questions are borrowed (Ricks 2004, pp. 330–5) or poems, such as Allen Ginsberg's declamatory poem *Howl* (1956) perhaps. It also echoes prophetic and apocalyptic Biblical passages. The use of precise numbers for no apparent reason, for example, coupled with the author's statement of what he has seen and done, are a marked feature of the *Book of Revelation* (12: 3):

> And I stood upon the sand of the sea, and saw a beast rise up out of the sea, having seven heads and ten horns, and upon his horns ten crowns, and upon his heads the name of blasphemy.

In addition, *A Hard Rain's A-Gonna Fall* resonates with other songs by the same author. Analysis of a corpus of all Dylan's songs[5] (hereafter the Dylan Corpus) shows that many of the significant words in this song ('ocean' and 'valley' for example) occur in other songs too, making a reading of their meaning in those songs potentially relevant here. In addition, a layer of ineffable meaning is added by the song's phonological patterns: the rhythm of the caesuraed lines, their parallel structures, the accumulation and release of each stanza, the alliteration ('stumbled'/'side', 'misty mountains', 'stepped'/'sad', 'dozen'/'dead') and assonance ('walked'/'crawled'). And all this is without treating it as a song and considering dimensions of meaning imbued by voice quality, accompaniment, and so on. In short, there is much more that could be said, for which we have no space here.

Public relations discourse

Let me recap the argument so far. We have considered two very different types of discourse: one striving to be precise, in which vagueness is a sign of failure; the other systematically imprecise, making vagueness a source of strength. Let us now turn to a third type, public-relations discourse, and try to see where it stands in relation to the other two. But before we do, a word about public relations in general.

Recent decades have witnessed an exponential growth in an activity defined by its own practitioners as public relations (PR), the major part of which is conducted through language which we may term public-relations discourse (PRD). PR has its own theory, a burgeoning workforce, a growing literature, thriving academic courses. It exerts a disturbing influence over both news reporting (Cottle 2003) and political campaigns (Franklin 2003). And it consumes a growing proportion of the budgets of organizations from businesses (which is where it originated and with which it is associated) to churches, political parties, trade unions, clubs and societies (for example the freemasons) universities and schools, charities and non-government organizations (NGOs), as well as individuals such as royalty, celebrities and high-profile criminals (Moloney 2000, pp. 17–18). Indeed it is hard to find people or organizations engaged in public life that are not also engaged in PR. This very catholicity makes the term extremely hard to define and therefore vague. Outside the commercial world, it is difficult to draw clear boundaries between 'PR' and 'propaganda', 'public information', and 'campaigns', while within business practice it is hard to distinguish PR from other related activities such as advertising, marketing and promotion, all of which may be defined as constituents but also precedents of PR. Given this, most definitions are very general. Moloney (2000, p. 60) regards PR as 'mostly a category of persuasive communications done by interests in the political economy to advance themselves materially and ideologically through markets and public policy making'. Yet, as he acknowledges, any such characterization is inevitably fuzzy at the edges, as almost any organizational communication might come under such a heading.

This indeterminacy as a genre is one of the many features PRD shares with literature, the boundaries of which are also notoriously slippery and difficult to define. PRD employs devices which have traditionally been associated with literary discourse, especially by formalist attempts to characterize a poetic function (Jakobson 1960) and in earlier stylistic work (for example, Leech 1969) focusing upon the effects of marked or deviant language choices. At the phonological and grammatical level there are instances of parallelism, not only in advertising (if that is regarded as a subgenre of PRD) where it is well documented (for example, Cook 2001, pp. 125–47), but in more general promotional prose as well. For example, a McDonald's (burger chain) press release[6] about the launch of a new low-fat salad dressing begins with two parallel noun phrases with the same premodifier, followed by three words with an internal rhyme and a pun: 'New Year, New Look – Dressing to Impress.' On the Imperial Tobacco web site, under the heading 'We value individuality and hard work',[7] are bullet-pointed sentences each beginning with the structure 'We' + present tense + predicate:

- We value people with good ideas who are willing to engage in constructive debate.
- We have created a culture where realism and open communication are valued.
- We acknowledge hard work, good cost control and goal achievement.
- We place strong emphasis on personal accountability.
- We encourage employees to voice their opinions.

This parallel grammatical structure occurs under all the other headings on the same page, creating a parallelism between different sections. In the section headed 'We work together for the good of the whole company', for example, we find:

We aim to deliver best-in-class financial results by each and every one of us contributing to outstanding business performance. What do we mean?

- We recognize that Group results are more important than individual success.
- We encourage cooperation with colleagues for the greater good of the business.
- We place strong emphasis on sharing information and resources and building relationships.
- We have developed a culture based on openness, trust and integrity where conflicts are managed maturely.

This self-answering structure is not unlike that of *A Hard Rain's A-Gonna Fall*. In the song, the question 'Where have you been?' is answered with a string replies in the form 'I have done X;' here 'What do we mean?' is answered by a string of replies in the form 'We do Y.'

At the lexical and semantic levels, PRD can have quasi-literary features too, using innovations whose very newness makes them resistant to precise interpretation. Consider for example the following publicity for the 'Milton Keynes Hub', a university unit offering support for businesses:[8]

> The Hub is designed exclusively to encourage and support knowledge-based pre-start and start-up companies during the early stages of their development, it provides a flexible easy-in, easy-out hatchery for embryo businesses.

Here we have word-class conversion ('start-up companies'), neologism ('pre-start'), and, at the semantic level, a host of metaphors: the 'hub' itself, and a 'hatchery' for 'embryo' businesses, as though they are eggs. Curiously, this farmyard imagery is rather common in British university jargon with its 'new blood' lectureships, 'pump priming' grants, 'seed corn' research, and 'drilling down' assessments. In such intensely metaphoric uses of language, connotational and symbolic meanings are foregrounded at the expense of denotative ones.

At the pragmatic level the voice of the sender in PRD, as in many literary narratives, is often ambiguous. 'Who is speaking thus?' asked Barthes (1977), when trying to disentangle the voices of author, narrator, characters and society in the Balzac short story *Sarrasine*. Looking at the 'we' of corporate web pages, we might well ask the same question. Just as we might ask who is speaking in *A Hard Rain's A-Gonna Fall*: a blue-eyed boy character, or the singer himself?

There are already some very significant studies of aspects of PRD such as service-speak (Cameron 2000), mission statements (Swales and Rogers 1995) and educational buzz-words (Mautner 2005), as well as more general critiques of obfuscatory institutional language which are relevant to PRD, such as Nash (1993) on jargon and Shuy (1998) on bureaucratic language. Nevertheless, given its growing social and political influence, there is still relatively little work specifically on the language of PRD, in contrast for example to the extensive work on the language of advertising, the press, or the law. It is sometimes assumed in some writing on PR (for example, Stauber and Rampton 1995) that the language of PRD, including its 'literary' devices, tends to provoke derision rather than praise and they are seen as superficial, pretentious, manipulative and insincere. And there is some research to suggest that PRD is indeed held in low esteem (Moloney 2000, pp. 75–88). Yet much more research is needed both into the linguistic and textual characteristics of PRD, and into public reactions to them, if these beliefs are to be validated. Detailed understanding of PRD has a contribution to make both to discourse analysis in general, and to language education, where the development of critical and discriminating responses to influential manipulative discourse could be a key component of both first-language and additional-language curricula. The analysis here aims to contribute to the understanding of the linguistic and semantic characteristics of PRD and the kinds of interpretation they may generate – but it should be borne in mind that it is confined to textual analysis, and based upon my own reading, rather than on the responses of other actual audiences.[9]

Food and tobacco PRD

One readily available source of PRD is the web pages of large corporations seeking to present a favourable view of themselves, both to the outside world (external PR) and to their own employees (internal PR). All major companies have such sites and they tend to have many features in common.

For the purposes of the following analysis I collected a corpus of web pages from (a) 14 of the world's biggest tobacco companies[10] and (b) the world's 14 biggest food companies.[11] Current PRD from these two industries is interesting for different but related reasons. Tobacco is now recognized as a killer and its promotion in many countries constrained by law, giving its manufacturers a particularly uphill task in presenting their activities in a favourable light. Food in contrast, far from being a killer is necessary to life. Yet food companies selling heavily processed food face similar if less extreme criticisms concerning the bad effects of their products on public health, particularly children's health. They too therefore face a difficult PR task, though not on the same scale as the tobacco industry. The discourse of contemporary food marketing brings together many of the key concerns of modern life: health and nutrition, quality of life, political decision-making, the environmental impact of agriculture, the relation of humans to other species, and continuity of tradition in both farming and food production (Cook 2004; Cook *et al.* 2004, 2006). It therefore engenders intense activity by marketing, and public-relations copywriters seek to connect their companies and products with beneficial causes and to influence public opinion and consumer behaviour.

From the websites of these two sets of companies I extracted the pages relating to description of the company (often entitled 'About Us'), social and environmental issues (often entitled 'Responsibility'), attitude to employees (often entitled 'People'), and its products and services (often entitled 'Our Products'). The last of these categories is necessarily a sample,[12] as product descriptions, especially in companies with numerous brands, can far exceed the other three in quantity of words. The whole amounts to a corpus of over quarter of a million words[13] which, stored in text-only format, can be searched using Wordsmith Tools for word frequencies, keywords in comparison with other corpora, collocational patterns. I shall refer to it as FTC (Food and Tobacco Corpus).

Keywords are words whose frequency is unusually high in one corpus in comparison with their frequency in another. They provide 'a useful way to characterize a text or a genre' (Scott 2005). Two words which emerge as unusually frequent[14] in the FTC when compared with the written component of the British National Corpus (BNC)[15] are 'our' and 'we'. They may be regarded, depending on how we define the term,[16] as part of a single lemma 'we/us/our'. This PR use of the first person plural echoes a similar one with first person singular in the Dylan Corpus where 'I', 'my', 'me' and 'I'm' all rank in the top ten keywords compared with the written component of the BNC.[17] Both then seem obsessed with the first person: 'What I/we think'; 'What I/we have done/will do' and so forth. But there is an important difference. While 'I' is relatively precise, meaning the sender of the message (unless the speaker is adopting a persona or repeating the words of someone else), 'we' has a notorious vagueness. Not only does it slip easily between 'exclusive we' ('us but not you') and 'inclusive we' ('us and you'), a difference which is not encoded in English,[18] but even within these two categories there is considerable ambiguity often exploited by politicians (Cook 2004, pp. 9–19) and advertisers (Cook 2001, pp. 157–9). In corporate PR 'we' can be either inclusive, meaning perhaps all humanity or all 'ordinary' people, or exclusive, meaning 'we the company' as opposed to 'you the customer'. But in this last case who exactly is included? Does the company mean the shareholders, the employees, some unnamed spokesperson, or all of these?

One manifestation of these frequent first person pronouns is in statements of what the company has done in the past. These are frequent in the FTC. There are 137 instances of the construction 'We have + PAST PARTICIPLE' including one from which I have taken the title of this chapter: 'However, where it makes business sense to seek external verification or auditing of our EHS systems, this we have done and will do.' Table 2.1 contains 20 randomly selected examples. Contrary to usual

Table 2.1 Twenty occurrences of 'We have + PAST PARTICIPLE' in the Food and Tobacco Corpus

1. We have implemented an active policy to prevent industrial accidents and to improve working conditions, notably through employee awareness and training programs.
2. We have included our 'Principles of Citizenship' to assist in the understanding of our core values.
3. We have acquired businesses with operations in numerous countries that brought more than 50 manufacturing plants into our system, which we have integrated and aligned with our environmental programs and practices.
4. We have intensified our efforts to increase efficiency and eliminate waste.
5. We have introduced significant improvements in our arrangements with effect from May 2004.
6. We have invested in state-of-the-art equipment, further improving our efficiency and competitiveness.
7. We have invested heavily in advanced techniques in this area with a view to improving quality, cutting waste and speeding production.
8. We have launched Bertolli pasta sauces and dressings.
9. We have listed Frito-Lay products according to specific dietary concerns here.
10. We have located our 24 worldwide processing facilities in proximity to our principal sources of tobacco.
11. We have met consumer demand for healthy foods by launching pro.active, a spread which contains ingredients that can help reduce cholesterol levels.
12. We have been at the forefront in developing and applying product-evaluation methods to assess the relative toxicity of cigarette smoke.
13. We have positioned The Coca-Cola Company for growth, guided by our mission to provide branded beverages that refresh people around the world, anywhere, any time, everyday.
14. We have reduced emissions of ozone depleting substances per tonne of product by 99%.
15. We have been at the forefront in developing and applying methods to assess the relative toxicity of cigarette smoke.
16. We have developed new cigarettes based on tobacco-heating technology.
17. We have set up resource development systems and tools, which work well.
18. We have worked to extend the approach embodied in our Social Responsibility in Tobacco Production programme to all our leaf suppliers, to reach those from whom we buy leaf on the open market.
19. We have focused our efforts thus far on commodities that are of both special importance to our business and associated with critical societal issues.
20. We have spent over $6 billion with women and minority businesses.

practice I begin the line with the search term as in most cases, the substance of what has been done follows this opening.

If we contrast these PRD 'have dones' with those of Dylan's first stanza, we can see that semantically and pragmatically they are very different indeed. In the song they conveyed a sense of helplessness, of being dwarfed and overpowered by the environment. There are words denoting physical actions (stepped, crawled, stumbled) and objects (mountains, oceans, valleys), but they seem to refer to the speaker's experience of the landscape rather than his influence upon it, and they are vague because we do not know what the objects and actions themselves denote, metaphorically. The PRD 'have dones' on the other hand refer to actions, in which the speaker ('we') has intervened decisively in their environment and claims to have changed it for the better. They are vague in a different way, not because they are metaphorical, but because they are abstract, and because the terms used denote evaluations of actions (for example, 'improve') rather than the actions themselves.

Let us take a few examples and in each case ask questions to test how precisely the statement tells us what actually happened:

> We have implemented an active policy to prevent industrial accidents and to improve working conditions, notably through employee awareness and training programs.

Who exactly is 'we': the management, the owners, the workforce? Did the policy actually reduce accidents? 'Improve' is a relative and often subjective term. What was the initial state from which there was an improvement? How much improvement was there and of what kind? Who viewed it as an improvement, the company or the workers, or both? How many training programmes were there? Were they voluntary or compulsory, in workers' own or paid time?

> We have intensified our efforts to increase efficiency and eliminate waste.

By how much? Did the effort yield results? If so, by how much did you increase efficiency? How do you define 'efficiency' and from whose perspective? How do you define waste? As waste surely cannot be eliminated in any industrial process, by how much have you actually reduced it?

> We have spent over $6 billion with women and minority businesses.

How much over? What proportion of your total expenditure is it? What do you mean by 'spend . . . with'? Do you mean firms with female employees or female owners or both? Could a reason for your choice be that female labour tends to be cheaper? How do you define 'minority businesses'?

If there were space I could make similar points for almost all the other 'have dones' in the corpus, with very few exceptions, such as 'We have launched Bertolli pasta sauces and dressings.' As an account of actual actions in the real (as opposed to a metaphorical or fictional world) it is all very vague indeed.

But of course, no such questioning is possible. Though these web pages adopt a dialogic and conversational tone, any implied opportunity for interaction is illusory.

Similarity and differences

What then are the similarities and differences between the 'have done' statements in the FTC and those in *A Hard Rain's A-Gonna Fall*? One similarity is merely formal: they deploy the same opening structure. Another is in overall effect: both are vague. But this vagueness seems to be very different in nature and quality and value. Why?

The humble emergency procedure text provides a useful point of comparison with both which may help to answer this question. Its success can be measured against a corresponding reality. We might say that it works if: (a) the procedure described is indeed the best one to adopt when confronted by a choking adult and (b) the writer succeeds in conveying the details of this procedure from their own mind to the reader's through the conduit of language. So any vagueness in the emergency text is a sign of failure. The song is quite different. Though there may be a reality which the speaker is trying to convey, its success is not to be measured against a preceding reality or successful outcome (Widdowson 1984). And this perhaps points to a profound difference between the discourses of poetry and PRD, which makes it seem absurd to compare them at all except at the formal and most general levels.

Being about the behaviour and impact of organizations in a real literal world, PRD can, like the emergency procedure text but *un*like the song, be measured against reality. 'Smoking', as the packets say, 'kills'. Obesity is rising among children eating processed food. Among US adolescents it has tripled since 1985 (Sperlock 2005, p. 11). Food retailers rely on poor labour conditions (Zacune 2005) and environmentally detrimental intensive farming (Carson 2000; Humphrys 2001). Food retail is part of a world of gross injustice, which can be expressed in quite precise statistics (Hart

2004). According to the United Nations Development Report (UNDP 1998, quoted in ibid.) the world's 225 richest men then owned more than a trillion dollars, the equivalent of the possessions of world's 47 per cent poorest people. According to the Institute for Food and Development Policy in 1999 (quoted in McGarr 2000, p. 85):

> The world today produces more food per inhabitant than ever before. Enough is available to provide 4.3 pounds to every person every day: 2.5 pounds of grain, beans and nuts, about a pound of meat, milk and eggs, and another of fruit and vegetable. The real causes of hunger are poverty, inequality and lack of access. Too many people are too poor to buy the food that is available, or lack the land and resources to grow it themselves.

In a real world of this kind, we the readers of PRD can ask questions of its producers such as the following, and educate our students to do the same. What have these companies done to prevent death and ill-health among consumers of their products? What changes did they make in their employees' working conditions? What did they do to diminish environmental pollution by their manufacturing and distribution processes? What have they done to address the injustices of wealth and food distribution? In short, 'What have you done' in precise and literal terms? In the FTC it is all very vague. PR writers may measure the success of their words by their aesthetic power as though they were poems, but the public may measure them by their truth as though they were emergency texts. There should be no confusion of the two. Vagueness in PRD should be evaluated in quite a different way from vagueness in literary texts. Despite some literary pretensions, it is its correspondence to the facts which matters.

Notes

1. Lobianco's study is of the texts as multimodal communication and also of readers' understandings of them. This particular procedure is in fact probably better demonstrated than explained, and the original is also accompanied by a picture.
2. The summary of approaches to literature in this section receives much fuller treatment in my book *Discourse and Literature* (Cook 1994, pp. 125–77)
3. William Blake's famous assessment of *Paradise Lost* in his *The Marriage of Heaven and Hell*. Quoted by Philip Pullman in 'Introduction', Milton (2005).
4. Included in the Martin Scorsese's 2005 film *No Direction Home*. The song was released in 1963, the year after the Cuban missile crisis, at a time of widespread and intense fear about nuclear war.

5. Part of a larger corpus of song lyrics 1955–2005 held by the author.
6. http://www.mcdonalds.co.uk/pages/global/dressing.html (accessed 17 November 2005).
7. http://www.imperial-tobacco.com/index.asp?pageid=78 (accessed 17 November 2005).
8. http://www.01908.co.uk/business/386?PHPSESSID=ac6d867292ecf 941a18d595d243971da (accessed 29 October 2005).
9. In other work on PRD I have combined textual analysis with interviews and/or focus groups eliciting responses from a range of readers to promotional material such a labels (Cook and O'Halloran 1999; Nyyssönen *et al.* 2000) arguments for GM agriculture and food (Cook *et al.* 2005) and for organic and non-organic foods (Cook and Robbins 2006).
10. Based on information provided by ASH and on the 'fortune 500' list of the world's largest corporations http://www.fortune.com/fortune/global500
11. Using the ranking given by the journal *Food Engineering,* available online at: http://www.foodengineeringmag.com/FILES/HTML/PDF/Top100chart.pdf (accessed 22 October 2005).
12. An amount taken from the beginning of the product description pages equal in size to each of the other categories.
13. 275,434 words in total: 122,875 from tobacco companies; 152,559 from food companies.
14. 'Our' ranks first and second, 'we' ranks eighteenth.
15. I used the BNC Baby, a 4-million word extract from the BNC comprising 3 million words of written and 1 million words of spoken data.
16. They would be by Francis and Kučera's (1982, p. 1) definition of a lemmas: 'a set of lexical forms having the same stem and belonging to the same major word class, differing only in inflection and/or spelling'.
17. Cautions is needed here, however, as the lemma (I/Me/My) ranks highly as a keyword in comparisons on spoken with written discourse. However, even compared with the spoken component 'My' is the first keyword and 'me' is the second keyword in the Dylan Corpus.
18. As it is in many other languages. In Malay the word 'kita' means 'we-inclusive-of-addressee', while 'kani' means 'we-exclusive-of-addressee.'

References

M.M. Bakhtin, *Problems of Dostoevsky's Poetics* (Manchester University Press, 1984). (Original Russian version published in 1929.)

R. Barthes, 'The Death of the Author', in *Image, Music, Text* (trans. by S. Heath) (London: Fontana, 1977). 142–9 (Original French version published in 1968).

D. Cameron, *Good to Talk? Living and Working in a Communication Culture* (London: Sage, 2000).

R. Carson, *Silent Spring.* (London: Penguin, 2000). (First published in USA in 1962).

G. Cook, *Discourse and Literature: The Interplay of Form and Mind* (Oxford University Press, 1994).

G. Cook, *The Discourse of Advertising,* 2nd edn (London: Routledge, 2001).

G. Cook, *Genetically Modified Language* (London: Routledge, 2004).

G. Cook and K. O'Halloran, 'Label Literacy: Factors Affecting the Understanding and Assessment of Baby Food Labels', in T. O'Brien (ed.), *Language and Literacies, BAAL Studies in Applied Linguistics 14* (British Association for Applied Linguistics in association with Multilingual Matters, 1999) 145–57.

G. Cook, E. Pieri and P.T. Robbins, ' "The Scientists Think and the Public Feels": Expert Perceptions of The Discourse of GM Food', *Discourse and Society* 15/4 (2004) 433–49.

G. Cook, P.T. Robbins and E. Pieri ' "Words of Mass Destruction": British Newspaper Coverage of the GM Food Debate, and Expert and Non-expert Reactions', *Public Understanding of Science* 14/1 (2005) 1–25.

G. Cook and P.T. Robbins, *The Discourse of Organic Food Promotion: Language, Intentions and Effects* (ESRC Research Project 000–22–1626, 2006).

S. Cottle (ed.), *News, Public Relations and Power* (London: Sage, 2003).

R. Dylan, *Bob Dylan Lyrics 1962–2001* (New York: Simon & Schuster, 2004a).

R. Dylan, *Chronicles Volume One* (New York: Simon & Schuster, 2004b).

M. Foucault, 'What Is an Author?' (trans. J.V. Harari), in J.V. Harari (ed.), *Textual Strategies: Perspectives in Post-Structuralism* (Ithaca, NY: Cornell University Press, 1988). (Original French version published in 1969.)

W.N. Francis and H. Kučera, *Frequency Analysis of English Usage* (Boston, MA: Houghton Mifflin, 1982).

B. Franklin, ' "A Good Day to Bury Bad News?": Journalists' Sources and the Packaging of Politics', in S. Cottle (ed.), *News, Public Relations and Power* (London: Sage, 2003).

E. Freund, *The Return of the Reader* (London: Methuen, 1987).

A. Ginsberg, *Howl and Other Poems* (San Francisco, CA: City Lights Books, 1956).

K. Hart, 'The Political Economy of Food in an Unequal World', in M.E. Lien and B. Nerlich (eds), *The Politics of Food* (Oxford and New York: Berg, 2004).

J. Humphrys, *The Great Food Gamble* (London: Hodder & Stoughton, 2001).

R. Jakobson, 'Closing Statement: Linguistics and Poetics', in T.A. Sebeok (ed.), *Style in Language* (Cambridge, MA: MIT Press, 1960.)

H. James, *The Turn of the Screw and Other Short Novels* (London: Penguin, 1995). (*The Turn of the Screw* first published in 1898.)

A. Jefferson and D. Robey, *Modern Literary Theory: A Comparative Introduction* (London: Batsford, 1982).

G.N. Leech, *A Linguistic Guide to English Poetry* (London: Longman, 1969).

T.M.F.B. Lobianco, *The Effect of the Interplay of Paralanguage and Language on the Accessibility of Written Texts: A Study of Emergency Procedures*, unpublished PhD thesis, London University Institute of Education (1999).

G. Mautner, 'The Entrepreneurial University. A Discursive Profile of the Higher-Education Buzzword', *Critical Discourse Studies* 2/2 (2005) 95–120.

P. McGarr, 'Why Green Is Red: Marxism and the Threat to the Environment', in C. Harman (ed.), *Anti-capitalism: Theory and Practice* (London: International Socialism Quarterly, 88 2000) 61–126.

J. Milton, *Paradise Lost* (ed. Philip Pullman) (Oxford University Press, 2005). (First published in 1667.)

K. Moloney, *Rethinking Public Relations: The Spin and the Substance* (London: Routledge, 2000).

W. Nash, *Jargon: Its Uses and Abuses* (Oxford: Blackwell, 1993).

H. Nyyssönen, A. Björkvall, G. Cook, F.X. Fernandez-Polo, B.-L. Gunnarsson, P. Haddington, K. Maryns, K. O'Halloran, S. Slembrouck, C. Suárez Gómez and A.-M. Vandenbergen, *Design and Accessibility of Baby-Food Labels from the Consumer's Point of View,* http://www.ekl.oulu.fi/babyfood/index.html (accessed 5 May 2005).

A. Pushkin, *Eugene Onegin* (trans. Charles Johnston) (London: Penguin, 2003). (Original Russian version published in 1833.)

M. Reddy, 'The Conduit Metaphor', in A. Ortony (ed.), *Metaphor and Thought* (Cambridge University Press, 1979).

C. Ricks, *Dylan's Vision of Sin* (London: Penguin, 2004).

M. Scott, 'Help Menu', in *Wordsmith Tools,* http://www.lexically.net/wordsmith/ (Oxford University Press, 2005).

R. Shuy, *Bureaucratic Language in Government and Business* (Washington, DC: Georgetown University Press, 1998).

M. Sperlock, *Don't Eat This Book.* (London: Penguin, 2005).

J. Stauber and S. Rampton, *Toxic Sludge Is Good for You: Lies, Damn Lies and the Public Relations Industry* (Monroe, ME: Common Courage Press, 1995).

J. Swales and P. Rogers, 'Discourse and the Projection of Corporate Culture: the Mission Statement', *Discourse and Society,* 6/2 (1995) 233–42.

S. Thorne, 'Second Language Acquisition Theory and the Truth(s) About Relativity', in J.P. Lantolf (ed.), *Sociocultural Theory and Second Language Learning* (Oxford University Press, 2000).

J.P. Tompkin (ed.), *Reader-Response Criticism: From Formalism to Post-Structuralism* (Baltimore, MD: Johns Hopkins University Press, 1980).

United Nations Development Program, *Human Development Report* (New York: UNDP, 1998).

H.G. Widdowson, 'Reference and Representation as Modes of Meaning', in *Explorations in Applied Linguistics 2* (Oxford University Press, 1984).

H.G. Widdowson, *Practical Stylistics* (Oxford University Press, 1992).

J. Zacune, 'ASDA WAL-MART: Cutting Costs At Any Cost' *Corporate Watch,* 19 October http://www.corporatewatch.org.uk/?lid=2102 (accessed 29 October 2005).

3

'About Twelve Thousand or So': Vagueness in North American and UK Offices

Almut Koester

Introduction

According to Drew and Heritage (1992 p. 22), workplace or institutional interaction 'involves an orientation /. . ./ to some core goal, task or identity /. . ./ conventionally associated with the institution'; that is, it is characterized by a focus of the discourse participants on accomplishing workplace tasks. Such a focus on workplace goals should result logically in a kind of discourse which is factual and precise, and does not contain too much vagueness or ambiguity. The use of vague expressions such as 'sort of', 'stuff like that', 'or something' is usually associated with informal, casual conversation, not with work-related talk.

It is therefore perhaps surprising that an investigation of spoken interactions across a variety of office environments found that vague language (VL) and hedging devices occurred regularly in interactions with focus on workplace tasks, such as meetings or training sessions. Koester (2006) investigated the frequency and function of interpersonal devices, including modals verbs, hedges, idioms and VL, in a corpus of interactions in North America and UK offices consisting of approximately 34,000 words. The results showed that modal items were extremely common; in fact, the 11 most frequent modal and semi-modal verbs in the corpus (verbs such as 'will', 'can', 'would', 'have to') accounted for about 4 per cent of all words. Adverbial hedges, such as 'sort of', 'really', 'just' occurred on average 10 times per 1000 words; and vague expressions, such as 'things', 'or something', about 6 times every thousand words. These findings show that such interpersonal devices, which qualify, hedge or introduce vagueness into a proposition, play an important role in work-related talk. This chapter investigates the specific functions of VL in workplace talk, and attempts to provide an explanation for its prevalence in this type of discourse, where VL intuitively seems out of place.

Here, only items which inherently make an utterance vague or imprecise (for example 'stuff', 'things like that') will be examined, and not those that also have other meanings and functions besides vagueness, such as adverbial hedges like 'sort of' or 'just'. The most complete examination of VL in naturally occurring discourse is Channell's (1994) study, which provides a good overview of the theoretical issues involved in defining what 'vagueness' is, and of the functions performed by VL. Channell restricts the notion of vagueness to *deliberately* vague uses of language (Channell ibid., pp. 20–2), and this definition will also be followed here.

The vague items examined here fall into three categories:

- Vague nouns, for example 'things', 'thing', 'stuff', 'bit'.
- Vague categories, for example: 'and stuff (like that)' and 'or something (like that)'.
- Vague approximators, for example 'about', 'around', 'or so'.

This chapter deals with the use of such items in a small corpus of North American and UK office conversations. Corpus linguistic tools were used to determine the frequency of the above items in the corpus, and these were examined in their discourse contexts to find the functions they performed. After briefly introducing the corpus, the chapter investigates the frequency and functions of the vague items in various types of interactions or 'genres'. VL is also contrasted with its 'opposite'–precise and explicit language–and we examine some of the contexts in which speakers choose to be explicit rather than vague. The final section of the chapter discusses the practical relevance of the findings, in particular to teaching English as a foreign language (TEFL).

Data

The data consist of naturally occurring spoken interactions recorded in the offices of a variety of organizations and companies in North America and the UK. The reason for including both North American and UK varieties was to provide a representative sample of workplace interactions in Englishes, thereby giving the corpus some international validity, which is of particular relevance for TEFL.

The organizations include university offices, publishers and small to medium companies in sectors such as the paper trade and advertising. From a total of about 30 hours of data, 66 conversations were transcribed (totalling just under 34,000 words), approximately half from the North American data and half from the UK data.[1] An attempt was made to find matching workplace settings in both; thus school or departmental university offices and editorial offices in a publishing company were chosen as venues in both. For data in the business sector, it was not possible to find strictly matching UK and North American settings. While all the companies were involved in sales, the area of business varied, ranging from paper, printing services, advertising to food retailing. While the primary purpose of the study was not to compare UK and North American English, ensuring that settings in both countries are similar, means that comparisons between the two varieties are also possible.

Most of the interactions were between co-workers (rather than with customers); and while the majority dealt with a variety of work-related tasks, some did not address workplace topics, and could be described as having more of a 'social' or 'relational' focus. Encounters occurring across the different office environments which had similar goals, for example making arrangements or giving instructions, were considered to belong to the same 'genre' (Hasan 1985; Eggins and Slade 1997; McCarthy 1998). The different genres found can be grouped into the following three broad categories or 'macro-genres'; the first two ('collaborative' and 'unidirectional') involve task-oriented or 'transactional' encounters, while the third ('non-transactional') consists of conversations with a social or relational focus:

- Collaborative genres, in which both (all) participants contribute more or less equally towards accomplishing the goal of the encounter. This includes the following types of task-oriented genres: planning and making arrangements, decision-making, discussing/evaluating.
- Unidirectional genres, where one of the speakers clearly plays a dominant role, in imparting information to the other participant, instructing/directing the other participant in action to be taken, or requesting action from the interlocutor. The unidirectional genres found in the corpus are: briefing, service encounters (involving information provision), procedural discourse (involving instructions and directives, for example in training new staff), requesting and reporting.
- Non-transactional genres–conversations which occur at the workplace, but where participants are not dealing with workplace tasks. Such conversations may involve office gossip, talk focusing on workplace topics, or small-talk, which is concerned with topics outside the workplace.

Many of the transactional encounters occur during prearranged meetings between two, sometimes three co-workers (only one is a formal multi-party meeting), but some also occur ad hoc, arising out of a specific query addressed to a colleague, and so on. While collaborative encounters are all between co-workers, some unidirectional encounters are between customers and suppliers, or, in the case of the university data, between members of staff and students.

As noted at the beginning of the chapter, VL has been associated with informal contexts of interaction. While one would expect non-transactional interactions to be more informal than transactional task-oriented ones, it should be noted that the notion of formality does not enter into the data classification. The interactions are classified first in terms of whether they are task-oriented or not (transactional or non-transactional), and second according to genre (that is the goal of the interaction).

As one of the purposes of the study was to identify differences at the lexico-grammatical level between the different genres, the occurrence of VL (and other devices) in the different genres was compared. The frequency of each of the types of VL described above (vague nouns, vague categories and vague approximators) was counted for each individual genre, using corpus-based methods (Scott 1999). Owing to the small size of the corpus, comparisons are often made between the three macro-genres, rather than individual genres.

General results

In total, 184 vague items were identified in the corpus. All three types of VL occur significantly more frequently in unidirectional genres than in the other two types of discourse. Table 3.1 shows the frequency of VL in each of the macro-genres normalized to frequency per thousand words (or 'density').[2]

Table 3.1 Frequency of vague language in the corpus of office conversations

Macro-genre	Density (frequency per thousand words)
Unidirectional	6.9
Collaborative	4.6
Non-transactional	3.5
Average density across corpus	5.5

As shown in Table 3.1, VL is much more frequent in unidirectional than in collaborative genres, which is statistically a highly significant difference.[3] It is least frequent in non-transactional discourse, consisting of small-talk or office gossip. This seems surprising at first, as vague and 'imprecise' language tends to be associated with more informal types of speech (Chafe 1982; Powell 1992; Overstreet and Yule 1997a). Unidirectional genres, such as briefing and procedural discourse, on the other hand, are concerned primarily with the transfer of information. Tasks such as briefing a co-worker, or giving instructions, involve frequent references to facts and figures, and one would expect precise information and specific details to be essential here. However, if one looks at how VL is used in these genres, it becomes clear that facts and information are often talked about in vague terms. This seeming contradiction can be explained if we explore in more detail the purposes for which speakers use the different types of VL, and the functions they perform.

The functions of vague language

In encounters where participants engage in a workplace task (collaborative and unidirectional genres), their goals are mainly transactional or task-oriented. Nevertheless, they orient simultaneously to interpersonal concerns, such as relationship-building, self-presentation or issues of power and identity, which will be referred to as 'relational' goals. While such goals are foregrounded in non-transactional genres (office gossip and small-talk), they are nevertheless present in transactional encounters, and evidence for this can be found a variety of surface linguistic features. VL can be used either for transactional or relational purposes:

- Transactional uses serve the task goal, and involve such specific functions as supplying the appropriate amount of information, obtaining information, or communicating effectively when specific information is lacking.
- Relational uses involve such functions as politeness, self-protection or showing solidarity (see Channell 1994, pp. 165–95).

These two different types of function can be illustrated with examples from the corpus. In many cases, vague reference conveys a sufficient degree of information for the participants involved; therefore it is not necessary for speakers to be more precise. In Example 1[4] between two North American co-workers, the speakers use only vague referents ('those things' and 'the monthly thing'), but they seem to understand each other perfectly:

Example 1[*]
Chris Did it also include by the way . . . uh those <u>things</u> that we talked about, that I- that I just called you up about,
Mike   Yeah. the- the monthly <u>thing,</u>

As co-workers, the speakers share a great deal of background knowledge. The vague nouns they use serve a transactional function, as they communicate the appropriate amount of information required in this situation.

However, the use of a vague noun like 'thing' may also have a relational function. In one conversation in a UK university office, colleagues frequently use vague referents in discussing a staff meeting:

Example 2
a I would say- I'm not disagreeing at all, I'm just saying that this <u>thing</u> uh it's complicated [laughing] . . . a- because people are complicated not because the <u>thing</u> is complicated.
b /. . ./ You don't really /hear/ about <u>things</u> . . . for a while before they happened

In these two extracts from different parts of the conversation, the speaker seems to avoid being precise, as the topic discussed is rather sensitive. She uses VL as a kind of shield, to avoid committing herself, and possibly saying something inappropriate.

The following section examines in more detail the transactional and relational functions of each type of vague item in the corpus, particularly in unidirectional genres, where such items are more frequent. VL is used in similar ways in both the North American and UK workplaces. Few differences were found in the relative frequency of vague items; any notable differences will be pointed out along the way.

Vague nouns

Vague nouns can be defined as vague words used to refer to entities; the ones found in the corpus are: 'things', 'thing', 'stuff', 'bit' (for example 'the extra bit'). Vague nouns are the most frequent type of vague item, accounting for 108 out of a total of 184 uses of VL. They are particularly

[*] See transcription conventions at the end of the chapter.

frequent in three of the unidirectional genres: briefing, procedural discourse and reporting. As these genres mainly involve the transfer of information, 'things' are of course frequently referred to; and there seem to be a number of reasons why vague references are often used for this.

Sometimes a vague referent is used cohesively to refer to a more specific item that is specified in the cotext, for example an assistant briefing her superior (this is an example from the North American corpus):

Example 3
It goes through all these different <u>things</u>, first? All these different little <u>processes</u>?

Other uses are deictic and refer to items in the physical environment (Kate, a secretary, is also briefing her boss in this UK example):

Example 4
Mary   ↑ D'you- d'you want to leave- leave <u>that</u>. <u>*stuff*</u>
Kate   ⌊It's just your post,

The most frequent reason for using a vague noun is because it is not necessary to be more precise, as the participants can easily identify the items or concepts referred to owing to the background knowledge they share from working together. This is illustrated in Example 1 above. Another North American example is the use of 'stuff' in the following extract from a procedural encounter, where a new employee is being trained:

Example 5
I don't know if I explained this already or not. but . . . the <u>stuff</u> that's already been pai:d: COD, ↓ which is indicated by that little green stub attached, . . . ↑ is no:t . . . that high of a priority

Although the addressee is new to the organization, and still needs to have many procedures explained to her, she already knows that 'stuff' here refers to the main job that she and her supervisor deal with, namely paying invoices. Such implicit uses of language can of course involve many other devices besides vague nouns: non-anaphoric personal and demonstrative pronouns, deictic adverbs, ellipsis, in-group expressions and jokes, and so forth (Cutting 1999, 2000).

The above examples show that vague nouns perform a number of different transactional functions, which are particularly useful when talking about facts and information. But vague nouns can also perform relational functions, as illustrated in Example 2 above. Many implicit uses simultaneously have a relational function, as they can project a sense of familiarity and group identity. Halliday and Hasan (1976 p. 276–7) point out that general nouns can convey attitude (for example sympathy or contempt). Such an attitude is clearly conveyed by the use of 'thing' in the following North American example, where the speaker responds to a colleague who wants something done, but (in the speaker's opinion) much too late:

Example 6
So it doesn't even have a . . . an HDS number. Nothing. No. <u>That</u> <u>*whole*</u> thing ought to go to: . . .

The use of the vague referent 'thing', pre-modified by the demonstrative 'that' (indicating emotional rather than physical distance; Lakoff 1974), and the prosodically prominent adjective 'whole', has the effect of distancing the speaker from the proposition, thus communicating her annoyance and impatience in this situation.

While the vague referents 'thing' and 'things' occur as frequently in the North American and the UK conversations, 'stuff' is much more frequent in the North American data, where it accounts for 34 of the 42 total occurrences. That this reflects a general difference between the two varieties of English is confirmed by comparing these findings with two larger spoken corpora: 'stuff' occurred only 690 times in one million words of CANCODE[5] (which consists only of spoken UK English), compared with 1000 times in 1 million in the North American segment of the Cambridge International Corpus (also consisting of spoken data).[6]

Vague categories

Speakers sometimes refer vaguely to categories of items, as in the following North American example:

Example 7
Because she's missing the servers <u>and things like that</u>

Such clause-final expressions, consisting of a conjunction and a noun phrase, have been referred to in the literature as 'generalized list completers' (Jefferson 1990) 'general extenders' (Overstreet and Yule 1997a, 1997b) or 'tags' (Dines 1980). Channell (1994) refers to whole expressions such as 'the servers and things like that' as 'vague category identifiers' made up of an exemplar ('the servers') + a vague tag ('and things like that'), where the exemplar is meant to allow the listener to identify the category referred to. Reference to vague categories was less frequent than the use of vague nouns, with only 49 instances in the corpus, but 14 different types were found, including 'or something/anything (like that)', 'and stuff (like that)', 'and things (like this/that)', 'and everything'. This kind of vague reference was also more frequent in unidirectional discourse, particularly in procedural discourse and service encounters. Again, it is interesting to look at some of the more specific functions that vague tags perform.

Let us begin with transactional functions. When speakers lack or are uncertain about information, using a vague tag is a useful way of getting or checking information, as in the following North American example:

Example 8
Chris   Oh the NC- the NCOA stuff won't be back until next week (or something)?
Mike   Right. Until . . . Wednesday or Thursday earliest,

In such cases, the tag is usually spoken with clause-final rising intonation, showing that confirmation from the interlocutor is sought, as in Example 8. Vague category identifiers (consisting of exemplar + tag) are often used in a similar way to vague nouns to refer implicitly to shared knowledge. In procedural discourse and briefing, instruction-givers or briefers often seem to use such expressions in order to cover a lot of ground, without having to go into too much detail. For example (9a from North America; 9b from the UK):

Example 9
a   /. . ./ An' that's just *page* after *page* after *pa:ge* . . . of . . . turnover orders . . . out of stock . . . update . . . you can *read* this if you want, it'll help acquaint you with . . . why stock keeps going out of stock, an' all tha:t
b   So it's gonna be four color. So you'll get photos coming down an' everything. I think it's only got- it's only /like ??/. It'll be A4 folded. Same size with the same border /. . ./

In the first of these, 'why stock keeps going out of stock' is given as just one exemplar of the type of thing, referred to by 'an' all that', which the addressee can read up on in the document (information is presumably also included on other topics mentioned earlier: 'turnover orders', 'updates'). In the second, where the speaker describes a brochure he is designing, 'an' everything' presumably refers to other elements (such as logo, text) that will be in the brochure besides photos; but as the focus here is on the layout of the brochure, not the details of what it contains, he glosses over this information by using a vague tag.

In some cases, instruction-givers use such expressions to exemplify their explanations, as in the following North American example:

Example 10
a   you can give a reason for the free, you know, like <u>gratis copy or something</u>
b   So instead of like the old way you know, we used to <u>fax and stuff</u>

A similar construction can be found in a meeting between a supplier and a customer, when the supplier explains the types of services he offers (UK example):

Example 11
The second thing is of course we can label it for what you want, if you want it /. . ./ you know: <u>/Abigail ?/ or something</u> uh m- m- um . . . whatever.

Referring to shared knowledge is a useful strategy in both procedural discourse and service encounters involving information provision, as this enables the addressee to link new information with pre-existing knowledge. According to Overstreet and Yule (1997a, 1997b), one of the major roles of general extenders is to convey such assumptions of shared knowledge or intersubjectivity. They note (1997a) that discourse markers such as 'you know' perform a similar function, and it is interesting that in the last examples the speakers introduce the exemplification with 'you know'.

Let us turn now to relational functions. In all the above examples, the vague tags refer to a category that the addressees are supposed to be able to infer themselves. But in some instances, vague tags do not actually seem to identify any category, as in this North American example:

Example 12
I don't have the SBN <u>or anything</u>

Here the speaker refers to a specific item, 'the SBN' (meaning the ISBN number of a book), therefore it is difficult to imagine what other items might come under the category of 'or anything'. Rather, the speaker seems to be apologizing for not having the ISBN number of a book she is requesting.

In such cases, vague tags often seem to have a relational function of downtoning or hedging an utterance, similar to the use of vague nouns in the second example above. In the same supplier–customer meeting as example above, Angus, the supplier uses a vague tag ('an' things') in referring to a business deal Paul, the customer, did with another company (the name is inaudible):

Example 13
Angus   Yes. Ah. I heard you did a deal with /??/ didn't you. to- take
        a lot of board in <u>an' things</u>
Paul   Yeah. I <u>think</u> we did. Yeah.

To make such an inquiry into a customer's business dealings with other companies could be seen as unwarranted interference; therefore the vague tag performs a negative politeness function in mitigating this potential face threat (Brown and Levinson 1987). It also gives Paul the option of remaining vague himself about this particular business, which is exactly what he does in his response: 'Yeah, I think we did.' Presumably he knows whether or not his company has actually made such a deal, but does not wish to discuss it with Angus. The use of VL by the supplier for negative politeness and by the customer to deliberately withhold information reflects the more powerful position of the customer.

Vague tags can function relationally not only as mitigators, but can also project intimacy and solidarity, as shown in another example from the supplier–customer meeting. In describing one of his services (UK example), Angus says:

Example 14
/. . ./ So we take all the funny sizes . . . an' all the- you know the-
odd: . . . bits an' pieces <u>an' things</u> /. . ./

The function of the vague tag 'an' things' is to create an atmosphere of informality, reinforcing the informality of the idiom 'the odd bits and pieces' (which is itself a vague expression). Such efforts on the part of the supplier, to make his sales talk more like an informal chat than a formal presentation, are evidence of his attention to relational goals in this encounter.

In a procedural encounter in a North American company between Mike, a junior manager, and Chris, his boss, Mike jokes about not being able to get a job done overnight by saying:

Example 15
[mock whiny voice] I'm sorry but I had to sleep first and eat breakfast

Later in the conversation, Mike and Chris talk about somebody who was supposed to get back to Mike with some information:

Example 16
1 Mike   Yup, [chuckles] An' I called an' talked to somebody else an' he said oh let me look into that.
2 Chris Heheheh. Still lookin' huh?
3 Mike   Yeah.
4 Chris Or did he go home an' go to sleep an' have breakfast an' stuff too.
5 Mike   ⌊Heheheheh

With his quip in turn 4, Chris refers back to the earlier joke, and in doing so uses a vague tag: 'an' stuff'. Like many other vague tags, it refers to shared knowledge; however in this case not to background knowledge needed to perform a transactional task, but to a private joke shared earlier in the conversation. Thereby it reinforces solidarity between the speakers and even projects a kind of intimacy. Overstreet and Yule (1997b, p. 256) highlight this solidarity function of vague tags: 'They represent a kind of implicit communication whereby speakers indicate an assumption of shared experience and hence closeness or common ground.'

Vague approximators

Vague approximators are used to refer vaguely to amounts, times and dates, and three types were found in the corpus ('about', 'around', 'or so'), with only a total of 27 occurrences. Like the other two types of VL, they occur most frequently in unidirectional genres; in fact they are nearly three times as frequent here as in collaborative genres. Again, this greater frequency can be linked to the fact that speakers are information-focused in these genres, and often refer vaguely to factual information, such as quantities and times, as demonstrated in the following (17a North American; 17b UK; 17c North American):

Example 17
a   An' I tried to do <u>about - about</u> twelve thousand <u>or so</u>
b   And I've got enough stock to last for <u>about</u> five months
c   we should have 'em . . . within <u>about</u> a week

As with other vague items, often the exact amount or time is not known, or it may not be relevant, as in the following from a North American procedural encounter, already shown:

Example 5
I don't know if I explained this already or not. but . . . the *stuff* that's already been pai:d: COD, ↓ which is indicated by that little green stub attached, . . . ↑ is no:t . . . that high of a priority

In this example, the approximate time period, not the exact one, is relevant for the procedure being explained.

In addition to such transactional functions, vague approximators can also perform relational functions, such as mitigating face-threatening acts. In the following UK example, when suggesting a time to meet, the speaker uses the vague approximator 'about' as a politeness device together with a number of other interpersonal markers:

Example 18
↑ I <u>was wondering</u> if . . . you an' I <u>could possibly</u> this ↓ week, at *about* eleven o'clock on Thursday morning, reinforce each other half an hour on- *just* to look through . . .

As becomes clear in the rest of the conversation, the speaker wants to meet at eleven o'clock, but by being vague about the time he avoids giving the impression that he simply expects the addressee to be free then.

Vague categories or approximators occurred as frequently in the UK as in the North American data, and no particular vague items were significantly more frequent in either of the varieties.

Summary of results

The above discussion of the three types of VL in the corpus has illustrated some of their most frequent functions, and we are now in a position to summarize the reasons for their much greater frequency in unidirectional genres. As we have seen, the more frequent occurrence of VL in genres like procedural discourse, briefing and service encounters can be linked to the speakers' focus on conveying information. It seems that discourse which is more information-oriented is also likely to contain *more* VL. When referring to facts and information, vague items are used for a number of reasons:

- They have a cohesive function, where the referent is specified in the cotext.
- The exact information may not be known.
- It is not necessary to be more explicit, because implicit reference conveys sufficient information, because of the knowledge shared by the discourse participants as members of the same professional discourse community (this is the most frequent use).

However, the greater frequency of VL in unidirectional discourse can also be linked to relational factors. Encounters involving unidirectional genres are always 'unequal' to a certain extent. At the very least there is a discursive imbalance in these genres, as one speaker always has a dominant role in controlling the discourse. Often, there is also a power imbalance, as many such encounters are between people of unequal status, for example manager–subordinate, customer–supplier. The risk of performing face-threatening acts is therefore higher than in collaborative discourse, where participants are on a more equal footing, at least discursively, even if they do not have an equal status. VL is therefore often used in such genres to mitigate potentially face-threatening acts. This function of VL is most evident in service encounters, where vague tags were noticeably frequent, most occurring during a meeting between a supplier and customer. This is a situation in which the risk of face threats is very great: there is a discursive imbalance (in favour of the supplier), as well as a power imbalance (in favour of the customer), and the cost of performing a face-threatening act is extremely high–the supplier may lose the customer's business. But, as most of these examples are from one particular encounter, it is of course important to be cautious with any generalizations.

VL can also be used with a different sort of relational function: to project solidarity and familiarity. Referring vaguely to items or categories means emphasizing the common ground that exists between the discourse participants, even if perhaps they do not know each other that well. This has the effect of making the discourse more friendly and informal, and allows discourse participants to reaffirm their existing relationship or establish familiarity in a new relationship.

All three types of VL are least frequent in non-transactional discourse (see Table 3.1). Vague categories and vague approximators are particularly infrequent here, as shown in Table 3.2.

Table 3.2 Frequency of vague languge in non-transactional genres in office conversations

Non-transactional genres	Density (frequency per thousand words)
Vague nouns	2.6
Vague categories	0.7
Vague approximators	0.2
Total density	3.5
Average density across corpus	5.5

Only vague nouns were fairly well represented (but still below average), probably owing to the relatively frequent occurrence of the informal vague referent 'stuff'. VL is usually considered to be a typical feature of informal, casual conversation (Chafe 1982; Powell 1992), therefore it is an unexpected finding that it occurred less frequently in the corpus during small-talk than work-oriented talk. It seems to contradict Overstreet and Yule's (1997b) finding that vague tags occurred more frequently in a corpus of informal compared to more formal spoken interaction.

However, this may also be due to a difference in classifying the data. Distinguishing between interactions simply in terms of formality, and not taking genre into account (which is the basis of the data classification here), may mean disregarding fundamental differences which can cut across such distinctions (Koester 2006). As the analysis shows, the occurrence of VL is not simply a question of formality or informality (in fact, none of the language in the corpus is very formal). The results for unidirectional genres seem to indicate that discourse which is information-focused and 'unequal' tends to contain more VL. The small-talk and office gossip in the corpus certainly does not fit into this category: it is not usually concerned with the transfer of information,[7] and the discursive roles tend to be equal.

Vague versus explicit language

What all the above examples demonstrate is that VL is a pervasive feature not just of casual conversation, but of much work-related talk as well. It is therefore interesting to ask when VL might *not* be appropriate: what kinds of situations require more precise and specific modes of expression?

An example from the corpus in which both vague and fairly explicit language is used may provide some clues here. As we saw in the above discussion, one of the reasons for using a vague tag is to show uncertainty about specific information. An example from a North American university office begins with such use of a vague category identifier. A young man, Ted, not a student himself, has just come into the office and is looking for a particular member of staff:

Example 19

Ted   Um . . . [5 seconds] Is there a list of . . . uhm . . . faculty assistants? [1 second] in <u>the handbook or something like that?</u> I need to try and /???/

Don   ⌊*No:*, there isn't a list in the *hand*book, I have a . . . typewritten list here,

It seems that Ted uses the vague category identifier 'in the handbook or something like that' because he is not sure whether he can find the information he is looking for in 'the handbook' or somewhere else (it turns out the information is on a typewritten list). Ted's use of VL here and his discourse throughout the conversation are symptomatic of someone who is not a member of the discourse community (he is not at the university himself) and therefore lacks the knowledge about and specific lexis of the organization. The rest of the discourse is characterized not by vagueness but by the extent to which the participants have to spell everything out. Ted's struggle to find the right word to designate the kind of person that he is looking for is a particularly good example of this:

Example 20

Ted   Ah . . . what about the um- you know the people that make ap*point*ments for people, the faculty . . . assistants, the um . . . uh-

Don   ⌊↑ Oh! I m- *those* are *se*cretaries.

Ted first uses a general noun, 'people', which he qualifies with the post-modifier 'that make appointments for people', and then attempts a more specific designation, 'faculty assistants', before Don supplies him with the appropriate word – 'secretaries'. Both the use of VL and the level of specificity chosen to designate referents are related to the information state of the speakers: they use such language to express lack of knowledge or to supply information the interlocutor lacks.

Therefore, one type of situation in which more explicit language is likely is when there is not much shared information between the discourse participants. Cutting's (1999, 2000) study of language in a developing discourse community demonstrates that implicit language increases over time.

Explicit language also sometimes occurs in the corpus in conversations between people who have a close working relationship. An interesting example is from the same university office, but this time between Don, and one of his co-workers, Andy. They are discussing how frequently they should check incoming applications. Don first makes a vague suggestion in turn 1, which he later reformulates much more explicitly (turn 5):

Example 21
1   Don   So I can do 'em . . . Let's say weekly. or something like
           that from here on out. I don't think it pays to do it any
           more often than that.
2   Andy   Well weekly, I mean you have to do it . . . [1.5] ah . . . more
           often than that right now, for this week an' next week,
           'cause we gotta- .hh . . . have 'em all entered into the system
           by a week on Friday.[1] so- any ones that are complete a-
3   Don   ⌊Yeah. but we're only talking about . . . a comparatively
           small number of *stray* . . . ⌊Andy: Yeah⌋ individual
           stray fo- you know you know you don't even *en*ter ↓ the
           individual letters an'- and transcripts do you? /. . ./
4   Andy   I'm holding off entering these- *this* week until they're
           complete. [3 seconds]
5   Don   Well then we'll check 'em at the end of this week or at the
           beginning of *next* week. that's what I'm *saying.*

In Don's initial suggestion in turn 1, he uses a hedge ('let's say') and a vague category identifier ('weekly or something like that'). His reformulation in turn 5, however, is much more explicit ('at the end of this week or at the beginning of next week'): not only does he not use VL or hedges, but he fully commits himself to the illocutionary force of his utterance by using metalanguage: 'that's what I'm saying'. According to Thomas (1984, p. 229) such 'metapragmatic comments' involve speakers commenting on 'the pragmatic force of his or her own utterance, thereby removing any polite ambivalence'.

Andy obviously understood what Don meant the first time, as he disagrees with his suggestion in turn 2. Therefore, the reason for Andy's more specific and explicit reiteration cannot be to clarify his initial utterance; but rather has to do with its function at that particular part of the encounter, where Andy and Don have been arguing about how often to do the task. The first proposal is made at a stage where the discourse has consisted of a simple exchange of information and consensus is assumed. It is thus made in a 'neutral' mode, whereas the reformulation is made within an argumentative, conflictual frame (Koester 2006).

This, and other examples in the corpus, indicate that very explicit language, particularly involving direct speech acts and metalinguistic devices, is typical of conflictual talk, but not of normal, consensual discourse between co-workers (Koester 2002, 2006). As discussed in Koester 2002, in cooperative discourse, the use of direct speech acts and metalanguage tends to be restricted to specific communicative functions, clarifying a misunderstanding, as in the following North American example:

Example 22
Yeah, I <u>understand</u> that. <u>What I mean</u> is /. . ./

Conclusion

This investigation into the frequency and function VL in a corpus of North American and UK workplace conversations shows that VL is not only a common occurrence in such interactions, but may even be the norm in interactions of many kinds. It performs a variety of important functions in discourse participants' transactional goals in getting the job done, and in building and maintaining workplace relationships. As the study was carried out on a relatively small corpus, the conclusions drawn from the findings must be seen as tentative. However, the findings are consonant with Channell's (1994 p. 196) conclusion that VL 'forms a considerable part of language use' and cannot be treated as 'the exception, rather than the rule'.

Applications of the findings

The received wisdom about VL is that it is 'sloppy', and reflects unclear thinking. Clearly this and other studies on VL (Channell 1994; Overstreet and Yule 1997a; Cutting 1999, 2000) demonstrate that this view does not reflect the way VL is actually used in naturally occurring interactions. This negative view of VL is also reflected in English language teaching, where the emphasis tends to be on 'correct grammar' and 'complete sentences'. While such an emphasis is often justifiable from a pedagogic and developmental point of view, it is nevertheless desirable for both teachers and students to recognize that VL makes up a considerable part of language use, even of business or work-oriented language. Whether native speaker fluency is the aim or not, language that is overly explicit can be inappropriate or even rude. This is particularly important for the teaching of Business English, as creating the wrong impression in business interactions can have serious consequences. Making learners aware of the relational functions of VL is of key importance here. As many of the above examples show, VL can convey subtle, but salient information about the speaker's attitude towards the interlocutor or the business at hand, and can be used strategically for politeness or solidarity. Successful use of such strategies can contribute towards a good business relationship, and ultimately successful business interactions.

Activities that teach students strategies for clarifying and checking information are quite common in TEFL, and such strategies are obviously useful. As illustrated in Example 22, one of the functions of explicit language is to perform exactly such a checking function. Activities could also be developed that encourage learners to find more vague, indirect or implicit ways of expressing information. Even for checking information, vague items such as vague tags can be useful devices (see Examples 8 and 19). But learners should also be made aware of some of the relational functions of VL for politeness and solidarity. A greater awareness of the form and functions of VL will give language learners a greater language repertoire to choose from in order to communicate in a variety of situations.

Directions for further research

Implications from the study point towards some directions for further research. The study indicates that VL plays an important role not only in informal casual talk, but also in workplace interactions. This suggests that spoken workplace discourse should be a rich area of further enquiry into the use and functions of VL.

Furthermore, the study also indicates that genre is a key factor influencing the frequency of VL (and many other interactive features of discourse). An examination of a variety of workplace genres could yield valuable insights into the genres that have a high density of VL, and those in which VL is infrequent, and thus contribute to our understanding of institutional and work-related discourse. It has been suggested here that a focus on facts and information results in an increase in VL. But is this also the case for other information-focused workplace and business genres, in particular more formal ones, such as business presentations? What about situations where the need for speed and accuracy would seem to discourage any discursive vagueness, for example on the factory floor or in certain medical situations? These are just a few examples of the types of genres and workplace contexts that might yield interesting and perhaps unexpected results about the use of VL.

Transcription conventions

,	slightly rising in intonation at end of tone unit
?	high rising intonation at end of tone unit
.	falling intonation at end of tone unit
!	animated intonation
. . .	noticeable pause or break within a turn of less than 1 second
-	sound abruptly cut off, for example false start
italics	emphatic stress
:	colon following vowel indicates elongated vowel sound
::	extra colon indicates longer elongation
↑	a step up in pitch (higher key[8])
↓	a shift down in pitch (lower key)
( )	parentheses around tone units spoken *sotto voce* (low-key intonation)
/ /	words between obliques show uncertain transcription
/?/	indicates inaudible utterances; one ? for each syllable
⌐	overlapping or simultaneous speech
⌐ ⌐	words in these brackets are utterances interjected by a speakers within another speaker's turn
=	latching: no perceptible inter-turn pause
[]	words in these brackets indicate non-linguistic information, for example pauses of 1 second or longer (the number of seconds is indicated), speakers' gestures or actions
/. . ./	ellipsis marks between obliques indicates that the speaker's turn continues, that the extract starts in the middle of a speaker turn, or that some turns have been omitted
.hh	inhalation (intake of breath)
hhh	aspiration (releasing of breath)
t°	tongue click
'Heheheh' indicates laughter; for each syllable laughed a 'heh' is transcribed	

Notes

1. The recorded and transcribed data were supplemented by field notes and interview data collected by the author using ethnographic methods (see Koester 2006).
2. Normalized rather than absolute frequencies are compared, as the non-transactional sub-corpus, with less than 5000 words, is much smaller than the two transactional sub corpora, unidirectional and collaborative discourse (which contain approximately 14,500 words each).
3. Significance was calculated using the chi-squared test: chi squared = 11.26318, degrees of freedom = 2, $p < 0.01$
4. All the data cited in the examples are the author's, except for Examples 7, 10 and 12, which are from the Cambridge International Corpus © Cambridge University Press. Some of the data examples were previously published in Koester 2000, 2002, 2004 and 2006. Transcription conventions are listed at the end of the chapter.
5. The Cambridge and Nottingham Corpus of Discourse in English
6. The Cambridge International Corpus was accessed by kind permission of Cambridge University Press.
7. Although non-transactional genres involve information inas much as they consist to a large extent of narratives, the focus is on the interest of such newsworthy events, rather than on specific facts.
8. The notion of 'key' is based on Brazil (1997).

References

D. Brazil, *The Communicative Role of Intonation in English* (Cambridge University Press, 1997).

P. Brown and S. Levinson, *Politeness: Some Universals in Language Use* (Cambridge University Press, 1987).

W. Chafe, 'Integration and Involvement in Speaking, Writing and Oral Literature', in D. Tannen (ed.), *Spoken and Written Language: Exploring Orality and Literacy* (Norwood, NJ.: Ablex, 1982).

J. Channell, *Vague Language* (Oxford University Press, 1994).

J. Cutting, 'The Grammar of the In-Group Code', *Applied Linguistics,* 20/2 (1999) 179–202.

J. Cutting, *Analysing the Language of Discourse Communities* (Oxford: Elsevier Science, 2000).

E. Dines, 'Variation in Discourse – "And Stuff Like That"', *Language in Society,* 9 (1980) 13–31.

P. Drew and J. Heritage (eds), *Talk at Work* (Cambridge Universtiy Press, 1992).

S. Eggins and D. Slade *Analysing Casual Conversation* (London: Cassell, 1997).

M.A.K. Halliday and R. Hasan, *Cohesion in English* (London: Longman, 1976).

R. Hasan, 'The Structure of a Text', in M.A.K. Halliday and R. Hasan, *Language, Context and Text: Aspects of Language in a Social-Semiotic Perspective* (Cambridge University Press, 1985), 52–69.

G. Jefferson, 'List Construction as a Task and Resource', in G. Psathas (ed.), *Interaction Competence* (Lanham, MD: University Press of America, 1990).

A. Koester, 'Getting Things Done and Getting Along in the Office', in M. Coulthard, J. Cotterill and F. Rock, (eds), *Dialogue Analysis VII: Working with Dialogue: Selected papers from the 7th IADA Conference, Birmingham 1999.* (Tübingen: Max Niemeyer, 2000) 197–207.

A. Koester, 'The Performance of Speech Acts in Workplace Conversations and the Teaching of Communicative Functions', *System*, 30/2 (2002) 167–84.

A. Koester, *The Language of Work* (London: Routledge, 2004).

A. Koester, *Investigating Workplace Discourse: Approaches to Analysing Spoken Interactions at Work* (London: Routledge, 2006).

R. Lakoff, 'Remarks on This and That', *Papers from the Tenth Regional Meeting of the Chicago Linguistics Society* (Chicago Linguistic Society, 1974). 345–356.

M. McCarthy, *Spoken Language and Applied Linguistics* (Cambridge University Press, 1998).

M. Overstreet and G. Yule, 'On Being Explicit and Stuff in Contemporary American English', *Journal of English Linguistics,* 25/3 (1997a) 250–8.

M. Overstreet and G. Yule, 'Locally Contingent Categorization in Discourse', *Discourse Processes,* 23 (1997b) 83–97.

M.J. Powell, 'Semantic/Pragmatic Regularities in Informal Lexis: UK Speakers in Spontaneous Conversational Settings', *Text,* 12/1 (1992) 19–58.

M. Scott, *Wordsmith Tools,* Version 3 (corpus analytical software suite), (Oxford University Press, 1999).

J. Thomas, 'Cross-Cultural Discourse as "Unequal Encounter": Towards a Pragmatic Analysis', *Applied Linguistics,* 5/3 (1984) 226–35.

4
Caught Between Professional Requirements and Interpersonal Needs: Vague Language in Healthcare Contexts

Svenja Adolphs, Sarah Atkins and Kevin Harvey

Vague language definitions: a brief introduction

Defining VL is a problematic endeavour, and VL is itself, arguably, a vague concept. A wide range of definitions exists, and the lexico-grammatical realizations and categories associated with VL vary considerably between researchers. For the purpose of this study, we adopt Channell's (1994) framework for describing and analysing VL, since it provides a systematic and rigorous description of VL used in real and varied contexts of communication, detailing how it is employed by real speakers and writers. Her framework has been applied effectively to a variety of contexts of interaction, ranging from studies into intercultural communication (Drave 2000) to adolescent talk (Stenstrom and Hasund 2002).

Channell (1994, p. 20) defines VL as language which 'can be contrasted with another word or expression which appears to render the same proposition' and which is 'purposely and unabashedly vague'. However, despite such a broad definition, the linguistic items Channell describes in her work form a closed set. Channell's work, moreover, is modelled on data which is taken typically from non-institutional contexts, and provides only limited fragments of healthcare interaction. Uncertainty, instantiated through the use of VL, particularly the use of hedges, is a typical feature of medical discourse (Bryant and Norman 1979; Prince *et al.* 1982; Varttala 1999; Sarangi and Clarke 2002). Consequently, in order to account for the character of our own data, we expand Channell's range of vague items to account for instances of language which, in the particular healthcare encounters that we investigate, take on a deliberately vague function and are a purposeful and characteristic feature of the discourse. Specifically, we include in hedges both 'approximators' and 'shields' (Prince *et al.* 1982), hedges which, respectively, signal a degree of fuzziness (Lakoff 1972) within utterances ('Her face was <u>somewhat</u> red') and hedges which signal speaker commitment to an utterance ('I <u>think</u> her face was red').

Health communication and VL

The need for effective communication between the health professional and the patient is of central importance to the health consultation. Channell (1994) highlights that any use of VL 'needs to be considered with reference to contexts and situations when it will be appropriate, or inappropriate' (p. 97). Several tensions emerge concerning the appropriateness of using VL in healthcare communication, illustrating the difficulty the healthcare professional faces in judging how best to deliver information about a patient's health. They must meet the institutional requirements of providing precise and clear information about a patient's medical problems and gaining precise understanding of a patient's symptoms, while at the same time they must elicit and deliver such medical information in a way that the patient can understand and not find unduly alarming.

Miscommunication and misinformation have been identified as key problems with healthcare communication (Kreps and Query 1990; Burnard 1997). Sontag (1991) for example argues against the mystification of illnesses, such as cancer and AIDs, through metaphoric explanation and encourages a 'truthful way of regarding illness', devoid of analogies and mystery (p. 97). Certainly the use of metaphor can be seen to create ambiguity and vagueness, 'hiding some features of the phenomena we apply them to and highlighting others' (Goatly 1997, p. 2) as well as creating more indirectness (Saville-Troike 1990, p. 34). In terms of presenting patients with a 'truthful' and clear account of their illness, therefore, the use of any vague and non-literal language would seem to be undesirable.

Nevertheless, in the health-professional–patient consultation, medical information, while it must be communicated accurately, must also be tailored to be understandable to the non-specialist patient (GMC 2001, p. 8). In an analysis of written medical research, Varttala (1999) finds that hedging devices which increase conceptual 'fuzziness' are used frequently in the popularization of medical research for the purpose of 'adjusting scientific information for a less scientific discourse community', thus meeting the interests of a non-specialist audience (p. 192). The use of hedges to this effect may therefore be particularly appropriate in the health-professional–patient interaction, in order to provide the patient with an account of their illness which is understandable.

Effective communication between health professionals and patients must also build 'relationships of trust' (GMC 2001, p. 8). The various stages of the medical consultation therefore, such as eliciting symptoms from the patient and delivering possible diagnoses, need to be conducted in a way that minimizes impositions and is non-threatening. Research by Channell (1994) highlights how VL can be used as a politeness strategy to minimize impositions on the other speaker as well as creating an informal, conversational atmosphere (pp. 190–1). The use of such VL items would therefore seem to be appropriate for the interpersonal communication required between the healthcare specialist and the patient. Indeed, a study of data from the NHS Direct phone-in, a 24-hour phone-in clinical advice service of the UK's National Health Service (Adolphs *et al.* 2004, p. 20), found that 'vagueness encoded by means of language items features prominently in the whole health professionals' corpus' and that this 'may serve as a deference strategy by softening the imposition on the caller and leaving room for elaboration or retraction from any particular question or suggestion'. In particular, the phrase 'or anything' featured frequently in the data, 'a vague expression mainly used as a tag question which again leaves room for a patient to add their own description of the situation' (Adolphs *et al.* 2004, p. 19). Here, then, is an example of VL performing two apparently conflicting needs, at once both being a marker of politeness and minimizing an imposition on the patient, but serving also as a strategy to elicit a fuller description of the patient's symptoms, thus fulfilling the institutional requirement of gathering all the necessary information on which to make a diagnosis.

However, the use of VL seems not only to benefit patients in terms of both interpersonal rapport with the health professional and ease of understanding of complex medical procedures and products. It may also be a misconception that medical communication, in terms of it being a scientific discourse, requires precise language. Prince *et al.* (1982) find that vagueness in medical discourse, in the form of hedging, features frequently and that this arises out of a professional, scientific need to express uncertainty within the medical subject-matter. They argue that this use of hedging by physicians 'demonstrates a scholarly orderliness in their representation of knowledge' (p. 96), rather than an undesirable imprecision. Many medical diagnoses and prognoses involve an inherent degree of uncertainty, especially with regards to diseases such as cancers that are still not wholly understood (Nicholson-Perry and Burgess 2002, p. 94). The language of the healthcare professional must necessarily reflect this degree of scientific uncertainty. There is perhaps a further institutional requirement placed upon the healthcare professional, therefore, to convey to the patient the uncertainty of some medical information through the use of VL items.

NHS Direct phone-ins and hospital-chaplain–patient interaction: two sites for analysing VL

Ultimately, just as the interpretations of what constitutes VL are many and varied, so too are the possible reasons for its use in the healthcare consultation context. As highlighted above, there are various contextual requirements acting at once that require different levels and types of VL from the healthcare professional.

The following analysis therefore looks at data from two quite different contexts of health-professional–patient interaction in an attempt to illustrate the range of VL items and their place in different healthcare contexts. The two contexts have been chosen because of the marked difference in requirements and goals associated with the respective interactions. The aim of this study is thus not to contrast the two data sets but to highlight the relationship between the prominent uses of VL and the institutional requirements of the discourse.

One set of data consists of the dialogue of NHS Direct phone-ins, where the institutional requirements from the health professionals are high in terms of the medical information they must obtain from the patient and the protocol they have to follow in the overall interaction. The other set of data consists of a series of conversations between patients and a hospital chaplain, where the requirements from the healthcare professional are to administer a spiritual and pastoral care rather than negotiate particular medical diagnoses and treatments. Though the chaplain might not be considered a health professional in the strict sense of someone who provides medical care, intervening in the physical treatment of patients, the chaplain is nevertheless an important figure in healthcare settings, responding to the spiritual and 'lifeworld' concerns of the patient (that is, the personal and social contexts of an individual's illness; see Mishler 1984). The chaplain's pastoral intervention is part of the total healthcare process – a unique social intervention which other professionals operating in healthcare are unlikely, if not unable, to provide. By analysing the healthcare discourse of NHS Direct practitioners and hospital chaplains, this study hopes to identify how the different contextual requirements of these two sets of interaction affect the use of VL.

The chaplain–patient discourse for this chapter was taken from data collected as part of a study into the communicative practices of spiritual and pastoral carers in healthcare (Harvey *et al.* unpublished MS). The data comprises a series of tape-recorded conversations between patients and a chaplain working from the Department of Spiritual and Pastoral Care located at a British hospital in the central region of England. The conversations were recorded in 2003 on various wards at the hospital. In order to obtain as authentic a discourse sample as possible, the data were taken from routine conversations conducted with patients in the course of the chaplain's regular spiritual and pastoral duties. The agreement of the hospital's ethics committee was obtained for the conduct of the study and subsequent publication. Other than obtaining patients' consent and providing them with an information sheet concerning the research, no other specific demands were made of the chaplain. He was, therefore, completely in charge of the data collection process and free to select whom to engage in recorded conversation.

The NHS Direct corpus was also collected in 2003, in collaboration with NHS Direct Nottingham. The corpus contains a range of caller interactions with NHS Direct health advisers and nurses (see Adolphs *et al.* 2004). It exceeds 60,000 words in total.

Our analysis below is based on samples of 1000 words from each of the two data sets. As such, it is qualitative in nature, aiming to highlight particular aspects of VL that seem pertinent to the different institutional contexts and requirements of the different situations, rather than attempting a comparative analysis.

Analysis: NHS Direct nurse–patient communication

Vague category identifiers

A particularly common phrase in the NHS direct data, observed by Adolphs *et al.* (2004), is the vague expression 'or anything', 'mainly used as a tag question which . . . leaves room for the patient to add their own description of the situation' (p. 19). For example, the following occurrences of 'or anything' can be noted within a few lines of each other in the data, at a stage where the health professional is attempting to elicit the patient's symptoms:

NHS Nurse: Er any intense headache or mental confusion or anything?
NHS Nurse: No shortness of breath or gasping for breath or anything?
NHS Nurse: And so there's no swelling anywhere to your face or anything?

These utterances are all of a similar formation and occur frequently throughout the NHS phone-ins. Typically they are clause-final, with the vague question taking the form of the health professional asking the patient if they have a particular symptom, often listing two similar symptoms, followed by a tag question, most commonly 'or anything?' Channell (1994) offers an analysis of this type of construction (exemplar followed by a tag), arguing that they direct 'the hearer to access a set, of which the given item is a member whose characteristics will enable the hearer to identify the set' (p. 122). These constructions are thus understood as designating a category encompassing a range of medical symptoms rather than a specific and discrete symptom, and the exemplar provided is 'understood to be a "good example" ' of that intended category (Channell 1994, p. 143). What particularly distinguishes these linguistic formations in the NHS Direct data is that often the NHS professional provides two exemplars rather than one, as in 'any intense headache or mental confusion'. These numerous binomials account for the frequency of the word 'or' in the data, the seventeenth most frequent word in the corpus. Adolphs *et al.* (2004) comment that these binomials 'add to the overall impression that the patient is being offered a range of possible scenarios' (p. 19). Specifically, the occurrence of such binominals signals categorical incompleteness, that the two symptoms listed are 'relevantly incomplete' (Jefferson 1990, p. 68) in that they do not exhaust the possible array of symptoms relevant to the medical assessment. As Jefferson (ibid.) points out, a third item (or, in this case, a third symptom) would not complete the list, the exhaustively wide and varied array of symptoms potentially experienced by or in some way relevant to the patient. Therefore, the occurrence of the vague category identifier 'or anything' indicates that it is not possible to list all the symptoms which might have been potentially experienced by the patient, with the effect of broadening the scope of the category. This, in turn, may encourage the patient to disclose symptoms which he or she might not otherwise have considered, nor thought relevant to the practitioner.

In the first example given above, 'any intense headache or mental confusion or anything', the patient is directed to understand this as a category of 'symptoms of ill health relating to the head and mental awareness'. The patient here is not simply asked to state whether they have a headache, or whether they are suffering from mental confusion, but directed to consider an entire category of symptoms similar to the two exemplars given. It is this that 'leaves room for the patient to add their own description of the situation' (Adolphs *et al.* 2004, p. 19), allowing them to describe how well their symptoms match the prototypical 'good examples' of the exemplars. Prompting information in this manner precludes the danger of the patient failing to provide what might be important information about their symptoms should they not display the prototypicality of the exemplars.

Categorization has long been thought to be an important cognitive process (Neisser 1987, p. 1). It is therefore 'not a surprise to discover that human language has several ways of referring to categories' (Channell 1994, p. 122), as in the ways outlined above. However, this does reveal an interesting feature of the way we conceptualize symptoms of illness, categorizing them rather generally, in terms either of parts of the body, such as the head, or of particular ailments, such as swelling.

However, it has also been suggested that this VL element, 'or anything', might serve as a deference strategy to reduce the imposition on the patient and also 'casualise the symptom reports so as to downgrade their seriousness' (Adolphs *et al.* 2004, p. 20). Indeed, Overstreet (1999) has emphasized that the referential and list-completing function of tags (what she calls 'general extenders') is not as important as their interpersonal function; she gives the example of speakers using them to mark an attitude towards hearers, specifically as a strategy of politeness and conversational cooperation. In the NHS Direct phone-ins it is certainly true that they seem to casualize the symptoms elicited, so as not to unduly alarm the patient. However, the fact these forms do not occur with the same high frequency in the chaplain–patient interactions suggests they are fulfilling a particular institutional objective in the elicitation of symptoms, as well as the more interpersonal politeness functions suggested above.

Softening potentially distressing subjects and mitigating demands on the patient

The dual functions of reducing the imposition on the patient and not alarming them unduly are often hard to distinguish between, in many of the health-professional–patient interactions, and without the input of the speakers themselves these functions are perhaps impossible to distinguish.

However, there is noticeable use of VL by healthcare professionals in the data when they are required to elicit or provide information which might be distressing for the patient, which would seem to suggest that it performs the function of reducing anxiety for the patient. This is particularly clear in the following NHS Direct example,[*] in which the nurse

---

[*] See transcription conventions at the end of the chapter.

must ask the patient about meningitis symptoms, leading to a potentially very dangerous diagnosis:

NHS Nurse: Cos we have to <u>kind of</u> un = we <\$=> We always do <u>like</u> the worst case scenario and work downwards.
Patient: All right. <$E> laughs <$E> Okay.
NHS Nurse: We always like look at the <u>meningitis type symptoms</u> first +
Patient: Yeah.
NHS Nurse: + okay and then we work downwards. So just bear with me.

The use of 'kind of' and 'like' makes the nurse's reference to meningitis less marked and in fact meningitis itself is not even mentioned within this speaker turn as the illness being considered. It is only in the following turn, after the nurse has elicited an 'All right' response from the patient (followed by laughter), that the name 'meningitis' is given. Even here, this is described vaguely as 'meningitis type symptoms'. The laugh and acceptances of 'All right' and 'Okay' elicited from the patient illustrate how the nurse's VL use works to make seriousness of this 'worst case scenario' tolerable for the patient. Thus we can see VL being used as a softening device to tone down the alarming nature of possible medical diagnoses. Only when the nurse is happy that the patient is comfortable discussing the possible 'worst case scenario' is diagnosis more precisely described as meningitis.

Chaplain–patient interaction

Before examining examples of chaplain–patient exchanges and the function of VL in them, it is necessary to outline the role of the healthcare chaplain and the communicative context in which spiritual and pastoral care operates. The primary function of the hospital chaplain is to meet the spiritual and religious needs of the healthcare community, which comprises patients, visitors and staff. Chaplains have to respond to a wide range of spiritual and pastoral requirements – to patients of particular faiths as well as to patients who do not profess any particular faith (Department of Health 2003). According to the Department of Health (2003, p. 5), the work of the chaplain, in meeting the spiritual and religious needs of patients, is fundamental to the care provided by the NHS.

Though an official framework exists for meeting the religious and spiritual needs of patients, it is a non-prescriptive, guidance-only document, encouraging flexible and innovative responses to the provision of chaplaincy spiritual care for patients. Consequently, concerning the actual day-to-day work of chaplaincy, the framework is relaxed, recommending, without defining or elaborating on, 'good communication'. Yet chaplaincy is a verbal practice, enacted through face-to-face communication with patients at their hospital bedsides. Chaplains encourage patients to disclose their anxieties and fears, to share feelings with someone who is not actively concerned with their medical treatment and care. The chaplain helps patients to understand and make sense of what is happening to them and, therefore, chaplaincy discourse is characteristically exploratory and non-programmatic (unlike many other institutional practitioner–patient encounters, such as GP consultations, which typically follow an 'ideal sequence' (ten Have 1989). Such an open format provides the patient with a significant degree of interactional space and freedom to discuss not only spiritual and religious issues and matters concerning medical treatment, but also social and emotional issues, talk salient to their own world of experience (Ribeiro 1996). As Cobb (2001) observes, the role of the chaplain exists primarily in relationships with patients, which in turn is accomplished in and through supportive talk and sympathetic hearing on the part of the spiritual practitioner (Harvey *et al.* forthcoming).

Communication, in short, is essential to chaplaincy spiritual care – to the emotional and interpersonal relationship between practitioner and patient, and to patient satisfaction. However, for chaplaincy practitioners, 'good (or appropriate) communication' is not linguistically, institutionally or otherwise defined. Therefore, when engaged in routine interaction with patients, chaplains have to depend on their own conversational strategies, using a personal repertoire of communicative practices without recourse to formal or institutional specifications. Consequently, in order to respond to the interactional and interpersonal demands of conversing with patients, chaplains are likely to deploy discursive practices from other genres of communication, typically counselling and therapy genres. However, the chaplain does have a formal institutional role to play and institutional goals to meet, both of which are accomplished through talk. To meet such requirements, the chaplain has to initiate interactional sequences and inevitably display a degree of conversational control. Yet such a demand necessarily produces a tension for the chaplain since he or she has to fulfil these institutional obligations while, at the same time, establishing and maintaining an empathetic, client-centred relationship with the patient, a relationship whose uniqueness relies upon closeness and informality through the chaplain's being independent of medical authority. It is not surprising, therefore, in managing this tension (and given the chaplain's relative autonomy) that chaplaincy spiritual discourse is underpinned by a pervasive reliance on ordinary informal conversation (Harvey *et al.* unpublished MS). Since an important feature of the vocabulary of informal conversation is lack of precision (Crystal and Davy 1975), one significant and recurring communicative provision deployed by the chaplain to get institutional work done, and to help construct a close emotional rapport with the patient, is the use of VL. The following extract reveals how the chaplain interactionally manages the activity of eliciting personal patient disclosure (necessarily a face-threatening task) while developing and maintaining a relaxed, supportive and intimate conversational atmosphere:

1	Chaplain:	You were saying that you were er feeling a bit bored today.
2	Patient:	<$G?>that's right yeah.
3	Chaplain:	Uh uh.
4	Patient:	Because it's pretty boring in the hospi=
5	Chaplain:	Yeah. <$=> Just lying in in in the <\$=>
6	Patient:	Bed fed up
7	Chaplain:	Uh hu yeah.
8		<$E> silence <\$E>
9	Chaplain:	<$=> You finding it a bit frustrating to be <\$=>
10	Patient:	Yeah because I had a stroke.
11	Chaplain:	Yes.
12	Patient:	That makes it a lot worse.
13	Chaplain:	Yes uh uh.
14	Chaplain:	Would you be able to tell me a little bit about how that affects
15		you? How having this+
16	Patient:	<$G?>
17	Chaplain:	+having had this stroke affects you?
18	Patient:	<$G?> It affects in just about everything honest.
19	Chaplain:	Yeah.
20	Patient:	I can't talk properly <$G?> <$H> speech got brain damage
21		<\$H> so I can't explain just like that.
22	Chaplain:	Yes uh uh. I understand. But it has always seemed to me that
23		you you you explain things very well.
24	Patient:	Oh if you say so <$E> laughs <\$E>
25	Chaplain:	Uh hu. Yeah.
26	Patient:	I try to+

27   Chaplain: Yes.
28   Patient: +explain as best I can.
29   Chaplain: Uh hu.
30   Patient: <$G?>
31   Chaplain: Yes.
32   Patient: See what happens.
33   Chaplain: Yes.

The exchange commences with the chaplain sensitively encouraging the patient to discuss his feelings in relation to the effects of his illness and his recent time spent in hospital. Of significance is the chaplain's use of the vague quantifier 'a bit' which is consistently deployed (lines 1, 9, 14) throughout the dialogue, helping to construct and maintain an informal tone of interaction. In line 1, 'a bit' is used adverbially to qualify the adjective 'bored', a modification which serves to reduce the negative assessment previously provided by the patient (though not recorded on tape by the chaplain). The chaplain, in fact, reformulates the patient's prior negative assessment of his day in hospital, packaging the utterance as a 'subjective expression' (Stubbs 1986, p. 3) of the patient's belief – therewith drawing attention to, and involving, the patient as the source of the original formulation: '<u>You were saying</u> that you were feeling a bit bored today.' In encouraging the patient to comment on its relevance and accuracy, the chaplain's reformulation provokes a more specific dis-closure and qualification from the patient (even if, owing to physical dif-ficulties with speech production, his turns at talk are somewhat restricted).

In line 9, 'a bit' is also used adverbially to quantify the extent of the frustration experienced by the patient. According to Channell (1994, p. 110), the adverbial use of 'a bit', when modifying an adjective for instance, is arguably non-vague since the qualification adds a degree of precision to the proposition so modified. Therefore, the alternative for-mulation of 'you finding it frustrating to be' would be propositionally less precise than the chaplain's actual 'you finding it a bit frustrating to be', which specifies a degree of experience and feeling. However, here the chaplain's use of the quantifier is principally interpersonal, func-tioning as a pragmatic device rather than as a semantic adjustment. Without the quantifier, the chaplain's utterance would be more emphatic, the illocutionary force significantly stronger. Attenuating the force of the speech act, quantifying the patient's feeling of frustration as 'a bit' rather than as unrestricted (and therefore bolder, more extensive) frustration, thus works to mitigate the possible distress the patient might feel in discussing his experiences by lessening the sense of their severity. While this almost appears as a severe understatement concerning the patient's emotional and physical response to his stroke, and potentially risks sounding meiotic, lessening the sense of severity of this emotion nevertheless appears to help the patient to talk about it with the chaplain (as the reformulation in line 1 helped engender further patient disclosures).

The use of 'a bit' also functions as a deference strategy, a marker to indicate that the chaplain does not wish to make bold assumptions and assertions about the patient's feelings or intrude too much into his private matters. In line 14, as part of the process of eliciting further personal and potentially painful, face-threatening disclosures from the patient, the vague formulation 'a little bit' in the chaplain's directive here serves to attenuate the request by minimizing the task of the directive speech act (Holmes 1984, p. 361). The demand on the patient to provide detailed personal information about the effects of his stroke is softened, allowing the patient the option to provide only as much information as he feels able to disclose.

Talking figuratively about illness

A particularly interesting interaction in the chaplain–patient data is a discussion with a patient who has undergone an amputation. In talking about how the amputation has affected the patient, the chaplain refers to the matter indirectly, through the concept of 'freedom'.

Patient: Be <u>free</u>.
Chaplain: Be <u>free?</u>
Patient: Yeah. <$E> silence <$E> To do what you want.
Chaplain: Uh hu. You mean yourself now?
Patient: Yeah.
Chaplain: Yeah?
Patient: Yeah.
Chaplain: Are you saying that being in hospital for you <$=> being in hospital now </$=> and for what you have gone through does that help you to be <u>free?</u>
Patient: No. I <$G?> even been in hospital <$G?> my freedom. I've not got the same <u>freedom.</u>
Chaplain: Yes. I understand. Yes.
Patient: You understand what I mean?
Chaplain: You don't have the same <u>freedom</u> now as you had before?
Patient: Yeah. Yeah.

The leg amputation and the fact that the patient will now have much less mobility are not overtly mentioned but discussed under this notion of 'freedom.' The patient desires to 'be free' and complains that staying in hospital and undergoing an amputation is restrictive: 'I've not got the same freedom.' However, the discussion of 'freedom' encompasses a broader, symbolic meaning than the literal freedom to walk. It acts as metaphor for how the patient feels that this medical treatment has affected life in general and the ability 'to do what you want'. This concept has to be carefully negotiated, with frequent questions by the chaplain in order for them to understand each other. It is only after this rather indirect reference to amputation that the they go on to talk more directly about walking, but even here it is about how the patient used to enjoy walking, and not directly about the current situation.

Discussion

The different data sets exemplify differences in terms of institutional requirements. The NHS Direct health professional has to elicit information from the patient in order to be able to prescribe a particular course of action. The chaplain, on the other hand, has to build up a relationship with the patient in order to provide spiritual support. The use of VL in the chaplaincy data is an important part of the chaplain's sensitive, informal management of the interaction, helping to facilitate the patient's conversational involvement, while mitigating the force of directives to such supply personal information. At the same time, it decreases the social distance between the speaker and hearer since, and by attenuating the force of an unpleasant speech act such as a request for potentially distressing information, the chaplain communicates positive feelings towards the hearer which helps to boost the solidarity of the relationship (Holmes 1984, p. 350).

The nurse's use of VL in the NHS Direct data adds a degree of tentativeness while still providing the patient with a clear idea of the serious nature of the topic she is attempting to broach. Given her intention to not alarm the patient, such tentativeness is understandable. However, the instances of VL in the NHS Direct data also help to maintain the relaxed atmosphere. As Aijmer (1984, p. 124) observes, vague elements such as 'kind of' function to prevent speakers from sounding too imposingly expert. Here the nurse prevents herself from sounding too technical and authoritarian, while contributing to the informal tone of the interaction. In short, the use of VL by the nurse allows her to establish an interpersonal relationship with the patient, while pursuing the necessarily intrusive institutional requirements of eliciting personal and sensitive responses.

One further reason for the differences in VL used in the two data sets might be related to the mode of interaction. The fact that the NHS Direct consultations are service encounters which are conducted by phone could be responsible for the higher level of VL in the elicitation process. Much of the information elicited by the nurse is linked to the physical appearance of a particular symptom, and the patient themselves, and the nurse's lack of the situational context to see it for himself or herself may be the cause of the VL. However, further research into the effect of the physical distance between speakers on the interaction is needed to confirm such hypotheses.

Application

There is a considerable need to train health professionals whose first language is not English in the use of communication skills relevant to the contexts of healthcare. The urgency of a global training programme for non-native speakers of English which focuses on successful communication in health contexts is further reinforced by projections according to which a considerable percentage of NHS staff will soon be non-native speakers of English (Grice 2004). Furthermore, there is now greater emphasis generally on language and communicative efficiency in the NHS, with communications skills programmes forming part of the initial training and continuing professional development of healthcare practitioners. However, current communications training in healthcare often relies on the pedagogies of fifty years ago. Training typically consists of a mixture of formal lectures, role-playing exercises and on-the-job observation of more experienced practitioners. Communication skills training materials (and corresponding lectures) typically make use of invented samples of spoken interaction that illustrate a theoretical insight or teaching point. These idealized, non-naturally occurring samples of language fail to reproduce important elements of everyday interaction (such as hesitations, false starts and VL use). As this study has sought to show, VL is not merely a symptom of disfluency or communicative uncertainty but strategically motivated by the goal of interactional convergence.

The use of real-life data in communication training offers a more fully evidenced-based and authentic approach to language use in different healthcare settings (Adolphs *et al.* 2004; Brown *et al.* 2003). It exposes learners to common features of discourse present in routine healthcare encounters, enabling them to explore its function. It also reproduces the contextual, institutional tensions and complexities which are inherent in professional–patient communication. Despite its significant function in managing tensions and minimizing impositions, VL is one neglected component of healthcare interaction. We argue that both native and non-native English-speaking practitioners might benefit from a practical knowledge and understanding of VL in naturally occurring everyday healthcare interaction. They could be trained to look closely at how participants produce meaningful actions (for example: requests for information, descriptions and listing of symptoms, diagnoses, and the provision of emotional support) and how participants interpret and respond to each other's meaning (Drew *et al.* 2001). Ultimately such an approach to the study of communication is able to assess whether a specific intervention or outcome has been successfully realized.

Conclusion

Our study has highlighted the differences in the use of VL between two diverse healthcare settings. We have shown how the institutional requirements influence the choice of VL items, and how VL facilitates the goals of the interactions. VL use has implications for the communications training of healthcare personnel. However, further research on more data and on more diverse healthcare settings is needed to gain a better understanding of the role of VL in health communication; VL is at the heart of the tension between interpersonal needs and institutional requirements.

Transcription conventions

<$=> . . . </$>	Unfinished sentence, repeat, or false start.
<$E> . . . </$E>	Transcriber's comments.
<$H> . . . </$H>	Guess.
<$G?>	Unintelligible.
=	Unfinished word or single letter.
+	Interrupted sentence.

Acknowledgement

We are grateful to Ronald Carter for comments on an earlier draft of this chapter.

References

S. Adolphs, B. Brown, R. Carter, C. Crawford, and O. Sahota, 'Applying Corpus Linguistics in a Health Care Context', *Journal of Applied Linguistics,* 1/1 (2004) 9–28.

K. Aijmer, ' "Sort of" and "Kind of" in English Conversation', *Studia Linguistica,* 38 (1984) 118–28.

B. Brown, P. Crawford and C. Hicks, *Evidence-Based Research: Dilemmas and Debates in Health Care* (Maidenhead, UK: Open University Press, 2003).

G.D. Bryant and G.R. Norman, 'The Communication of Uncertainty', in *Proceeding: Eighteenth Annual Conference on Research in Medical Education* (Washington, DC: Association of American Medical Colleges, 1979) p. 205–7.

P. Burnard, *Effective Communication Skills for Health Professionals,* 2nd edn (Cheltenham: Nelson Thornes, 1997).

J. Channell, *Vague Language* (Oxford: Oxford University Press, 1994).

M. Cobb, 'Walking on Water? The Moral Foundations of Chaplaincy', in H. Orchard (ed.), *Spirituality in Health Care Contexts* (London and Philadelphia, PA: Jessica Kingsley, 2001).

D. Crystal and D. Davy, *Advanced Conversational English* (London: Longman, 1975).

Department of Health, *NHS Chaplaincy: Meeting the Religious and Spiritual Needs of Patients and Staff* (London, 2003).

P. Drew, J. Chatwin and S. Collins, 'Conversation Analysis: A Method for Research into Interactions between Patients and Health Care Professionals', *Health Expectations,* 4 (2001) 58–70.

N. Drave, 'Vaguely Speaking: A Corpus Approach to Vague Language in Intercultural Conversations', in P. Peters, P. Collins and A. Smith (eds), *Language and Computers: New Frontiers of Corpus Research. Papers from the Twenty-First International Conference of English Language Research and Computerised Corpora* (Amsterdam: Rodopi, 2000) p. 25–40.

A. Goatly, *The Language of Metaphors* (London: Routledge, 1997)

GMC (General Medical Council) *Good Medical Practice,* 3rd edn (London: GMC, 2001).

A. Grice, *Everyday English for Nursing* (London: Baillière Tindall, 2004).

K. Harvey, P. Crawford, B. Brown and S. Candlin. ' "Elicitation Hooks": A Discourse Analysis of Chaplain–Patient Interaction in Pastoral and Spiritual Care' (forthcoming).

J. Holmes, 'Modifying Illocutionary Force', *Journal of Pragmatics,* 8/3 (1984) 345–65.

G. Jefferson, 'List Construction as a Task and Resource', in G. Psathas (ed.) *Interaction Competence* (Lanham, MD: University Press of America, 1990).

G.L. Kreps and J.L. Query, 'Health Communication and Interpersonal Competence', in G.M. Phillips and J.T. Woods (eds), *Speech Communication: Essays to Commemorate the 75th Anniversary of the Speech Communication Association* (Carbondale: Southern Illlinois University Press, 1990).

G. Lakoff, 'Hedges: A Study in Meaning Criteria and the Logic of Fuzzy Concepts', *Proceedings of the Chicago Linguistic Society,* 8 (1972) 183–228.

E. Mishler, *The Discourse of Medicine: Dialectics of Medical Interviews* (Norwood, NJ: Ablex Publishing Company, 1984).

U. Neisser (ed.), *Concepts and Conceptual Development: Ecolological and Intellectual Bases of Categorization* (New York: Cambridge University Press, 1987).

K. Nicholson-Perry and M. Burgess, *Communication and Cancer Care* (Malden, MA: BPS Blackwell, 2002).

M. Overstreet, *Whales, Candlelight, and Stuff Like That: General Extenders in English Discour* (Oxford, New York: Oxford University Press, 1999).

E.F. Prince, J. Frader and C. Bosk, 'On Hedging in Physician–Physician Discourse', in R. di Pietro (ed.), *Linguistics and the Professions. Proceedings of the Second Annual Delaware Symposium on Language Studies* (Norwood, NJ: Ablex Publishing Corporation, 1982) p. 83–97.

T.B. Ribeiro, 'Conflict Talk in a Psychiatric Discharge Interview', in C.R. Caldas-Coulthard and M. Coulthard (eds), *Texts and Practices: Readings in Critical Discourse Analysis* (London: Routledge, 1996).

S. Sarangi and A. Clarke, 'Zones of Expertise and the Management of Uncertainty in Genetics Risk Communication', *Research on Language and Social Interaction,* 35 (2002) 139–71.

M. Saville-Troike, *The Ethnography of Communication,* 2nd edn (Oxford: Blackwell, 1990).

S. Sontag, *Illness as Metaphor: AIDS and Its Metaphors* (London: Penguin, 1991).

A-B Stenstrom and I.K. Hasund, *Trends in Teenage Talk: Corpus Compilation, Analysis and Findings* (Amsterdam: Benjamins, 2002).

M. Stubbs, ' "A Matter of Prolonged Fieldwork": Notes Towards a Modal Grammar of English', *Applied Linguistics,* 7/1 (1986) 1–25.

P. ten Have, 'The Consultation as a Genre', in B. Torode (ed.), *Text and Talk as Social Practice* (Dordrecht: Foris, 1989).

T. Varttala, 'Remarks on the Communicative Functions of Hedging in Popular Scientific and Specialist Research Articles on Medicine', *English for Specific Purposes,* 18/2 (1999) 177–200.

5

'Well Maybe Not Exactly, but It's Around Fifty Basically?': Vague Language in Mathematics Classrooms

Tim Rowland

It may come as something of a surprise to find a mathematician (albeit in the guise of a mathematics educator) writing about vagueness, since it is commonly supposed that precision is the hallmark of mathematics. Such a point of view is reflected in the landmark 1982 Report of the Committee of Inquiry into the Teaching of Mathematics in Schools (the *Cockcroft Report*), which asserted that, 'mathematics provides a means of communication which is powerful, concise and unambiguous' (Department of Education and Science 1982, p. 1), and proposed the communicative power of mathematics as a 'principal reason' for teaching it. There was refreshing novelty in such a claim, which seemed to be justifying the place of mathematics in the curriculum in much the same way that one might justify the learning of a foreign language, and it did much to promote and sustain interest in the place of language in the teaching and learning of mathematics. Such a view of mathematics is in contrast, however, with that expressed in a contemporary pamphlet issued by the Association of Teachers of Mathematics (ATM 1980, pp. 17–18), whose authors argued that:

> Because it is a tolerant medium, everyday language is necessarily ambiguous. /. . ./ Now, mathematising is also a form of action in the world. And its expressions, however carefully defined, have to retain a fundamental tolerance /. . ./ Because it is a tolerant medium, mathematics is also necessarily an ambiguous one.

This description emphasizes mathematics as human activity, and language as a social means of working towards mutual understanding and agreement. Furthermore, it offers the radical proposal that ambiguity is a beneficial ingredient in the formulation, the 'expression', of mathematics. As a 'product' (polished, final), mathematics may be presented, particularly in writing but also in speech, as though it lacked ambiguity, representing truths about the world – or at the very least, about itself – in a sure, exact and unequivocal kind of way. By contrast, the 'process' of mathematics production ('mathematizing') is characterized by a number of forms of vagueness.

Consider the following brief episode from a mathematics lesson in a secondary school. The teacher, Judith, is working with a class of 13- to 14-year-old pupils, who have marked a number of dots (points) on paper. The pupils' task is to connect them, by drawing line segments joining two points. They are asked, 'What is the smallest number of segments necessary to join all of the points?' It is rather like a cluster of towns and a network of roads that joins them all. One pupil, Allan, starts with a 3×3 array of dots, and counts eight line segments. Judith enquires:

Judith: All right then, so what're you going to do now?

Allan: I'll try a, um, 4 by 4 grid.

Judith: Right. Can you make any predictions before you start? (3 seconds' pause)

Allan: The maximum will probably be, er, the least'll probably be about 15.

Judith: So why did you predict 15?

Allan: Uh . . . because I thought there might be a pattern between . . . if there was um a certain amount of, um . . . if it's 3 by 3 say . . .

Judith: Uh-hum.

Allan: If you ti-, 3 times 3 is actually 9.

Judith: Uh-hum.

Allan: But as, if you went round all the dots, it would only come to about, if you did it once it would come to one, uh less than 9, 'n' you got, uh, because, because there's o-, there's only . . . 'cause you only have, y- . . . you can miss out a line exactly, 'cause you, you can miss out a gap, c- 'cause you um, y'd 'ave to go all the way round the whole dots.

Judith: OK . . . So why did that make you say 15?

Allan: Because uh, f- for the same reason, 'cause if you um w- tried to go round the whole all the dots you'd get 16 but if you just did it once all the way round the dots but missing out gaps you'd still come to uh, you just minus one basically and just . . .

Judith: So what would happen in some other squares?

Allan: Probably if you minus one from the s-, if you square the num-
        ber you'd probably find that if it was actually, if you minus
        one from that you'd probably find that that would be the
        answer.

Allan would hardly win a prize for clarity or precision or conciseness,
nor for the elegance of his mathematical articulation. His utterances are
fragmented throughout, and when he is asked to generalize to 'some
other squares', he invokes 'probably' three times. It requires some effort
to make sense of what he is trying to tell Judith. We might infer that
Judith is working hard towards the same end. Many teachers find the
'lust' to clarify and explain irresistible, but Judith's contributions are
limited to requests for Allan to explain his reasoning, and to assurances
that she is listening to his answers ('uh-hum'). She does not attempt to
correct or improve Allan's expression of his thinking. Again, we might
infer that Judith believes that there is something to be gained by
encouraging Allan to struggle to use language as he progresses towards
articulating the generalization in the last of his utterances above.

A personal and contextual note

Research in mathematics education seeks to improve the teaching and
learning of mathematics, and to understand better the various contexts
and conditions within which they take place. For many years, my
research focused on learners. My principal method was the 'clinical
interview', devised and developed by Piaget (1929). 'Clinical' is a reference to the origins of the method in Freudian psychoanalysis. I used a
version of the clinical interview (Ginsburg 1997) in which the interviewer offers a task to the participant, and encourages them to talk
aloud as they respond to it.

   When I began this research, my aim was located in mathematics education: to access and describe the mathematical frameworks and private
constructions locked away in the minds of learners. My concern was to
uncover what they 'knew', and how they structured that knowledge. In
other words, I began with my attention focused on what Brown and Yule
(1983) call the 'transactional' functions of language, that is 'that function
which language serves in the expression of content' (p. 1). I had no
explicit knowledge and little awareness of VL as a linguistic phenomenon. However, close examination of the transcripts of these clinical
interviews drew me towards the tentative, provisional character of many
of the participants' utterances, and in time I came to recognize their

inherent vagueness. My focus shifted towards the ways that they used language to communicate 'propositional attitude' (Russell 1919, Jaszczolt 2000; Rowland 2004), and thus to 'interactional' functions of language (Brown and Yule 1983, p. 3). My awareness of these pragmatic language dimensions was first prompted by the participants' use of the 'hedges' that are the principal theme of this chapter. Allan's last utterance above is an example of hedging; he uses 'probably' to convey the fact that his commitment to the stated generalization is less than complete.

The emergence of VL in mathematical situations involving the articulation of a 'generalization' is significant, although vagueness has no place in the official register of mathematical generalization. Generalization is a case of inductive reasoning that is recognizing what a number of particular cases have in common. Inductive reasoning takes the thinker beyond the evidence, by somehow discovering by generalization some additional knowledge inside themselves. No wonder, then, that it entails not only creative satisfaction, but uncertainty too. In this chapter, I shall describe and analyse some ways in which this uncertainty is coded in spoken language, with reference to a mathematical study carried out with children aged 10 and 11, drawing attention to the presence of a vagueness in the mathematical discourse, and showing how it served the pragmatic purposes of the speakers.

Hedges

Some recent[1] approaches to the problem of vagueness within the field of linguistics originate in consideration of the meaning and function of a class of words and phrases called 'hedges'. These include words such as 'sort of', 'about' and 'approximately', which have the effect of blurring category boundaries or otherwise precise measures, as well as words and phrases such as 'I think', 'maybe' and 'perhaps', which hedge the commitment of the speaker to that which she or he asserts. The work of Zadeh (1965) and Goguen (1969) laid the foundation for fuzzy interpretation of VL, setting the scene for work by Lakoff (1973, p. 471), who concluded that:

> one need not throw up one's hands in despair when faced by the problems of vagueness and fuzziness. Fuzziness can be studied seriously within formal semantics /. . ./ For me some of the most interesting questions are raised by the study of words whose meaning implicitly involves fuzziness - words whose job is to make things fuzzier or less fuzzy. I will refer to such words as 'hedges'.

While much of Lakoff's paper is taken up with technical details in mathematical logic, he begins from and frequently returns to the issue of the meaning of VL in use.

Hedges can be usefully separated into four basic types. This observation was initially made in a study (Prince *et al.* 1982) of paediatric clinicians, whose spoken language in case conferences turned out to be unusually rich in hedging. The following representative examples of physician–physician talk (ibid., p. 85) have an authentic ring to them:

> Well, I think he's uh – I think he's always se- I still think he's seizing a- a little bit.
> There is evidence that's been presented that makes me think that it might be a little risky.

The first major type of hedge, a 'shield', is exemplified in Prince *et al.* (1982) by 'Well. I think that . . . ' and 'There is evidence that's been presented . . . '. These indicate some uncertainty in the mind of the speaker in relation to some proposition. The marker (such as 'I think that') lies outside the proposition itself, which may be unequivocal. Prince *et al.* subdivide shields into two kinds. The first of these is termed a 'plausibility shield', typified by 'I think', 'probably' and 'maybe'. The second kind type of shield involves attribution of information to some third party, specified or unspecified. A favourite 'attribution shield' with the clinicians, with evident attendant suspicion, was 'According to the mother . . . '

The second major category of hedge, an 'approximator', includes 'about' and 'a little bit'. In distinction to shields, these approximator hedges are located inside the proposition itself. The effect is to modify, as opposed to comment on, the proposition, making it more vague. A sub-category of approximators – called 'rounders' – consists of the standard adverbs of estimation, such as 'about', 'around' and 'approximately', which are commonplace in the domain of measurements and quantitative data. Another type of approximator is called an 'adaptor'. These words or phrases, such as 'a little bit', 'somewhat' and 'sort of', attach vagueness to nouns, verbs or adjectives associated with class membership. These adaptors exemplify the hedges which are the subject of Lakoff's semantic work (1973), and the issue here is class membership.

The notion of 'conversational implicature' (Grice 1975) offers illuminating insights into the semantics associated with each of these hedge types. Briefly, Grice proposed that ordinary conversation is posited on a 'cooperative principle', embodied in four 'maxims' of conversation, which specify what participants need to do in order to converse rationally and cooperatively. The requirements are, essentially:

- 'Maxim of Quality': let your contribution be truthful: do not say what you believe to be false.
- 'Maxim of Quantity': let your contribution be as informative as is required (for the current purposes), and not more informative than is required.
- 'Maxim of Manner': let your contribution be clearly expressed – for example be brief, orderly, unambiguous.
- 'Maxim of Relevance': let your contribution be relevant to the matter in hand.

Grice proposed that while speakers do not always observe the maxims at the surface level, hearers interpret the contributions of other participants in conversation as if they were intended to observe the maxims at some level of meaning other than that contained in the truth-semantic content of the utterance. 'Conversational implicature' is rather like a hint. Speakers are either overtly cooperative because they observe the maxims, or else they are covertly cooperative by ostentatiously breaching or, as Grice puts it, 'flouting' the maxims.

Hedges can flout the maxims of manner or quantity, or both, and thereby imply some deficiency or lack of precision in the speaker's knowledge, or some doubt that what is being claimed will be fulfilled by events or stand up to evidential scrutiny. With the hedge, the speaker indicates that they are not being as clear as they might have hoped. For example, a man who says that his wife's dress size is 'around 12 or 14' is neither sufficiently informative nor adequately unambiguous for someone wanting to buy her a dress for her birthday. On the other hand, it cautions them to ask someone else. Hedges enable the speaker to observe the maxim of quality.

'Make ten'

I now proceed to an account of my study with twenty 10- and 11-year-old children. I chose to work with them on a task – I call it 'Make Ten' – that required them to predict, generalize and explain. Each interview was with two children. I began by asking them for two numbers (such as 3 and 7) whose sum is 10. Typically, they offered me several such pairs. I then asked them in how many ways 10 can be 'made' as a sum of two numbers. In most of the interviews the children listed all the possible sums, orally or on paper, and then counted them. Then I would say something like:

> Now, just as you eventually decided about that question for 10, I'd like you to decide between you how many different ways are there of doing that for 20?

I then proposed other numbers to be 'made' in this way, my choices depending, in keeping with the essential contingency of the clinical interview, on the children's earlier responses to my questions about 'making' 10 and 20 – in particular, on the facility they displayed, and whether they opted to view reversals such as '2 plus 8' and '8 plus 2' as distinct solutions. (The mathematical consequences of such choices are summarized in a note.[2])

The next phase would then involve my proposing a further target number – say 30, 50 or even 100, beyond the range of those already counted, and inviting a 'prediction' of the number of ways this number could be made. Subsequent phases, contingent on preceding ones, would involve my probing for the reasoning, inductive or otherwise, behind this prediction and discussion of perceived 'rules' – conjectures about what might happen with 'any' number.

In some interviews, there was an additional phase in which the children were asked to test the generality of such conjectures, and to consider (and explain) why they might be true 'in general'.

I worked with ten pairs of children, for about 30 minutes with each pair, and encouraged peer discussion of the task. As will be seen, I was very much a participant in these clinical interviews. Each of the 'Make Ten' interviews was audio – taped and transcribed – a corpus of about 24,000 words.

Each of the four categories of hedge identified by Prince *et al.* is in evidence in the Make Ten transcripts, and is associated with particular kinds of goals. Here I take a first look at how some of these hedge-types were used in the Make Ten interviews.

'Plausibility shields' are typified by 'I think', 'maybe' and 'probably', as in this excerpt from the 'Make Ten' interview with two girls, Frances and Ishka:

T6:16[3]	Frances:	4 and 6, 5 and 5, 6 and . . . oh that's the same.
17	Ishka:	5 ways?
18	Frances:	<u>Maybe.</u>
19	Ishka:	Mm, <u>maybe</u> . . . <u>I think</u> . . .

Ishka proposes an answer to the 'how many' question, but it is tentative. Frances believes that Ishka may be correct, but is not entirely sure. The provisional nature of their answer (five ways) is conveyed by the plausibility shields 'maybe' and 'I think', and also by the rising intonation in Ishka's 'Five ways?'. These hedges provide the two girls with a means of offering an idea without the obligation of commitment to its truth.

In the 'Make Ten' data there are relatively few 'attribution shields', and these tend to be used by me rather than the children, as a teacher-like device for metacomment (Pimm, 1992) on the activity.

'Rounders', which constitute the first subcategory of approximator, are usually associated with estimation in the domain of measurements, of quantitative data (Channell 1994). Association with prediction and generalization does not readily come to mind, yet rounders occur frequently in the Make Ten corpus, to qualify a prediction, as in the interview with Frances and Ishka:

> T6:26   Frances: Shall we just say 5 ways?
> 27   Ishka: There's <u>about</u> 5.

and later:

> T6:105   Ishka: I think there'll be <u>around</u> . . .
> 106   Frances: 15?
> 107   Ishka: Yup.

The children's use of 'adaptors' is exemplified in the following fragment from the Make Ten interview with Jubair and Shofiqur. Shofiqur has just indicated what a list of ways of 'making' 20 would look like, and predicts 21 different ways.

> T5:66   Shofiqur: It's just <u>a bit</u> the same, like this (indicating the list for 10).
> 67   Tim: Shofiqur is <u>pretty</u> convinced that it's 21. Right, are you persuaded by his argument?
> 68   Jubair: Not <u>really</u>.
> 69   Tim: Have a go at - I'm <u>fairly</u> convinced what you said Shofiqur, have a go at convincing Jubair that there are 21 ways. I mean, take it slowly.
> 70   Jubair: Come on then!
> 71   Shofiqur: I only took a guess.

Adaptors suggest, but do not define, the extension of categories, concepts and so on. Thus, Shofiqur uses an adaptor phrase 'just a bit' with respect to same(ness); I myself use two adaptors here, 'pretty' and 'fairly' (lines 67 and 69), to suggest that, first, Shofiqur's conviction, then mine, is not simple and unreserved, but of a fuzzy kind. I might reiterate, here, that my use of these hedges did not arise from any explicit awareness of their linguistic significance. I was necessarily a participant in the interview, but my perception of my role was that of researcher in mathematics education. I recognize that the pupils were more likely to perceive me as some kind of teacher.

A sift through the transcripts suggests that it is I, rather than the children, who makes most use of adaptors. I use them, like attribution shields, as a means of commenting on the children's contributions. Specifically, I use them to make indirect comments on their predictions, generalizations and explanations.

The taxonomy provides a setting for studying the significance of a few of the hedges used in my Make Ten interviews. The framework is useful in making distinctions and providing starting-points. In conjectural mathematics talk there is an affective subtext just below the surface of the propositional text. It is there because mathematics is a human activity: the participants care about the mathematics, but they also care about themselves, their feelings and those of their partners in conversation.

Particular hedges in mathematics talk

The children I interviewed were being encouraged to make mathematical predictions and generalizations. When they hedge, it is more often than not in order to imply uncertainty of one kind or another. In other words, their hedges predominantly are, or have the same effect as, plausibility shields, deployed at significant and identifiable stages in the interviews. For the sake of maintaining coherence while sampling from the data, I shall examine when and how two particular pairs of hedges are used.

'Maybe', 'think'

'Maybe' and 'think' are paradigm plausibility shields which can successfully convey a speaker's lack of full commitment to a proposition under consideration. It is necessary here to give more detail from the Frances/Ishka interview, for immediate and future reference. I asked the two girls to come to an agreement about the number of ways of making 10. Their discussion proceeds:

T6:12	Frances:	There's 1 and 9.
13	Ishka:	Yeah.
14	Frances:	So that's one. 2 and 8 . . . and then there's
15	Fra and Ish:	3 and 7.
16	Frances:	4 and 6, 5 and 5, 6 and . . . oh that's the same.
17	Ishka:	5 ways?
18	Frances:	Maybe.
19	Ishka:	Mm, maybe . . . I think . . .
20	Frances:	What do you think?
21	Ishka:	We haven't had 5–5 have we?
22	Frances:	We have!
23	Ishka:	Oh OK, erm . . .
24	Frances:	The others are like if you do 6–4, we've already done 4–6.
25	Ishka:	Mm (sighs)
26	Frances:	Shall we just say 5 ways?
27	Ishka:	There's about 5.
28	Tim:	Erm, I'd like you to be more convinced Ishka. I mean if it's about 5 then it's 4 or 6 or 7 or whatever . . . the number's sufficiently small that I think you should be sure one way or another.
29	Frances:	I think it's 5 ways.
30	Ishka:	But I'm sure.
31	Tim:	You are sure.
32	Frances:	Me too.

Having enumerated 5 ways, Frances begins to repeat herself (T6:16) – 'oh that's the same'. Rather, she offers me (and Ishka) the first insight into what sameness means to her in this context. She has an implicit criterion, which surfaces when she withdraws '6 and . . . '. Ishka evidently shares or accepts the view that reversals will not count separately, and she asserts (T6:17) that there are 5 ways. The fact that Ishka's claim is tentative is indicated by rising intonation ('5 ways?'), a prosodic hedge which transforms her statement (that there are 5 ways) into a question.

Frances (T6:18) perhaps echoes Ishka's uncertainty; or perhaps she may feel that Ishka's answer is offered prematurely, before she has exhausted all the pairs she can bring to mind. In any case the pair now seem to have an understanding that it will be productive to assert their uncertainty, and reconsider the '5 ways' claim. Ishka effectively conveys this (T6:19) in the form of two shields without a substantive proposition. Frances encourages her ('What do you think?') to articulate her position. However, having encouraged Ishka, she is impatient at Ishka's next contribution, which only suggests that Ishka has forgotten what has already been listed. Frances indicates (T6:24) that she is now satisfied that no further possibilities have been overlooked. There follows (T6:26, 27) an apparent reversal of the earlier roles (T6:17, 18) of Ishka and Frances in relation to the claim that there are 5 ways. On each occasion one has sought agreement with a hesitant assertion that there are 5 ways; the other has given hedged assent – Frances with a shield, Ishka with a rounder. The second time (T6:26, 27), however, I inferred that Frances was fully committed to the claim, whereas Ishka was not – 'I'd like you to be more convinced, Ishka'. I had, after all, introduced the dialogue above with a clear request for common consent:

T6:10   Tim: I'd like you two to agree between you, how many different ways there are of doing that. Right? Two numbers that add to 10, and I'll just be quiet for a moment.

My repeated request for agreement is complied with by Frances and Ishka to a remarkable degree. Ishka is not yet, however, prepared to concede unqualified agreement (T6:27). The function of her chosen hedge, 'about', will be considered later in this chapter. In any case, she has successfully implied the fragility of her commitment, borne out by the fact that I press her quite explicitly on the matter of being more convinced, urging that she 'should be sure'. Frances responds (T6:28) with an apparently hedged indication of where she stands. Ishka's response is unhedged, fully committed; but is it genuine, or have I blackmailed her into renouncing doubt in order to please me? After all, what I have demanded is not 'the answer' but rather for Ishka to be 'more convinced'. At this stage of the interview I am encouraging the children to generate valid instances of a generalization-in-waiting. That there are 5 ways of making 10 is such an instance. I readily accept Ishka's assurance that she is 'sure' (T6: 30, 31) without comment as to whether or not she is correct.

'Maybe' is a modal form which seems to be user-friendly, in that it is favoured by the children in comparison with the apparently synonymous 'perhaps' and 'possibly', which occur not once, in the children's speech or in mine, in the whole corpus. The following transcript data, from the interview with Rebecca and Runi, illustrates the appearance of 'maybe' within hedged predictive statements:

T9:133   Tim: Alright um, supposing, we've done, we've done 10, 20, 30, 16. /. . ./ I'd just like you to sort of say how many you think there would be, say for the number 24. /. . ./

136   Rebecca: /. . ./ 22? No, not 22 ways. 12 ways?

140   Rebecca: Oh yeah, on the 20 there were more ways than the 16, so on 24 . . . must be more then the 20, because that was less, because it was a lower number.

141   Tim: Right, how many more?

142   Rebecca: I'm not sure.(pause)

143   Runi: (whispers) 11 and 12, (inaudible, presumably 'forty') ways.

144   Rebecca: Not 40, 14.

145   Runi: Yeah, that's what I was going to say.

146   Tim: Let's just see. Runi thinks <u>maybe</u> 14 ways, and I think you suggested 12 Rebecca, yeah?

147   Rebecca: Yeah.

148   Tim: Um, what was your reason for suggesting 12?

149   Rebecca: Well, it was 4 off than 20 and then 22 (?20 . . . 2) was 2 less than 4 so you've 12. Have 12 because, if you had, 20 had 10 ways and 24 was 4 more than 20 then <u>maybe</u> it would be 12 because it's um . . . halfway in between.

150   Tim: 'cos it's halfway in between. OK. And what do you think Runi, are you saying it's 4 more, so it's 4 more ways?

151   Runi: Yeah, that's what I was thinking of.

When Rebecca explains (T9: 149) her reason for suggesting 12 (as I put it in T9: 146), she seems to be reasoning that what happened in the increase from 16 to 20 might happen again with a further increase to 24. But, by hedging (T9:149) 'maybe it would be 12', she seems to be signalling an awareness that she might be jumping to conclusions. It is an honest and straightforward expression of doubt, as to the validity of the reasoning and the conclusion. By contrast, I double-hedge (attribution and plausibility, respectively) in (T9:146) 'Runi thinks maybe . . . '

as a device to cast doubt on Runi's unhedged and incorrect ('14 ways') which is beginning to take over from Rebecca's interrupted but correct train of thought. We are some way into the interview; this is the fifth example I have asked them to consider and I am getting impatient. My reaction to Runi's off-course prediction is to undermine it by attributing doubt where there may have been none. Thus, my 'Runi thinks . . . ' (T9:146) is intended to imply 'but that's only what Runi thinks'. Furthermore, 'Runi thinks <u>maybe</u> 14' was intended to convey 'even though Runi said 14, she wasn't really sure about it, and you shouldn't be either'.

'About', 'around'

Channell (1994) observes that 'about' and 'around' appear to be inter-changeable approximators, and that the first is more common in speech. I shall examine here their use by three different children, in two extracts from the data. The first is with Harry and Alan:

T4:39   Tim: So how many ways is it Alan?
   40   Alan: 9.
   41   Tim: 9, right. (pause) What if instead of saying two numbers adding up to 10 I said two numbers adding up to 20?
   42   Harry: That would be <u>about</u>, yeah I think . . . that would be 18
   43   Alan: (simultaneous) . . . 18 ways. <u>About</u> 18 probably.

The second, from the Frances/Ishka interview, includes use of 'around'. In fact, the pragmatic analysis of 'about' which follows could be applied equally well to 'around', and be illustrated from this extract and else-where in the corpus:

T6:129   Frances: 50?
    130   Ishka: <u>About</u> 50 yeah.
    131   Tim: <u>About</u> 50. Now are you saying <u>about</u> 50, Ishka, because you're sort of playing safe or I mean do you really think it is 50?
    132   Ishka: Well maybe not exactly, but it's <u>around</u> 50 basi-cally? /. . ./
    134   Frances: Maybe <u>around</u> 50.

In each case a prediction is being made about the number of ways of making 20 (T4:42, 43) and 100 (T6:130), and each time the hedge is an approximator (a rounder) at the surface level. Channell (1994,

p. 46) has found that respondents typically understand 'about *n*' to designate a range of possibilities, symmetrical about the exemplar number *n*. So the boys predict that the number of ways to make 20 is in the region of 18, maybe more, maybe less. I suggest, however, that the purpose and function of the hedge is to shield against possible error in the cognitive basis of their prediction. This suggestion is supported by closer inspection of the data in context. Harry and Alan have already listed ways of making 10, and decided on 9 positive integer possibilities, allowing reversals but not including 0 as a summand. On being presented with the second problem (making 20) it was more common for children to list and count again. Harry, however, is a confident boy. He is a risk-taker,[4] and goes straight for a prediction for making 20, avoiding the tedium of listing and counting. The basis of Harry's prediction seems to be proportional reasoning (doubling) – there are 9 ways for making 10, so there are 18 for 20. For fuller insight into Harry's thinking, his next contribution (following T4:43 above) is:

> T4:44   Harry: No I think 19.
>   45   Tim: 18, 19?
>   46   Harry: I should write that again. (laughs)
>   47   Alan: What's that?
>   48   Harry: Up to 20.

Harry begins a list '10 plus 10', '9 plus 11', '8 plus 12'. Later, and before the list is complete, he ventures:

>   76   Harry: I think that'll be 19.

From the outset, then, Harry is uncertain as to whether the 'answer' to my question is 18 or 19. It is unclear how he arrives at these two possibilities. If his prediction is an extension of his experience of making 10, then doubling would produce Harry's first prediction. A more detailed awareness of the nature of his list of ways of making 10, which I tried to prompt in the later episodes of some Make Ten interviews, could have led to the second prediction. The fact that he articulates it ('No, I think nineteen') is all the more remarkable because his first, incorrect prediction is confirmed by Alan, albeit with something less than total commitment (T4:43). It seems, then, that Harry may be entertaining these two different predictions from the moment that I ask about making 20, and he seems (T4:42) to be testing out the first possibility, not just for my consideration, and possibly Alan's, but also for his own:

> T4:42   Harry: That would be <u>about</u>, yeah I think . . . that would be 18.

The effect of the initial hedging is to allow himself some space for further consideration, and to declare uncertainty in the assertion which completes the sentence. In the end he resorts to listing and counting, presumably since he lacks sufficient confidence in either of his predictions to choose between them when I ask him to do so ('18, 19?').

My conclusion is that the hedge 'about', although a paradigm approximator, is being used by Harry in T4:42 principally to assist the communication of his propositional attitude; in particular, to serve shield-like ends. Harry's attitude to his prediction, and my interpretation of it, is further reinforced by his use of the prototypic shield 'I think'.

Ishka implies the same attitude with 'about' in T6:130. My next turn in that conversation is evidence that I (as interviewer) suspected this intention:

> T6:131   Tim: <u>About</u> 50. Now are you saying <u>about</u> 50, Ishka, because you're sort of playing safe or I mean do you really think it is 50?

What I infer from Ishka's 'about' (T6:130) is not that she has approximated the actual number of ways to the 'round' number 50, rather that she is in possession of a generalization, a conjecture which would lead to exactly 50 as a prediction. In fact, it is normal practice to use round numbers as vague numerical reference points (Channell 1994, p. 78); indeed, a round number on its own may serve as a rounder (that is without a prefix like 'about' or 'approximately'), as in, for instance:

A suit like that would cost you £300.

The fact that round numbers are normally chosen with numerical rounders is further evidence in support of my suggestion that Harry and Alan (T4:42, T4:43) are deploying 'about' as a shield, and not as a rounder. If their intention had been to approximate rather than to hedge commitment, then Channell's findings would lead me to expect 'about 20' rather than 'about 18'.

My spoken contribution, then, in T6:131 is designed to test out Ishka's commitment to 50, asking 'do you really think it is'. Ishka's reply indicates her discomfort:

132   Ishka: Well maybe not exactly, but it's around 50 basically?
        /. . ./

This (my chosen title for this chapter) was the most elaborately hedged utterance in the whole Make Ten corpus. Even the word 'well' is described by Brockway (1981) as a 'maxim hedge', suggesting that the speaker is serving notice to the hearer that the contribution about to come will in some respect fall short of the requirements of one or more of Grice's maxims of cooperation. It is therefore a fitting preface to Ishka's virtuoso performance in hedging (T6: 132), by means of which she skilfully sidesteps my demand ('do you really think . . . ?') for commitment to her claim.

Conclusion

Hedges play an important part in the communication of propositional attitude, and this is of vital importance in the formation and articulation of predictions and generalizations. What began as a study of mathematical thinking became a way of looking at ways of learning and styles of teaching through the particular perspective of VL. What stands out from this pragmatic analysis is that vagueness is not a deficiency, but an essential ingredient of communicative competence in mathematical interaction. In a conjecturing atmosphere, VL is the means of saying what you want to say, while conveying the extent to which you are committed to what you say, in the context in which you speak.

The power relationships between participants are part of that context. In the school classroom, and even in the clinical interview, the child is obliged to conform to the expectations and demands of the teacher/interviewer. VL is one way he or she can redress the power imbalance while observing the social norms that constrain their actions and responses. Those of us who teach and learn mathematics can benefit from learning how to recognize such vagueness, and knowing how to use it.

An application of this knowledge about VL in mathematics classrooms, and a direction for future research, will therefore be through initiatives to enhance teachers' awareness and sensitivity to the function of vagueness in the – perhaps unexpected – context of mathematics teaching. My efforts in this direction to date have been encouraging. A group of 12 teachers, whose pupils were aged between 4 and 18, began working with me to investigate pragmatic aspects (for example hedges, politeness, indirectness) of the language in their own mathematics lessons. My own research participants had also included university undergraduate students. The teacher 'Judith', whose classroom we visited earlier in this chapter, was one of the 12. Their assessment of the value of their new set of linguistic 'lenses' was positive. In terms of the specific focus of the group on VL, it appeared that the phenomenon of hedges was one they could readily identify. In fact, it was the only one. This may be a consequence of the difficulty of attending to language in the classroom as distinct to attending to the business of teaching mathematics. Nonetheless, the teachers' feedback suggested they had been sensitized, or believed that they had been, to the use of hedges by children as an indicator of propositional attitude, principally of uncertainty. One wrote, for example:

> I am now more aware of the effect of using vague language in the classroom so I can use it in a positive way. /. . ./ My knowledge of hedges has helped me to spot that some statements made by children are less certain than they appear. /. . ./ I can then respond to them at an appropriate level.

Future research might also explore the vague features of mathematics classroom language in other countries, languages and cultures, and the use of hedges in particular. This could usefully build on the seminal investigations of Brown and Levinson (1987) into the issue of linguistic universality, as opposed to cultural particularity, in the case of 'politeness'. Their account includes the use of hedges in politeness strategies, but makes no reference to formal classroom contexts, nor to mathematics teaching in particular. It would be important to know how learners give voice to their propositional attitude about mathematical conjectures in Greece, Hong Kong or Brazil, for example, and how their linguistic and cultural affordances and constraints compare with those in the UK and the USA. Furthermore, it would be valuable to know whether and in what ways VL is used in classrooms where other subjects are being taught and learned, and whether it is associated with uncertainty.

Notes

1. Recency is relative, of course, but philosophical enquiry into vagueness can be traced back at least to 400 BC, in disputes and attempted resolutions of the 'sorites' paradox (see for example Goguen, 1969). The first definition of vagueness is due to Peirce (1902, p. 748).
2. The mathematical consequences of such choices may be summarized as follows. Let n be a positive integer and $f(n)$ be the number of pairs (a, b) such

that $a + b = n$, where a, b belong to a set A of 'numbers'. If (b, a) is taken to be distinct from (a, b) (unless $a = b$) and A is the set $N = \{1, 2, 3, \ldots\}$ of natural numbers, then $f(n) = n - 1$; if A also includes zero then $f(n) = n + 1$. If, however, (a, b) is always identified with (b, a), and A = N, then $f(n) = \frac{1}{2}n$ when n is even, and $\frac{1}{2}(n - 1)$ when n is odd. With zero included in A these become $\frac{1}{2}n + 1$ and $\frac{1}{2}(n + 1)$ respectively. Of course, if A includes negative as well as positive integers, then $f(n)$ is not finite.

3. This refers to the 16th turn in the transcript of the 6th 'Make Ten' interview.
4. These claims concerning Harry's personality ('confident', 'risk-taker') are based on the testimony of his class teacher, supported by several anecdotes.

References

ATM, *Language and Mathematics* (Nelson: Association of Teachers of Mathematics, 1980).

D. Brockway, 'Semantic Constraints on Relevance', in H. Parrett, M. Sbisa and J. Verschueren (eds), *Possibilities and Limitations of Pragmatics: Proceedings of the Conference on Pragmatics at Urbino, July 8–14, 1979* (Amsterdam: Benjamins, 1981) 57–78.

G. Brown and G. Yule, *Discourse Analysis* (Cambridge University Press, 1983).

P. Brown and S. Levinson, *Politeness: Some Universals in Language Usage* (Cambridge University Press, 1987).

J. Channell, *Vague Language* (Oxford University Press, 1994).

Department of Education and Science, *Mathematics Counts* (London: Her Majesty's Stationery Office, 1982).

H.P. Ginsburg, *Entering the Child's Mind: The Clinical Interview in Psychological Research and Practice* (Cambridge MA: Cambridge University Press, 1997).

J.A. Goguen, 'The Logic of Inexact Concepts', *Synthese,* 19 (1969) 325–73.

H.P. Grice, 'Logic and Conversation', in P. Cole and J.L. Morgan (eds), *Syntax and Semantics: Speech Acts 3* (New York: Academic Press, 1975), 41–58.

K.M. Jaszczolt, *The Pragmatics of Propositional Attitude Reports* (Oxford: Elsevier Science, 2000).

G. Lakoff, 'Hedges: A Study in Meaning Criteria and the Logic of Fuzzy Concepts', *Proceedings of the Chicago Linguistics Society,* 8 (1972) 183–228.

J. Piaget, *The Child's Conception of the World.* (New York: Harcourt Brace, 1929).

C.S. Peirce, 'Vague', in J.M. Baldwin (ed.), *Dictionary of Philosophy and Psychology'* (London, Macmillan, 1902), p. 748

D. Pimm, 'Classroom Language and the Teaching of Mathematics', in M. Nickson and S. Lerman (eds), *The Social Context of Mathematics Education: Theory and Practice* (London: South Bank University, 1992), 67–81.

E.F. Prince, J. Frader and C. Bosk, 'On Hedging in Physician-Physician Discourse', in R.J. di Pietro (ed.), *Linguistics and the Professions. Proceedings of the Second Annual Delaware Symposium on Language Studies* (Norwood, NJ: Ablex, 1982) 83–96.

T. Rowland, 'Propositional Attitude', paper presented at the Tenth International Congress on Mathematical Education, (ICME10), Copenhagen, 2004.

B. Russell, 'On Propositions: What They Are and What They Mean', *Proceedings of the Aristotelian Society,* supplementary volume, 2 (1919) 1–43.

L. Zadeh, 'Fuzzy Sets.' *Information and Control,* 8/3 (1965) 338–53.

6
'I Think He Was Kind of Shouting or Something': Uses and Abuses of Vagueness in the British Courtroom

Janet Cotterill

The legal system, in all its guises, is characterized by a desire for precision and clarity. From contract law (dealing with enforcement of written agreements) to criminal law (dealing with crimes and their punishments), it is possible to observe an inherent conflict and tension between the formal textualized types of documents, for example wills, contracts and statutes, and the oral practices which underpin their negotiation and implementation. Tiersma (1999, p. 71), himself a lawyer, writes under the heading of 'The Quest for Precision' that 'much of the linguistic behavior of the legal profession is geared towards speaking and writing as clearly and precisely as possible', as in the following extract taken from a last will and testament (www.languageandlaw.org/nature.htm):

> I give, devise and bequeath all of rest, residue and remainder of my property which I may own at the time of my death, real, personal and mixed, of whatsoever kind and nature and wheresoever situate, including all property which I may acquire or to which I may become entitled after the execution of this will, in equal shares, absolutely and forever, to ARCHIE HOOVER, LUCY HOOVER, his wife, and ARCHIBALD HOOVER, per capita, to any of them living ninety (90) days after my death.

This is an example of explicitness of each referring expression and explicitness of adding all possible referring expressions to cover all possible referents. This brief illustrative extract encapsulates the comprehensive and inclusive nature of texts of this type, which aim to encode in definitive form, a version of an individual's, an institution's, or even a nation's wishes. This is not to say that there are not vociferous and protracted debates around the precise meaning of terms and the extent of their application, which can extend into many years and many millions of dollars. Solan (1993) has written extensively about such debates, and the legal and linguistic battles which ensue from disputes over even apparently explicit and unambiguous terms and conditions.

The same search for precision is present in the courtroom, with trial lawyers and judges (who defend/judge clients before a court of law where the facts of a case are decided) attempting to elicit testimony from witnesses and defendants which will fulfil the law's need for detail, clarity and exactitude. In a seminal work on the nature of legal language, Mellinkoff (1963, p. 22) notes that, 'opposing themselves to the "inherent vagueness of language", lawyers make many attempts at precision of expression [in both speech and writing]'. The nature of this clash – between lawyers and the legal system on the one hand, and layperson witnesses on the other – is the focus of this chapter. In this chapter, I attempt to address three key questions: What constitutes vagueness, construed through the lens of the adversarial trial context? What kinds of vagueness do witnesses and defendants produce in the course of giving their evidence (and why)? and thirdly, What are the judicial reactions to these vague responses, as illustrated by lawyers' follow-up moves in the interaction? In order to engage with these issues, I will draw on my COURTCORP corpus of 12 million words of UK trial talk,[1] recorded in the UK courts in the late 1990s.

Dimensions of vague language

VL comes in many forms, and is sometimes identifiable as such only in retrospect. However, there is a well-developed body of research (which this volume consolidates) that has addressed the taxonomic and definitional issues associated with vagueness, and which has sought to identify categories and contexts of occurrence, as well as the consequences of its use.

There is relatively little terminological consensus on vagueness; in fact the boundaries of these categories are frequently blurred in the literature. In short, it is fair to say that the terms used to refer to VL are somewhat vague themselves; indeed Cheng and Warren's article in 2003 entitled *Indirectness, Inexplicitness and Vagueness Made Clearer* attempts to delineate these interconnected terms. They conclude that 'while terminology differs, the realizations of vagueness are more consistent across the various studies'. It is not my aim in this chapter to tease apart the definitional minutiae of the various terms which describe VL, but rather to see how vagueness as construed below plays out in the courtroom setting.

The current analysis draws on the seminal work of Channell (1994), as well as Wang's (2005) system of categorization. The analysis carried out here ultimately reflects the more applied approach of Jucker *et al.* (2003), who see vagueness as an 'interactional strategy', a resource which speakers have at their disposal to draw upon in their talk. Channell (1994, p. 18) divides her taxonomy into three main areas:

- 'Vague additives' – approximators such as 'about' and 'approximately' and tags referring to vague category identifiers such as 'and stuff like that'.
- 'Vagueness through lexical choice' – 'thingy' and 'whatsit' and vague quantifiers such as 'tons of'.
- 'Vagueness by implicature' – the sentence 'Sam is 6 feet tall' is potentially vague, as it is possible that Sam is actually 6 feet and a quarter of an inch tall.

Wang (2005) usefully combines the categorizations of Chafe (1982) and Zhang (1998), producing the following series of groupings:

- 'Impression' indicators: vague quantifiers ('a lot', 'many') and approximators ('approximately', 'about', 'roughly').
- 'Unspecificity' indicators ('after 10 o'clock', 'at six-ish').
- 'Fuzziness' indicators: approximators ('sort of', 'kind of').
- 'Etcetera' indicators: additives ('and so', 'and things like that').
- 'Uncertainty' indicators: vague adverbs ('maybe', 'probably').

The primary focus of attention in this study will be 'fuzziness' and 'etcetera' markers. I will not be focusing in this chapter on markers of certainty and doubt, although these also have clear implications in a forensic context for the credibility of a witness's account. Instead, I focus on the way in which witnesses, in the majority of cases, defendants, use these kinds of markers, particularly vague category markers such as 'something like that' and 'whatever', to resist providing evidential detail required by the cross-examining lawyer and to strategically downgrade the significance of their alleged (criminal) actions, a process termed 'downtoning' or 'detensifying' by Hübler (1983).

VL is everywhere in casual conversation. McCarthy and Carter's (forthcoming) top 20 three-word clusters in CANCODE[2] include the vague quantifying expressions 'a lot of' (at number 2 in the list), 'a bit of' (at number 14) and 'a couple of' (at number 18). The 20 most commonly occurring five-word clusters include 'this, that and the other' (at number

8), with terminal tags 'all the rest of it' (at number 10), 'and that sort of thing' (at number 14) and 'all that sort of thing' (at number 18). McCarthy and Carter note that vagueness is both necessary and desirable in informal interaction, since 'its absence can make utterances blunt and pedantic'. From a pragmatic politeness point of view, vagueness is in many ways the norm, a default position not only enabling speakers to fulfil requirements of face, but also permitting the sharing of real-world knowledge; speakers, they argue, 'need only allude to the shared cultural knowledge and may assume their listeners can fill in the detail'.

Such interactional behaviour may be entirely appropriate in the casual conversational domain. However, in the adversarial trial context, as I have argued elsewhere (Cotterill 2003), there is a need for a high degree of explicitness in exchanges between speakers, and the usual assumptions about cooperation (Grice 1975) and politeness (Brown and Levinson 1987) cannot be taken for granted, particularly during cross-examination. In addition, the dynamics of the courtroom setting are such that in dialogic exchanges between lawyer and witness, the jury as ratified recipient is signalled less explicitly. Rather than overt acknowledgements of the jury as the addressee, in the form of direct address forms or eye contact, the dialogue of lawyer-witness questioning, which makes up much of the trial, takes on instead the characteristics of display talk. Goffman (1981, p. 137) discusses the notion of 'display' talk, referring to the jury as the 'encircling hearers', and likening them to the audience of a TV talk show, positioned outside the immediate questioner–respondent dyad, but nonetheless the intended addressee or 'target' in Levinson's (1983) terms. This means that a high degree of explicitness is required of both lawyer and witness and, as we will see, VL is not well tolerated in this setting.

The following extract illustrates the protracted nature of this pursuit of precision, and the nature of the problem:

Extract 1 – And you are sure about that? – examination-in-chief
Q. Mr S, can you help us at all as to which year this was?
A. 1996.
Q. In 1996?
A. Yes.
Q. Can you tell us, please, as to what month it might have been?
A. Roughly, to be honest, I can't know. At the time I was receiving treatment for depression.
Q. When you made your statement about this matter, you did indeed say that buds were handed to you *by* Mr M.

A. That's correct.
Q. <u>And you are sure about that</u>?
A. I'm 100 per cent sure of that.
Q. <u>What is your relationship</u> with Sandra Mitchell,[3] the Defendant.
A. A friend.
Q. <u>How long have you been a friend</u> with Mrs Mitchell for?
A. At least 17 years.
Q. What about the Defendant, Mr G? Do you know Mr G?
A. Yes, I do.
Q. <u>How long have you known Mr G</u>?
A. About 7 years. I'm not really too sure. Quite some time.
Q. <u>Would you also describe him as a friend</u>?
A. An acquaintance. Somebody that I know. Not a friend, friend.
Q. <u>Do you remember Wednesday, 13 March of last year</u>?
A. Yes, I do.
Q. Did you see either of the two Defendants on that day?
A. I think that was the day Sandie phoned me up, yes.
Q. <u>When you say 'Sandie', do you mean Mrs Mitchell</u>?
A. Sandra Mitchell. Sorry, Sandra Mitchell, yes.

This extract shows the necessarily protracted and 'pedantic' nature of courtroom questioning, in this case during examination-in-chief (questioning of a witness under oath). The questions in this segment relate to a number of details which the lawyer is trying to elicit from the witness by means of a series of detailed Wh- and Wh-type questions. He first addresses the timing of the alleged incident, asking about both the year and the month in which the alleged incident occurred ('Mr S, can you help us at all as to which year this was?' and 'Can you tell us, please, as to what month it might have been?'). He then turns his attention to both the topic of the witness's friendship with the defendant and Mr Gardiner, asking 'how long' the witness has known them 'How long have you been a friend with Mrs Mitchell for?' and 'How long have you known Mr G?') and the precise nature of his relationship with them ('What is your relationship with Sandra Mitchell, the Defendant?' and 'Would you also describe him as a friend?'). The lawyer moves on to ask about the actual day of the crime itself ('Do you remember Wednesday, 13 March of last year?') before seeking clarification on the precise name of the defendant. Thus, this brief but representative extract clearly illustrates attempts by the lawyer, on behalf of the 'fact-finding' jury, to ascertain precise details about the individuals and relationships between them, as well as exact dates relating to the crime itself.

If we turn our attention to the witness's responses to these questions, we can see that this typical witness demonstrates many levels of uncertainty and imprecision in his answers. He is able only to approximate which month the crime took place, justifying his response of 'Roughly, to be honest, I can't know' with an explanation of treatment for depression which he suggests has clouded his powers of recall. He is also unsure about how long he has known the two individuals – 'At least 17 years' for the first person and 'About 7 years. I'm not really too sure. Quite some time' in three attempts to respond about the second person, each response displaying considerable vagueness. Finally, he prefaces his otherwise affirmative response about seeing the defendants on the day in question with the hedge 'I think' ('I think that was the day Sandie phoned me up, yes'). Even when the witness does provide precise, unambiguous and uncontroversial responses, apparently lacking in vagueness, the lawyer on two occasions nevertheless asks for confirmation, first by repeating the response provided by the witness (A. '1996.' Q. 'In 1996?'. A. 'Yes.') and later by: 'And you are sure about that?' A. I'm 100 per cent sure of that'.

The need for precision, and its importance in the courtroom setting, is clearly shown in the next data extract, taken from a trial involving an allegation of causing death by dangerous driving. During examination-in-chief evidence, the defendant uses the seemingly innocuous (though somewhat obscure) word 'bibbing', presumably meant to indicate short bursts of the car horn. The precise intended meaning of the word is crucial, since it indicates how clearly a driver on the opposite side of the road was signalling danger to the defendant. This provides the jury with a sense of the extent to which he was aware of the potential danger of the situation and therefore his alleged level of disregard for safety.

Extract 2 – I don't wish to be pedantic about this – examination-in-chief
Q. And was Mr S flashing his headlights at you?
A. He did, yes.
Q. And I think you have said he also was <u>bibbing</u> on the car horn.
A. He was.
Q. Yes. <u>I don't wish to be pedantic</u> about this: you've talked about quarter- and half-second bursts.
A. You know, it, it wasn't for a long period of time.
Q. Right. It's not a long "Mmmmmmmmmmmm"?

A. No, sort of "Beep, beep, beeep", sort of – you know, that sort of thing.
Q. Okay, I just wanted to be clear about that, yes. And as far as you're aware, you were never breaking the speed limit?
A. No, I had no reason to.
Q. No. So there is nowhere on the Main Road where you would have been going at between 50 and 60 mph.
A. Definitely not.

The cross-examining lawyer in this extract asks the witness to eliminate or at least reduce the amount of vagueness in this term by estimating the exact length of time each 'bib' lasted. He makes reference to an earlier statement made by the defendant, where he suggests it may have been 'quarter- and half-second bursts'. He makes a pseudo-apology for insisting on such precision 'I don't wish to be pedantic about this', 'pseudo' since a pedantic attention to detail is exactly what is prescribed in this situation. The next two turns make it clear that the only way to resolve the vagueness of 'bibbing' is to demonstrate it in action. First the lawyer and then the defendant resort to a demonstration, which results in a resolution of the conflict, albeit with the witness using 'sort of – you know, that sort of thing'.

There are many reasons why a witness or defendant may be imprecise or vague in their responses; in addition to the usual social pressures to show cooperative behaviour and politeness common to all speakers, there are additional pressures on witnesses to 'be responsive' in the power asymmetry of the courtroom, in fact they can be reprimanded, fined or even imprisoned if they are held to be evasive or avoidant in providing appropriate evidential responses. Even when witnesses do provide 'an answer' to 'a question' in simple adjacency pair terms, and these answers appear to provide 'type-confirming' responses (Raymond 2003), there is still the potential for these responses to fall short of fulfilling the lawyer's interrogative agenda.

The responsibility for this incongruity is not necessarily the fault of the witness. Although lawyers are generally skilled communicators, they are also on occasion responsible for producing unclear, ambiguous and vague questions which are often mirrored in the responses produced by witnesses. There is also the potential element of deliberate obfuscation on the part of the lawyer, who may produce complex and confusing questions so as to bamboozle the witness. Witnesses, on the other hand, may produce vague responses because they:

- Don't know, because of a lack of knowledge, comprehension.
- Can't remember, because of their memory or cognitive issues.
- Are not allowed to answer fully, because of coercion, threat, taboo, lack of permission.
- Are inarticulate, because of their lack of communicative competence.
- Are intimidated by proceedings, because of their inhibitions.
- Have learning difficulties or because of communicative problems and communication disorders.

Many of these cognitive, linguistic and affective factors may result in responses which could be interpreted as 'vague'. The power dynamic of the courtroom is such that, for the essentially 'cooperative' witness at least, the pressure to produce 'an answer' is considerable, perhaps accounting for vagueness of the kind we see in Extract 1 above, where the witness makes three attempts at providing an adequate answer, each one as vague as the previous one: 'About 7 years. I'm not really too sure. Quite some time.'

It is important however to be cautious in any attempt to interpret a speaker's motivation for producing VL. This is true especially in forensic contexts such as the courtroom or the police interview, where the possibility of deliberate deception is relatively high compared to most other settings. The potential for deception must clearly be added to the list above as a possible motivational factor. As O'Keeffe (2004a, p. 9) notes, without access to the speakers for personal reflection, and only then assuming sincere responses, 'we cannot know for certain whether they chose to take linguistic shortcuts: a) to be "deliberately and unresolvably vague" (Powell, 1985: 31), or b) to be expeditious and adhere to conversational norms of quantity.'

This is a somewhat different list of reasons from that proposed by O'Keeffe in her (2004b) comparative analysis of vagueness in radio phone-ins and casual conversational data from the Limerick Corpus of Irish English (LCIE). Her categories included 'expression of group membership', 'marking shared knowledge', and 'talking about unpleasant things that both the speaker and listener would rather under-specify'. The stakes are clearly much higher in court, where rights to group membership are to a large degree abandoned, 'shared' knowledge about events is disputed and very many 'unpleasant things' have to be explored in great detail.

Having established what vagueness is (at least seen through a forensic linguistic lens), why witnesses may be vague in their responses to lawyers' questions, and why this matters, I will now address the remaining two questions: What kinds of vagueness do witnesses and defendants produce in the witness box in the COURTCORP corpus, and how do lawyers react to this in court?

Extract 3 – 'and everything' – examination-in chief
Q.   What did you tell him on that occasion about C C?
A.   What on the 23rd?
Q.   Yes in the pub in Anytown.
A.   I spoke to him about 4 or 5 times on the phone before. I told him the full story. I think on the Thursday we had gone through *the whole story of what had happened and everything*.
Q.   He was a supporter of yours, a friend of yours and you had told him how effectively you were the subject of an attack. Is that right?
A.   Yeah.
Q.   Put your side of the story completely?
A.   Yeah.
Q.   At the pub on the Saturday what did you say to him about C C?
A.   I can't remember. We had already spoke about it, because it is the sort of thing you are going to speak about, but I can't remember what I said.
Q.   Was it words to the effect that he was worthless. He was nothing but a fucking skin-head?
A.   No, because C wasn't a skin-head. V wouldn't know that because he has never met him, but C has long gelled back hair. He has never been a skin-head as long as I have known him, so I wouldn't have described C as a skin-head, but V not having seen C would not have known that.
Q.   Did anything pass between you and S V, did anything occur that you can now think of that might have made V turn against you?
A.   No.
Q.   Nothing at all?
A.   No. I have never had an argument with him or nothing. No.

Extract 3 is a piece of examination-in-chief testimony which illustrates the use of vague expressions as a kind of evidential shorthand, a means by which both lawyers and, particularly, witnesses are able to cover a large amount of evidential ground in only a few turns, presenting the crime narrative in abbreviated terms. This is only possible because of the fact that both lawyer and witness have a fund of shared knowledge about the crime on which to draw. This means that the witness is able to summarize the context of the incident as 'the full story' and the 'whole story'. This becomes transposed into the vague anaphoric expression 'what had happened and everything'.

This apparently imprecise response to the specific wh-information-seeking question 'What did you tell him on that occasion about C C?' is nevertheless accepted by the lawyer, who himself helpfully fills in the missing narrative detail in the next turn, in the form of a declarative statement: 'He was a supporter of yours, a friend of yours and you had told him how effectively you were the subject of an attack,' followed by the tag 'Is that right?' which invites the witness to confirm.

The exchange continues with a further request for specific information: 'At the pub on the Saturday what did you say to him about C C?' The witness does not provide a suitably detailed response, claiming he 'can't remember'. He tells the court he can recall 'the sort of thing you are going to speak about' but says he does not remember 'what I said'. Once again the direct-examination lawyer is required to step in and fill the informational void, by suggesting what he might have said, and in fact, what the prosecution claim he did say: 'Was it words to the effect . . . ?' The sequence of exchanges ends with a series of question–answer adjacency pairs which seem to resolve the matter, at least from the defence's perspective, with a succession of definitive (and negative) responses – 'no', 'never', 'or nothing'.

In a parallel, contrastive example, this time taken from a cross-examination extract, the witness is not allowed to get away with using this type of shorthand. In Extract 4, below, the witness uses the vague summarizer 'this, that and the other', in response to a question about why he had not told the police he had a weapon (a baseball bat):

Extract 4 – 'this, that and the other' – cross-examination
Q. Why did you tell the police it was your bat?
A. Because I didn't, I don't know who these people are, do you understand me? <u>If I start telling the police things, oh, this, that and the other,</u> then that's what I told him it was mine because I didn't want to say nothing. I didn't want to tell the police anything because of what might happen, if you like.

Q. <u>You apparently told the police everything.</u> You say in your evidence, oh, no sooner does L C appear at the doorstep than he has told you he has been involved in a robbery at Y Way, yes?

A. (No answer)

The defendant in this assault case equates telling the police 'this, that and the other' with opening himself up to potential problems; he tells the court he was afraid of 'what might happen'. The cross-examining barrister (lawyer in the higher courts, in England and Wales) in this instance uses the witness's vagueness to contrast it with the comprehensive nature of his subsequent police interview, where the - defendant is alleged to have 'told the police everything', including, significantly, an attempt to incriminate one of the other defendants.

The COURTCORP corpus contains many examples of this type of courtroom discourse, where witnesses produce vague and unspecific evidence relating to their memories of evidentially significant conversations. This vagueness is of course important in the forensic context because the jury was not present at the crime, its origin or its aftermath, and so speech evidence must be recalled and reconstructed by witnesses. Such evidence frequently includes forensically significant speech acts such as threats or confessions, and as such can be key in evidential terms. The vagueness of tags such as 'and everything' 'this, that and the other' and, in Extract 5, below, 'something like that' cannot be left undisturbed in court, and the barrister's role is to explore and if possible explore its component elements. If unsuccessful, for the examination-in-chief case, this could mean that valuable evidence is not conveyed to the jury; equally for the cross-examination, a vital opportunity to pursue evidential inconsistency could be missed.

In Extract 5, the concept of inconsistency, and therefore the suggestion that the witness is at best unreliable and at worst deceptive, is pursued by the cross-examining lawyer:

Extract 5 – 'something like that' – cross-examination

Q. Was not this a remarkable series of events?

A. Yes, it was.

Q. Did not Mr S come into the lavatory and say, for example, 'Give us those buds back, P'?

A. <u>He may have said something like that</u>. I can't remember.

Q. You cannot help us as to what he said?

A. Not exactly, no.
Q. Down at S's house, 'Here we are, L. These are for you.' Cannot
    remember?
A. Not exactly what was said, no.
Q. Because of that, you would rather not mislead the jury by get-
    ting it wrong?
A. I don't know exactly what was said.

The witness presents his recall of the conversation concerned as a vague
'something like that' and goes on to claim that he is unable to assist further with the exact content of the exchange. Even though the lawyer
produces what he insists is the exact wording (recorded in the court
transcript reproduced above including direct quotation marks), the witness is adamant that he cannot remember what was said, a claim he
repeats on three separate occasions ('Not exactly, no,' 'Not exactly what
was said, no,' and 'I don't know exactly what was said'). The lawyer
ends this line of questioning with the suggestion that the witness does
in fact recall the conversations, but is being evasive in his responses. It
later emerges that the reason for the direct quotation marks is that these
utterances reflect directly statements made earlier by the same witness,
when interviewed by the police and suggesting that this vagueness may
have been motivated by deception.

The second set of extracts discussed here illustrate a different kind of
forensic linguistic vagueness. These extracts are all taken from the testimony of defendants and eyewitnesses giving evidence about violent
offences against the person – assault, both physical and sexual, and
attempted murder – all of which clearly represent 'talking about
unpleasant things that both the speaker and listener would rather
under-specify', to echo O'Keeffe (2004b). In the courtroom setting,
however, such conversational concessions are available to neither
defendant nor lawyer; in order for due process to be seen to be done,
these topics must be explored exhaustively.

In Extract 6, dealing with an allegation of sexual assault, the prose-
cuting barrister cross-questions the defendant, attempting to elicit his
version of events. The lawyer begins by laying out some of the specific
allegations in detail: that the defendant put his hand on her breast and
that he cupped her breast with his hand:

Extract 6a – cross-examination
Q. I suggest that Mrs S made a comment and you did not say any-
    thing; do you remember that?

A. No.

Q. Then another occasion, <u>you put your hand on her breast, on S's breast over her clothes and cupped her breast with your hand;</u> do you remember doing that?

A. No.

Q. And Mrs S told us that she was very angry at this time and made some comment; do you remember?

A. No.

The defendant claims to have no knowledge or recollection of these events occurring, responding to each of the accusations with a bald 'no'.

The lawyer then attempts to separate out the actual events themselves with the defendant's recall of them, with the result that the evidence descends from specific allegations to more vague and indirect suggestions:

Extract 6b – 'sort of thing' – cross-examination

Q. <u>Are you saying that none of these things ever happened or they might have happened but you just do not remember?</u>

A. I didn't do <u>them</u>.

Q. You did not do <u>them?</u>

A. No.

Q. So <u>this</u> never happened?

A. <u>I can't promise 100 per cent but I wouldn't have done that sort of thing.</u>

Q. <u>Well is it the sort of thing you might have done?</u>

A. Yes.

Q. Are you sure?

A. Yes.

The questions and answers begin with anaphoric declarative exchanges: A. 'I didn't do <u>them</u>.' Q. 'You did not do <u>them?</u>' As the discourse progresses, however, both lawyer and witness shift away from the specific incidents themselves to more oblique references. The defendant first shifts from responding to the question '<u>this</u> never happened', to reformulate it as a more vague and more global 'that sort of thing'. In the next turn, a further shift in the direction of hypothetication is reflected in the grammar of the exchange, moving from 'wouldn't have done' to 'might have done'. The lawyer moves away from specific allegations, which the defendant denies outright, to more general and more hypothetical suggestions, which the defendant is prepared to admit, thereby portraying himself as the kind of individual who may have committed the offences he is charged with.

The final pair of extracts show a process of lexical negotiation in court which result in the naming of alleged acts and actions being up- and downgraded in terms of specificity and vagueness, a phenomenon discussed in more detail in Cotterill (2001). In Extract 7, a case of attempted murder, the defendant is resisting the formulation of his actions as causing the victim to 'splutter' and 'choke':

Extract 7 – 'a bit/some sort of' – cross-examination
Q. You loop this noose around his neck. It is loose and he does not try and get it away from his neck?
A. I put some pressure on it and Mr F has grabbed my hand, sir.
Q. You pulled it as tight as you could, did you not?
A. Sir, that is not correct. No.
Q. He was spluttering and choking, was he not?
A. I could see that once I had put pressure on with my hand that Mr F was going a bit red and making some sort of noise from his throat. Yes.
Q. He was choking, was he not?
A. No, sir. I would not say it was life threatening. No.
Q. He was not choking?
A. I am not saying that he was not choking. There was some noise coming from his throat, yes.

Instead, the defendant suggests that the victim was 'going a bit red' and 'making some sort of noise from his throat'. The defendant then resists two further attempts by the barrister to suggest that the 'sort of noise' coming from his throat constitutes 'choking' although he does eventually concede that 'some noise coming from his throat' may in fact be construed as 'choking'.

In Extract 8, this process of negotiation in the lexical specificity and vagueness of accounts becomes more protracted, producing a lengthy exchange of possible lexical formulations. This eyewitness is providing an account of the behaviour of a nightclub bouncer:

Extract 8a – '. . . sort of ' – cross-examination
Q. So, the bouncer was to the side of him. What? Effectively carrying this person along, was he?
A. Well, literally, yeh. He had hold of his scruff and the bottom of his jeans, or whatever he had on.

Q. Then threw him out of the door.
A. Well, just let go of him.
Q. Well, there is a difference, you see. You have described the man being flung. That is the word that you used.
A. <u>When I say he just – well, not exactly threw him, like somebody flew through the air, but, I mean, threw him sort of.</u>
Q. The bouncer just let go of the man, did he not? Just let go of him.
A. Just slumped him to the floor.
Q. Just let go of him.
A. Let go of him.

The negotiation taking place in this extract concerns the precise nature of the bouncer's physical behaviour when ejecting the alleged victim of the assault. The lawyer asks the witness to confirm that the defendant 'threw' the victim out of the door, a formulation which the witness resists, rephrasing the action as a more vague 'just let him go', complete with the minimizer 'just'. The lawyer then goes on to question the witness about his original version of events, which described the man as 'being flung', a more precise (and more violent) formulation . The witness, who by this stage is floundering, then tries to backtrack by suggesting a hedged and indeterminate version of events: 'When I say he just – well, not exactly threw him, like somebody flew through the air, but, I mean, threw him sort of.' This vague depiction leads the cross-examining lawyer, at the end of the extract, to produce a series of three challenges to the witness's version, which end when the dejected witness simply concedes, 'Let go of him,' thereby effectively diffusing the initial sense of violence conveyed by the use of 'flung'.

The lawyer follows up with a triplet of verbs which form further nails in the coffin of the witness's account:

Extract 8b – cross-examination continued
Q. He did not <u>throw</u> him, did he? Did he?
A. No.
Q. He did not <u>push</u> him?
A. No, he just let go of him.
Q. Did not <u>fling</u> him. He did not <u>fling</u> him, did he?
A. No.

By this point, the lawyer appears to have effectively completed the destruction of the witness's credibility as illustrated by the final pair of turns in the exchange:

Extract 8c – cross-examination continued

Q. Now, you appear to be agreeing with me and what I am saying, and disagreeing with what you said yourself earlier. Why is it that you seem to be changing your mind?

A. I'm not changing my mind. I was just – Well, I mean, that was a year ago, weren't it, so –

Conclusion

The extracts chosen for discussion in this chapter attempt to illustrate a widespread phenomenon found in courtroom discourse. Witnesses and defendants use markers of vagueness of many kinds, but particularly those which express fuzziness in the form of approximators ('some sort of', 'kind of', 'a bit', 'whatever', 'this, that and the other') and 'etcetera' additives or tags ('and everything', 'sort of thing', 'something like that'), are particular sites of interactional trouble in the courtroom, and are invariably picked up by lawyers on both sides of the legal divide. Witnesses and defendants also overtly alude to the vagueness of their knowledge and memory: 'I'm not sure', 'I can't remember', 'I don't know exactly' and 'I can't promise 100 per cent'. This is both VL in substitution of more precise expressions and VL used as padding round other vague terms, in order, perhaps, to mitigate the very vagueness of the other term, vaguely covering up vagueness.

For the barrister conducting an examination-in-chief, the use of vague expressions can present him or her with an account which lacks precision, detail and therefore potentially, a challenge to their witness's credibility; for the cross-examiner, such expressions represent an opportunity for confrontation, since vagueness may be seen to stem from witness failings in memory, expression or integrity in the eyes of the cross-examiner. Exploitation of any of these shortcomings may pay dividends in the destruction of the witness's evidential credibility.

Applications

For the majority of witnesses, such cross-examination strategies are seen as legitimate and necessary for the rigour of the criminal justice system. For some researchers in forensic linguistics, however, such hostile interactional strategies may lead to the mistreatment of some types of witness in particular, including vulnerable witnesses such as children, the disabled, those with learning disabilities or communication disorders, or limited-English-speakers who do not qualify for the services of an interpreter. For them, vagueness may be a necessary linguistic resource which forms a part of their linguistic repertoire, and does not necessarily indicate a deliberate avoidance of detail. Whereas vagueness has traditionally been seen as a negative phenomenon in the legal setting, it should be considered common and necessary in witness examination and cross-examination. It is clearly important that such witnesses do not suffer adversely from the aggressive cross-examination techniques described above, and that lawyers, judges and jurors need to be sensitive to the potential uses and abuses by all sides of vague expressions in court.

The findings in this study could possibly be used to help barristers and cross-examiners to detect when there is vagueness because of witness failings in integrity and when it is because of language limitations. A discussion of these language issues could be included in the syllabus of a law degree.

Notes

1. The corpus was developed at the University of Nottingham, and funded by Cambridge University Press, with whom sole copyright resides. CANCODE forms part of the larger Cambridge International Corpus. The corpus conversations were recorded in a wide variety of mostly informal settings across the islands of Britain and Ireland, then transcribed and stored in computer-readable form. Details of the corpus and its design may be found in McCarthy (1998).
2. CANCODE stands for 'Cambridge and Nottingham Corpus of Discourse in English' and is a 5-million-word corpus of transcribed conversations. It was established at the Department of English Studies, University of Nottingham, and was funded by Cambridge University Press.

References

P. Brown and S. Levinson, *Politeness: Some Universals in Language Use* (Cambridge University Press, 1987).

W. Chafe, 'Integration and Involvement in Speaking, Writing and Oral Literature', in D. Tannen (ed.), *Spoken and Written Language: Exploring Orality and Literacy* (Norwood, NJ: Ablex, 1982) p. 35–55.

J. Channell, *Vague Language* (Oxford: Oxford University Press, 1994).

W. Cheng and M. Warren, 'Indirectness, Inexplicitness and Vagueness Made Clearer', *Pragmatics*, 13/3), (2003) 381–400.

J. Cotterill, 'Domestic Discord, Rocky Relationships: Semantic Prosodies in Representations of Marital Violence in the Courtroom', *Discourse and Society*, 12/3 (2001) 291–312.

J. Cotterill, *Language and Power in Court* (Basingstoke: Palgrave, 2003).

E. Goffman, *Forms of Talk* (Philadelphia, PA: University of Pennsylvania, 1981).

H.P. Grice, 'Logic and Conversation', in P. Cole and J. Morgan (eds), *(Syntax and Semantics: 9)* Speech Acts (New York: Academic Press, 1975).

A. Hübler, *Understatements and Hedges in English* (Amsterdam: Benjamins, 1983).

A.H. Jucker, S.W. Smith and T. Lüdge, 'Interactive Aspects of Vagueness in Conversation', *Journal of Pragmatics*, 35/12 (2003) 1737–69.

S.C. Levinson, *Pragmatics* (Cambridge University Press, 1983).

M. McCarthy and R. Carter, *'This That and the Other: Multi-Word Clusters in Spoken English as Visible Patterns of Interaction'*, Teanga, 21 (2004).

D. Mellinkoff, *The Language of the Law* (Boston, MA: Little, Brown, 1963).

W.M. O'Barr, *Linguistic Evidence* (New York: Academic Press, 1982).

A. O'Keeffe, '"Like the Wise Virgins and All That Jazz" – Using a Corpus to Examine Vague Categorization and Shared Knowledge', in U. Connor and T. Upton (eds), *Applied Corpus Linguistics: A Multidimensional Perspective* (Amsterdam: Rodopi, 2004a) pp. 1–20.

A. O'Keeffe, 'How to Be Vague and That Kind of Thing', presented at the 38th International Association of Teachers of English as a Foreign Language (IATEFL) Conference, Liverpool, (2004b).

M.J. Powell, 'Purposeful Vagueness: an Evaluative Dimension of Vague Quantifying Expressions', *Journal of Linguistics,* 21 (1985) 31–50.

G. Raymond, 'Grammar and Social Organization: Yes/No Interrogatives and the Structure of Responding', *American Sociological Review,* 68 (2003) 939–67.

L. Solan, *The Language of Judges* (Chicago: Chicago University Press, 1993).

P. Tiersma, *Legal Language* (Chicago: Chicago University Press, 1999).

A. Wang, 'When Precision Meets Vagueness: A Corpus-Assisted Approach to Vagueness in Taiwanese and British Courtrooms', presented 7th Biennial Conference of International Association of Forensic Linguists, Cardiff (2005).

Q. Zhang, 'Fuzziness – Vagueness – Generality – Ambiguity', *Journal of Pragmatics,* 29/1 (1998) 13–31.

Part III
Psychology of Vagueness

7
Vague Language as a Means of Self-Protective Avoidance: Tension Management in Conference Talks

Hugh Trappes-Lomax

Introduction

> Then she left. The navy guy and I said we were glad to have met each other. Which always kills me. I'm always saying 'Glad to've met you' to somebody I'm not at all glad I met. If you want to stay alive you have to say that stuff though.
>
> J.D. Salinger, *The Catcher in the Rye*[1]

Polite behaviour is not the same as a sincere desire to make the other person feel good. This is self-evident and the point has been made by others (Thomas 1995, p. 150). We say 'Glad to've met you' not – or at least not usually – out of loving-kindness but because it is the kind of thing that is expected at the closing stage of a certain type of interaction, because we tend to act in accordance with the politeness maxim 'Make the other person feel good', and because we 'want to stay alive'.

We thereby manage to avoid three kinds of trouble which might otherwise arise in our encounters with our fellows:

- Interactional trouble (misunderstandings, misalignments, omissions).
- Interpersonal trouble (threats to the self-esteem or autonomy of the addressee which may damage the relationship of the participants).
- Personal trouble (threats to the self-esteem or autonomy of the speaker).

Though mismanaging the speech events that we take part in may not often result in physical death (fortunately the days of duels on matters of honour are long past), nevertheless it may have consequences for us as *social* beings which are, or may appear to us to be, almost as serious.

Avoidance of such 'personal trouble' in communication is thus an interactional imperative.

In this chapter, I look at the contribution of VL to this aspect of the communication process, drawing on concepts of face, conflict and avoidance in order to do so. I focus first on tension management devices, then describe the features of VL that interest me, and finally exemplify my argument with data from a variety of sources, looking especially at the language of conference talks.

Positive and negative communication goals

When we enter a communication situation with an interlocutor, an audience, a reader, or a readership, there are things that we want to achieve (positive communication goals) and things that we want to avoid (negative communication goals).

For a framework for describing positive goals, we may look to theories of functions of speaking and speech acts (Austin 1962; Hymes 1972; Searle 1979) which define categories for describing things speakers want to achieve. The much-cited distinction posited by Brown and Yule (1983, pp. 1–4) between a transactional and an interactional function conveniently encapsulates in the most general way the two main positive goals of human communication. The former relates to the achievement of efficiency and effectiveness in delivery of content, to getting the business in hand successfully done; the latter to 'the expression of social relations and personal attitudes', through conventional routines of phatic communion and signalling of solidarity.

For a framework for describing negative communication goals, we need look to theories of face, politeness and conflict, with, as a common thread in all of these, the concept of avoidance. In one sense, avoidance is merely the obverse of positive action; it is an act of not doing something. To adhere to the maxim of quantity (Grice 1975), I should avoid violating it; to respect the positive face wants of my addressee I should avoid causing offence. Holden Caulfield, the teenage protagonist in Salinger's novel, is doing this kind of avoidance: he is avoiding causing offence to the navy guy. But in so doing he is accomplishing another kind of avoidance: he is reducing a potential threat to himself.

This latter type of avoidance is observed in animal species other than our own and is therefore of interest to biologists, for whom avoidance is 'behaviour that tends to protect an animal by reducing its exposure to hazard' (Allaby 1999). To increase its chances of physical survival, an animal may freeze, flee, camouflage itself and so on. In saying 'Glad to've met you' to the navy guy, Holden is doing something similar (a kind of camouflage behaviour, perhaps). He is trying to increase his chances of survival. Focused as they are on the face wants of the other, theories of politeness and tact (to which some VL theory relates) tend to overlook, or at least underemphasize, the defensive motivations of the self. Brown and Levinson (1987, pp. 67–8) devote approximately one page plus a footnote to threats to the face of the speaker, and, understandably in view of the topic of their book, pay little or no attention to strategies for dealing with such threats. We cannot, after all, be impolite to ourselves.

Such defensive motivations are, however, well described and explained by sociologists of self-presentation and interaction management, theorizers of social survival, such as Goffman (1981, 1999) and Garfinkel (1973). Key to this understanding is Goffman's (1999, p. 306) concept of face:

> the positive social value a person effectively claims for himself by the line others assume he has taken during a particular contact. A person tends to experience an immediate emotional response to the face which a contact with others allows him

The way events turn out – sustaining, enhancing or damaging face – will result in feelings of indifference, in feeling good or in feeling bad, as the case may be.

Interested as he is in interaction management generally (that is, not just in politeness), Goffman (ibid., p. 309) provides an account of face and of 'face-work' that is concerned both with the face of the speaker and with that of the hearer. A person

> may want to save his own face because of the emotional attachment to the image of self which it expresses /. . ./ [He] may want to save the other's face because of his emotional attachment to an image of them, or because he feels that his co-participants have a moral right to this protection, or because he wants to <u>avoid the hostility that may be directed towards him if they lose their face</u> [my emphasis]

Avoidance motivations are thus both defensive (of the face wants of the speaker – S) and protective (of the face wants of the hearer – H). As we have seen in the Holden Caulfield example, the wish to be (or at least appear) protective may be motivated by considerations that are purely defensive. Face-saving of H (politeness) can be seen as a defensive stratagem of S (avoidance of personal trouble).

For Garfinkel, survival depends on 'the successful management of situations of risk and uncertainty' (1973, pp. 87–8). Garfinkel records the experience of a transsexual (Agnes) convinced that she was 'naturally, originally, really, after all, female', that is the face she is impelled to present is one of never having been male:

> Can you imagine all the blank years I have to fill in? Sixteen or seventeen years of my life that I have to make up for, I have to be careful of the things that I say, just natural things that could slip out /. . ./ I just never say anything at all about my past that in any way could make a person ask what my past life was like. I say general things. I don't say anything that could be misconstrued.

As Argyle (1967, p. 167) observes, anyone who takes part in social encounters must present some kind of face or self-image, and this must be realistic or there is a danger of it collapsing. We can try to 'avoid embarrassment by presenting a face that cannot be invalidated'. This, however, is not always possible, and Agnes must resort to 'management' devices – for example speaking vaguely ('saying general things') – to protect her vulnerable self-image.

Another way of understanding Agnes's situation is as one of conflict. The conflict arises from the situation she is in, one which presents her with two outcomes she equally wants to avoid: on the one hand telling the truth (about the 'blank years'), and on the other telling a lie. Such 'avoidance-avoidance' conflicts (Lewin 1952, pp. 260–4) have been posited (Bavelas *et al.* 1990, pp. 54–63) as the cause of interpersonal equivocation – use of 'intentionally vague, ambiguous or non-straightforward communication' (Bello 1998).

Though the research of Bavelas and her colleagues 'strongly supports the theory that avoidance-avoidance conflict (AAC) routinely leads to equivocation, it does not /. . ./ rule out many other conceivable causes of equivocation' (Bello 1998). One such cause, studied by Bello, is level of situational formality. The present study suggests a third possible cause, namely 'approach-avoidance' conflict, a situation in which a single goal has both positive and negative qualities.

One response to negative communication goals is to avoid the risky encounter altogether. Another, and opposite, response is, either through possession of 'a face that cannot be invalidated' or through indifference to the consequences, to engage in the encounter, to 'face up to it'. It is in the area between complete avoidance and uninhibited engagement that the perception of risk arises, where tension is created, and where tension must be managed (Figure 7.1).

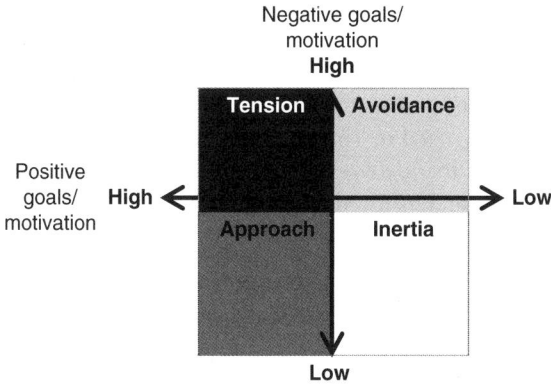

Figure 7.1   Approach and avoidance

Tension management devices

Figure 7.1 represents part of our everyday experience of tension in interaction in terms of an 'approach-avoidance' model, capturing the fact that 'positive' and 'negative' are not poles of a single dimension of motivation but are orthogonal dimensions of the motivational 'space'.

Where negative motivation (what is feared) is maximum and positive motivation (what is wished for) is minimum, we are keener on avoiding than on achieving, and so we are in the area of 'avoidance': the outcome will be, in Brown and Levinson's (1987) terms, 'Don't do the FTA'. Where negative motivation is minimum and positive motivation is maximum, we are keener on achieving than on avoiding, so we are in the area of 'approach': the outcome will be 'Do the FTA bald on record.'[2]

It is when the level of motivation on each dimension is moderate to high that, linguistically, things become especially interesting: the conflict between what the speaker wants and does not want produces a tension which is reflected in the language used to cope with the situation. The speaker is as keen to avoid something as they are to achieve something. If asked in an interview, for example, to say whether I would quickly move to another job if offered a better salary, I may be torn between displaying commitment to my prospective employer (positive goal) and avoiding telling a lie (negative goal). I may therefore equivocate with 'Well, of course it would depend on the circumstances' or 'I don't think so but I suppose a situation might arise . . . ', or attempt to deal with the problem through some device of indirectness, for example by denying that I am interested in any other job. In such a situation, therefore, it seems to be the case not that 'equivocation is avoidance' (Bavelas *et al.*

1990, p. 54) but rather that equivocation is a symptom of avoidance in conflict with approach. Both are needed to explain the tension and the need for the management of the tension, expressed in equivocation or indirectness – 'a mechanism for dealing with *conflicting* intentions and desires' (Pyle 1975, cited in Thomas 1995, p. 179; my emphasis).

These particular manoeuvres do not, of course, exhaust the repertoire of what we may call 'tension management devices', a list which includes 'off-record' vagueness (such as hints), violations of Gricean maxims (quantity, quality and the others), implicitness, conventional indirectness, category and quantity approximation, hedges, modal expressions, stance adverbials, questions and conditionals, euphemisms, softeners and downtoners, metaphors and idioms; including, it will be noticed, a large part of the repertoire of items listed by Brown and Levinson as strategies for dealing with various kinds of threats to positive or negative face. I include under hedges expressions such as 'I think', 'I suppose' and 'maybe', but it is important to note that the term has been used by others to cover a wide variety of the items in the list above, and in its broadest definition – 'any linguistic device by which a speaker avoids being compromised by a statement that turns out to be wrong, a request that is not acceptable, and so on' (Matthews 1997) – is almost synonymous with 'tension management devices' (TMD).

Vague language

Which of the above should be included under the heading of VL is a matter of some dispute. Some (for example Channell 1994) take a rather restrictive view of VL, limiting it to vague quantification ('approximation'), vague categorization (for example tags such as 'or something like that') and 'placeholder words' (for example 'thingy', 'whatsisname'). Others, notably Brown and Levinson, take a much less restrictive view, including hedges such as 'I think' (Brown and Levinson 1987, p. 116), which Channell (1994, p. 17) explicitly excludes, and ambiguity and violations of the quantity maxim.

I tend to the more inclusive approach, taking as an instance of VL any purposive choice of language designed to make the degree of accuracy, preciseness, certainty or clarity with which a referent or situation (event, state, process) is described less than it might have been. This definition excludes forced vagueness (where there is no word, or the speaker does not know or cannot remember the word, which precisely denotes the referent or situation) and intrinsic vagueness (labelled by Channell 1994, p. 194) 'displacement', where there is no precise true way of referring to the situation because it is inherently vague, for example the outlook for the weather.

For language use to be recognized as VL, it must be purposive, but it need not, in my view, be 'unabashedly vague', since disguising a vague intent may be, in itself, a self-protective device. If we accuse an interlocutor of 'being very cagey', or using 'weasel words', we are recognizing their vague intent and expressing some degree of disapproval of it. Of course, from an analyst's point of view, the more disguised the vagueness the more difficult it will be to recognize and to describe, but this should not deter us from taking an interest in behaviour which is 'abashedly vague' or, as we may say, vaguely vague.

As to the particular purposes of VL, these have been fully, if not yet perhaps exhaustively, discussed in the literature (Brown and Levinson 1987, pp. 116–17; Channell 1994, p. 194; Cheng and Warren 1999, p. 296). I shall not review these accounts here, but for the time being simply note what is perhaps obvious, that some but not all VL has avoidance (defensive/protective) purposes, and some but not all avoidance behaviour is expressed through VL. What is particularly of interest here, therefore, is the area of overlap between avoidance behaviour and VL.

In the remainder of the chapter I shall apply the ideas outlined above to the case of conference talks, a genre in which the making of evidence- and argument-based claims and criticisms, to an audience of professional peers, in a face-to-face and formal situation, creates high motivations for both avoidance and approach, and thus for tension and its management.

Giving a talk at a conference

At a postgraduate conference a speaker began her talk with the words, 'I'm sure you've heard most of this before, so I hope you don't fall asleep.' Why the modesty? Is it excessive?

As Thomas (1995, p. 176) has observed, 'simply by speaking we trespass on another's space'. In public speaking the trespass is greater and more than usually noticeable. The speaker is imposing not just on a single interlocutor but on many people as an audience, making claims on their time, their attention and their interest. In formal situations (sermons, conference talks, news conferences) escape is difficult for the audience and is impossible for the speaker. The anxiety generated by being about to speak in public is thus easily understandable. Being in front of an audience (Argyle 1967, p. 207) 'makes people feel "observed" and it increases the level of arousal. The performer is aroused and anxious because his esteem and image are exposed to the risk of being damaged.'

The risks to face arise out of the fact that in any formal situation of public speaking there are recognized goals and norms, accepted by both audience and speaker. By standing in front of an audience, a speaker presents a certain face: as someone able to perform before this audience and is worth attending to. 'How can audience anxiety be reduced? If [a public speaker] does not claim a self-image that cannot be invalidated he is less vulnerable; while he must put on a performance, he can do it in a modest way' (ibid.).

The modesty referred to by Argyle is but one possible tactic in the kind of face-work Goffman calls the 'avoidance process', and which involves both defensive and protective manoeuvres. Defensively (Goffman 1999, p. 310), a speaker

> will often present initially a front of diffidence and composure, suppressing any show of feeling until he has found out what kind of line the others will be willing to support for him. Any claims regarding self will be made with belittling modesty, with strong qualifications or with a note of unseriousness; by hedging in these ways he will have prepared a self for himself that will not be discredited by exposure, personal failure, or the unanticipated acts of others.

Protectively, he will 'show respect and politeness /. . ./, employ discretion, leave unstated facts which may contradict and embarrass the positive claims made by others, /. . ./ employ circumlocution' (ibid.).

Goffman is (or appears to be) thinking of conversational encounters, but his account of the avoidance process can be applied with little modification to the situation of public speaking, including that of academic conference presentations. Though the latter may vary considerably in style and content, depending on conference discipline (humanities, sciences, social sciences), conference situation (plenary, parallel, colloquium), research focus (recent empirical, overview, theory/speculation) and the individuality of the speaker, we may suppose that there is something like an avoidance repertoire of which all speakers – and their audiences – are, more or less consciously, aware.

In Table 7.1, I set out some of the more obvious defensive and protective motivations we may expect a speaker at a conference to have.

Table 7.1 Conference presentations: things to avoid

Mainly defensive:
- Revealing what you don't know but ought to know.
- Being inaccurate; saying more than you have evidence for.
- Saying less or more than is needed to make the point.
- Revealing what you haven't done but ought to have done or have done but oughtn't to have done (displaying technical incompetence).
- Being responsible for future failures (commitments, predictions).
- Looking ignorant or misguided; being held responsible for unsustainable opinions.
- Being uninteresting; having nothing much which is both new and relevant to say.
- Overstating/understating the importance of the topic or message.
- Claiming undue credit.
- Seeming self-important, pompous or pretentious.

Mainly protective:
- Imposing unduly (on A's goodwill, freedom of thought or action).
- Threatening self-worth of A, for example by disagreeing, by not valuing a question from the audience.
- Causing offence (through omission or commission).

The list is intended to reflect two realities: that the conference presenter is doing public speaking and that the conference presenter is doing academic work. In addition to the face-work requirements of public speaking, discussed above, the normal requirements of academic text-making – objectivity, acknowledgement, caution and politeness (Myers 1989, pp. 1–35; Salager-Meyer 1994, pp. 150–1; Hyland 1996, pp. 433–5; Crompton 1997, pp. 274–6) – must be observed, though modified of course by the constraints of time and oral delivery.

A prospective conference presenter conscious only of the list of things to avoid would never make it to the podium. Balanced against these fears are of course equally (more or less) powerful 'approach motivations': among them, to advance knowledge, to be seen to be doing one's job, to enhance one's own and one's institution's reputation. Out of this conflict comes tension (Figure 7.1), and from this the extensive repertoire of means to manage it.

Some TMDs in a sample of conference talks

The data here analysed was transcribed from a group of five very short (10-minute) presentations with discussion, at a medical congress held in

Edinburgh in 2000 (sample A, total words 5667),[3] with one more extended (30-minute) presentation given at a medical conference held in Edinburgh in 1998 (sample B, approximately 3700 words).[4] This longer talk was included to provide an element of comparison, on the assumption that more time creates more scope for discursiveness and risk-taking, and thus more TMDs.

My approach is qualitative. My interest has been to explore – identify, describe, explain – some of the phenomena of tension management (tension arising from the conflict between approach and avoidance motivations as illustrated in Figure 7.1), in particular where these overlap with the phenomena of equivocation (or VL). My method is, for each suspect instance of a TMD, to describe the apparent positive goals (approach motivation), the apparent negative goals (avoidance motivation), and the nature of the TMD utilized by the speaker. Taking my cue from Channell (1994, p. 20), I apply the test that language is VL if it 'can be contrasted with another word or expression which appears to render the same proposition', by producing a hypothetical alternative utterance, one that might have been used if the speaker had perceived no 'tension' or if they had simply failed to 'manage' it.

Openings and closings

These we might expect to be rich sites for TMDs, with the speaker both claiming attention (positive goal) and disclaiming immodest ambitions (negative goal). Of the five short talks, four restrict themselves to the minimal conventional routines – thank the chairman at the beginning, thank the audience at the end – while one (from text A1) displays TMDs in the opening:

> [A1]   Madam Chairman, ladies and gentlemen thank you for giving me the opportunity of speaking today. My name is [name] and I am working as a research associate at [institution]. I would just like to bring to your attention the efforts of the research team: [names].

All these examples (Table 7.2) can be seen as manifesting one or another kind of category vagueness in the service of tension management; we

Table 7.2 Openings – belittling modesty

No.	Text	Positive goal	Negative goal	TMD	Non-TMD alternative
A1.1	thank you for giving me the opportunity of speaking today	Claim attention of audience (A).	Avoid appearing to claim the unfettered right to speak	Shift power to A.	thank you
A1.2	I am working as a research associate at	Claim competence.	Avoid claiming undue credit	Convert role into process: working as.	I am a research associate
A1.3	I would just like to bring to your attention the efforts of the research team . . .	Claim tellability reportability of research work.	Avoid appearing to overstate the research achievement	Conventional indirectness: would like to Downtoner: just euphemism: bring to your attention Focus on process not outcome: efforts	I shall report on the work of . . .

see claim-making with 'belittling modesty' through fudging of the nature of the relationship between speaker and audience (A1.1), the work status of the speaker (A1.2) and the speaker's assessment of the weightiness of the work accomplished (A1.3).

The B speaker, with more time at his disposal, provides a somewhat more elaborate display of TMDs in his opening. There is an array of euphemistic, hedging and approximating devices here ('plan to', 'half hour or so', 'present to you', 'partly drawing on', 'from the point of view of') that are so much part of the ritual of conference talk openings that we hardly notice them. B.4 is the familiar ploy of the expert in alien territory: in this case the research scientist (neurochemist) among an audience of clinicians. The only non-TMD alternative in this case would be to make no reference to the academic cultural divide at all (Table 7.3).

Table 7.3   Openings – euphemisms, hedging and approximating

No.	Text	Positive goal	Negative goal	TMD	Non-TMD alternative
B.1	What I plan to do over the next half hour or so	Claim attention of A.	Avoid appearing to impose unduly on A by giving a rigid scheme or time frame	plan to substitute for euphemist will/shall approximator or so	What I shall do in the next half hour
B.2	is to present to you the major theories for . . .	Inform A of outline of talk.	Avoid appearing to underestimate existing state of knowledge of A	present substitute for euphemist tell	is to tell you about the major theories for
B.3	partly drawing on results from my own research lab . . .	Claim competence.	Avoid claiming undue credit[5] or being over-precise about source	Approximator: partly	drawing on results
B.4	And I should say I am presenting this very much from the point of view of a neurochemist	Claim competence.	Avoid displaying lack of relevant expertise or insight	Hedge: I should say. stance emphasis: very much from the point of view of	—

B's closing likewise goes some way beyond the minimal 'thank you for your attention' of the A presenters:

> [B.5]   And on that point I should finish. I have really just glossed over some of the neuronal bases of /. . ./ and I think this rather superficial review of /. . ./ really reflects our very limited understanding of /. . ./. Thank you very much.

We see B protecting himself against the possible thought that there are things known to the audience that he may be ignorant of, or of which he may appear not have appreciated the full importance. He implies that the glossing over is due to lack of sufficient time (euphemistically choosing 'should finish' in preference to 'must stop') and cushions his own admission of 'glossing over' with a softening 'really just' and an approximating 'some of'. He mitigates 'limited understanding' with the robust academic vague-ism 'our': possibly referring (in order from less to more damaging) to himself and the audience, or himself and all other neurochemists, or himself and his colleagues.

Research background, methods and results sections

There is a great deal of VL in these sections, much of which can be straightforwardly explained in terms of normal adherence to the maxims of quantity and quality.

[A3.1]   <u>Often</u> the patient is elderly, the defect <u>might</u> be larger, the patient has <u>several</u> general diseases <u>perhaps</u>, and also will <u>perhaps</u> receive radiation therapy afterwards.

[B.6]   Although there are *slight* deviations from that, that correlation <u>it seems to generally rule</u> that <u>almost all</u> anti-psychotic drugs are *likely* to work by blockade of dopamine D2 receptors.

[A1.4]   The psychological status of the patient <u>can</u> be just as important as the physical as they <u>can</u> influence each other.

[A5.1]   As far as the surgical treatment [is] concerned segmental resection is reserved <u>mainly</u> for the invaded mandibles, as should be self-explanatory, and second rim/ring dissection is <u>mainly</u> for the dentate jaws, whereas the edentulist mandibles are treated mainly with a segmental resection.

Here we see a range of vagueness devices motivated by inherent uncertainty: A3.1 speculating about a hypothetical typical patient, B.6 summarizing the current state of knowledge on the effects of drug in question. A4.1 and A5.1 make generalizations about strong tendencies while leaving open the possibility of cases that fall outside the generalization; in the absence of justification for providing detailed frequencies for such cases, 'can' and 'mainly' secure adherence to the maxims of both quantity and quality.

In most cases quantitative approximation (use of round numbers, imprecise quantifiers and so on) functions similarly.

[A1.5]   Treatment for oral cancer has become increasingly aggressive in order to achieve better survival statistics with <u>2900 people a year</u> diagnosed in the UK.

[A1.6] Patients were seen <u>every two weeks to a month for up to eight</u> months.

But the next example does not seem so easily explained in this way:

[A1.7] The themes here are just a selection of the issues we concentrated on in the interview with <u>approximately eight</u> of the themes discussed.

The use of 'approximately' with a precise small number, one for which the presenter as researcher is himself the source, suggests tension, possibly arising in this case from the negative goal of wishing to avoid a commitment to present and analyse a precise number of themes (Table 7.4).

Nominalization and passivization are both used with the apparent intention of being inexplicit about agency:

[A1.9]   Fear of recurrence was always present.
[A1.10] Patients were evaluated . . .
         Patients were seen . . .
         The interviews were structured . . .
         Patients . . . were recruited . . .
         very substantial data were produced
         patients will be randomised
[A1.11] The interviewer developed close relationships with patients and their families.

The nominalizations in A1.9 leave implicit the subjects of 'fear' (patients) and 'recurrence' (cancer), thereby, since the audience can be

Table 7.4 Methods/Results – using 'approximately'

No.	Text	Positive goal	Negative goal	TMD	Non-TMD alternative
A1.8	with <u>approximately eight</u> of the themes discussed	Report on research activity (methods, results)	Avoid making a commitment to look at a precise number of distinct themes	Approximator: <u>approximately</u>	with eight of the themes discussed

assumed to be able to work them (the subjects) out for themselves, maintaining adherence to the maxim of quantity. A self-protective explanation for the examples in A1.10 is not necessarily compelling but is conceivable. Whereas in academic written text such deletion of agency may be seen as part of the framing of the research activity as scientifically objective, in the case of an oral presentation, with its more immediate exposure to risk (questions from the floor), it may be seen as (alternatively or additionally) shielding the speaker from attribution of personal responsibility: being blamed for imperfections in the research process or being blamed for taking undue credit. The noun phrase 'the interviewer' in A1.11, open as it is to a generic interpretation ('whoever and however many did the interviews'), may likewise have a wholly or partly shielding function (compare other conventionally inexplicit or impersonal descriptions such as 'the researcher', 'the investigator').

Much of the protective work found in these sections of the talks is motivated by modesty and by respect for the assumed prior knowledge of the audience (Table 7.5). The tension between the wish to inform and the wish to avoid underestimating the knowledge of the audience is reflected in the examples below. A3.2–4 illustrate conventional routines for signalling to A that it is not assumed that they do not possess the information being provided, thereby respecting A and protecting S. A1.12 achieves the same avoidance effect, not by what is said but by what is omitted – namely any specification of the 'systems crucial to life' referred to – presumably eating, drinking, and so on – which the speaker must assume that the audience can infer (Table 7.5).

Defensive-protective ambiguity is frequently produced by the use of 'just' (Table 7.6). The following examples all involve episodes where the speaker is signalling that findings are about to be presented:

The interpretation section

In the interpretation section of the presentation, tension arises from the conflict between wanting to make confident statements on research outcomes and wanting to avoid well-founded challenges on validity. Merely to present methods and results would be to fall short of the conventional expectations for an acceptable performance: it is the interpretation of results that makes the presentation as a whole worth while. Though Howard (1998, p. 13) is no doubt right in arguing that one explanation for vagueness – he is looking specifically at non-exact quantification presented on slides – is 'to initiate the process of generalizing from the particular results of the research to scientific truths', it also seems to be the case that this vagueness arises out of the fundamental tension between

Table 7.5   Methods/Results – respecting assumed prior knowledge

No.	Text	Positive goal	Negative goal	TMD	Non-TMD alternative
A3.2	Now we all know that there are several problems	Wish/need to inform (provide relevant medical context)	Avoid appearing to underestimate the relevant knowledge of the audience	Audience inclusion: we all know	There are several problems
A3.3	And you are all familiar with these problems that occur sooner or later like the plate fracture			Audience inclusion: you are all familiar with	And problems occur sooner or later like . . .
A3.4	We resected the mandible, after scrubbing *of course* and anaesthesia			Audience inclusion: of course	We resected the mandible, after scrubbing and anaesthesia
A1.12	as side effects of the treatment are so visible and affect systems crucial to life			Inexplicit general noun phrase	affect systems crucial to life such as eating, speaking

the need to be interesting and the need to be true. This tension is managed most straightforwardly through the routinized use of attitude/belief expressions ('believe', 'think', 'seem') and of epistemic modals:

[A3.6]   So we believe /. . ./ should be done
[A4.3]   In conclusion it appears that /. . ./ seems to be . . .
[A4.4]   we see here that we thought that we had . . .
[A5.2]   we may say – may be able to say . . .
[A1.14] This [qualitative methodology] should provide us with a solid framework . . .
[A1.15] It appears health professionals underestimate . . .
[A1.16] [reluctance to eat] in public /. . ./ was thought to be caused by . . .

with frequent use in this particular sample of data of 'indicate'/'indication':

[A2.1]   From these data proposed indications for /. . ./ is roughly like this

[A1.17]   the qualitative data has indicated possible themes for further investigation.

Table 7.6   Methods/Results – 'just' minimizing imposition

No.	Text	Positive goal	Negative goal	TMD	Non-TMD alternative
A4.2	This is a slide just to summarize our results	Signal forthcoming information about research process/ results	Protective: . minimize weight of imposition defensive: avoid the suggestion that there is nothing more that could be said (if imposing were not a problem)		This slide summarizes . . .
A1.13	The themes here are just a selection of the issues we concentrated on in the interview				The themes here are a selection . . .
A3.5	And just shortly about the results of this study.			Minimizer: just	And shortly about . . .
B.7	And just to summarize it for you . . .				And to summarize it for you . . .
B.8	Just to take – developing this a little further – the role of dopamine /. . ./				To take /. . ./ the role of dopamine

Here, again, the B presentation provides instances of more elaborate TMDs.

Table 7.7 Interpretation – avoiding challenges on validity

No.	Text	Positive goal	Negative goal	TMD	non-TMD alternative
B.9	Now, now although there's some dispute as to the origin of this change it's perhaps generally interpreted as primarily a change in response to /. . ./ and not particularly associated with the disease process	Present interpretation of research outcomes	Avoid challenges on validity	Acknowledge counter-interpretation: some dispute Disguise agency: interpreted, associated Hedging adverbs: primarily, generally, not particularly	This change is in response to /. . ./ and not the disease process
B.10	And this thought came from several further experiments			Euphemisms: thought, come from	We concluded from several further experiments that . . .
B.11	How might that be? Well, here I've just listed a few of these receptors and how they might be implicated . . .			Rhetorical question and answer with conversational well modal might	These receptors are implicated . . .

Here the speaker's efforts at self-protection are more transparent, distancing him as they do, through use of passivization, euphemism and an interrogative, from plain responsibility for the interpretation.

It is important to make clear that I am not here offering a variant of the research presenter (speaker or writer) using VL as a 'cover-up' tactic. In response to the question 'Imprecision and Vagueness: Courtesy, Coyness or Necessity?' (Salager-Meyer 1993, pp. 1–13) my reply is: not necessarily 'courtesy', or 'coyness', but by and large, 'necessity'. The presenter is doing no more or less than presenting 'the true state of [their] understanding, the strongest claim a researcher can make' (ibid., p. 9). My argument is that this activity is inherently, unavoidably, tension-inducing, that this tension has to be managed, and that the means of this management is, in large part and in the broadest understanding of the term, VL.

Conclusion: applications and further research

Politeness theory has given us a clearly articulated, evidence-supported, account of the causes and kinds of politeness behaviour, with an extensively detailed repertoire of stratagems for face-saving. It has been criticized on various grounds, among these that it focuses too much on the speaker at the expense of hearer (on production rather than reception) and that the universality of politeness has been overemphasized at the expense of a proper recognition of the constitutive role of cultural and situational appropriateness (Eelen 2001).

A principal part of my argument in this chapter has been that one consequence of the success of politeness theory has been an excessive focus on that part of face-work that attends to the face needs of the hearer and a corresponding lack of interest in its counterpart, that part of face-work that attends to the face needs of the speaker. There are two strands to this argument: first that defensive (self-protective) face-work constitutes an important part of the normal repertoire of communicative competence; and second that other-protective face-work (politeness) can also be seen, as Holden Caulfield saw it, as serving a self-protective function.

The other main part of my argument has been that self-protective (avoidance) motivations interact with positive goal motivations to create approach-avoidance conflict, and that it is, in part, through the stratagems of equivocation, realized in one kind or another of VL, that the consequential tensions are managed in day-to-day communication.

The range of possible applications of this kind of analysis is the same as those of the broad field of interaction management, politeness and face taken as whole: greater understanding of, and potentially more effective intervention in, processes of language use in teaching and learning (not only of languages), academic discourse, language in the workplace, political and other public language, and so forth.

In looking at medical research presentations in conferences, I have explored VL as part of tension management within a specific oral – public speaking – genre: both a culture and a situation of tension-prone language use. Further work on these lines would offer, I suggest, a practical framework for analysis (including comparative analysis), unfettered by claims or implications of cultural universalism, of many varieties of institutional discourse. In particular, the apparent differences between the two samples of data studied in this chapter suggest that attention to the effects of different subgenres (mentioned above) and different styles of academic speaking on use of VL would be worth while. By different styles I have in mind the 'reading', 'conversational' and 'rhetorical' styles identified by Dudley-Evans and Johns (1981, p. 34) and Goffman's (1981, pp. 171–2) 'three main modes of animating spoken words': 'memorisation', 'aloud reading' and 'fresh talk'. The extent to which the lecture 'is processed by the speaker in real time or is read' and 'allows for any spoken interaction with the audience or is pure monologue' (Dudley-Evans and Johns ibid.) may well turn out to be variables in perceived levels of tension and consequent tactics, including VL, for tension management. Such work could lead to better understanding not only of genre and style but also of cross-cultural differences in talk presentation and reception, and thence, especially in an era when the 'conversational' and the 'fresh' are favoured in public discourse, to more effective modes of education and training for the next generation of scholars.

Notes

1. J.D. Salinger, *The Catcher in the Rye* (London: Penguin Books, 1994).
2. If both negative and positive motivation are low, we are driven neither to achieve nor to avoid; we are in a state of inertia.
3. The data were collected and transcribed by Ron Howard (formerly of the Medical English Section, IALS, University of Edinburgh), whose contribution to the work that lies behind this chapter I gratefully acknowledge.
4. Data from the Medical English Archive, held at IALS University of Edinburgh.
5. See Goffman (1981, p. 167) on the 'troublesome' term speaker (in the lecturing context): a person who, among other things, is seen as the 'principal' and who personally believes in what is being said.

References

M. Allaby (ed.), *Dictionary of Zoology* (Oxford University Press, 1999).
M. Argyle, *The Psychology of Interpersonal Behaviour* (Harmondsworth: Penguin, 1967).
J.L. Austin, *How To Do Things With Words* (London: Oxford University Press, 1962).
J.B. Bavelas, A. Black, N. Chovil and J. Mullett, *Equivocal Communication* (Newbury Park, CA: Sage Publications, 1990).
R. Bello, *Causes and Psycholinguistic Correlates of Interpersonal Equivocation* (National Communication Association, New York: NY, November 1998).
G. Brown and G. Yule, *Discourse Analysis* (Cambridge University Press, 1983).
P. Brown and S. Levinson, *Politeness: Some Universals in Language Use* (Cambridge University Press, 1987).
J. Channell, *Vague Language* (Oxford University Press, 1994).
W. Cheng and M. Warren, 'Inexplicitness: What Is It and Should We Be Teaching It?' *Applied Linguistics*, 20/3 (1999) 296.

P. Crompton, 'Hedging in Academic Writing: Some Theoretical Problems', *English for Specific Purposes,* 16/4 (1997) 271–87.

T. Dudley-Evans, 'A Team Teaching Approach to Lecture Comprehsion for Overseas Students', in *The Teaching of Listening Comprehsion,* ELT Documents special, (London: British Council, 1981).

G. Eelen, *A Critique of Politeness Theories* (Manchester: St Jerome's Press, 2001).

H. Garfinkel, 'Time Structures the Biography and Prospects of a Situation', in M. Douglas (ed.), *Rules and Meanings* (Harmondsworth: Penguin Education, 1973).

E. Goffman, 'The Lecture', in *Forms of Talk* (Philadelphia, PA: University of Pennsylvania, 1981).

E. Goffman, 'On Face-Work: An Analysis of Ritual Elements in Social Interaction', in A. Jaworski and N. Coupland (eds), *The Discourse Reader* (London: Routledge, 1999).

H.P. Grice, 'Logic and Conversation', in P. Cole and J. Morgan (eds), *Syntax and Semantics: Speech Acts 31* (New York: Academic Press, 1975).

R. Howard, 'Non-Exact Quantification in Slide Presentations of Medical Research', *Edinburgh Working Papers in Applied Linguistics,* 9 (1998) 1–16.

K. Hyland, 'Writing Without Conviction? Hedging in Science Research Articles', *Applied Linguistics,* 17/4 (1996) 433–54.

D. Hymes, 'Models of the Interaction of Language and Social Life', in J. Gumperz and D. Hymes (eds), *Directions in Sociolinguistics: The Ethnography of Communication* (New York: Holt, Rinehart & Winston, 1972) 35–71.

K. Lewin, *Field Theory in Social Science* (London: Tavistock, 1952).

P.H. Matthews, *Concise Dictionary of Linguistics* (Oxford University Press 1997).

G. Myers, 'Politeness in Scientific Articles', *Applied Linguistics,* 10/1 (1989) 1–35.

C. Pyle, 'The Function of Indirectness', presented at N-Wave IV, Georgetown University, Washington, DC (1975).

F. Salager-Meyer, 'Hedges and Textual Communicative Function in Medical English Written Discourse', *English for Specific Purposes,* 13/2 (1994) 149–70.

F. Salager-Meyer, 'Imprecision and Vagueness (Hedging) in Today's Medical Discourse: Courtesy, Coyness, or Necessity?', *ESPecialist,* 14/1 (1993) 1–15.

J.R. Searle, *Expression and Meaning* (Cambridge University Press, 1979).

J. Thomas, *Meaning in Interaction: An Introduction to Pragmatics* (London: Longman, 1995).

8
'Looking Out for Love and All the Rest of It': Vague Category Markers as Shared Social Space

Jane Evison, Michael McCarthy and Anne O'Keeffe

Introduction

Carter and McCarthy (2006, p. 202) assert that VL expressions are a strong indication of an assumed shared knowledge and that they mark in-group membership, in so far as the referents of vague expressions can be assumed to be known by the listener. This is consistent with Cutting (2000), who illustrates how discourse communities use VL as a marker of in-group membership. It is this interactive aspect of VL that we will focus on in this chapter. We examine one particular manifestation of vagueness: the creation of vague category markers (hereafter VCMs), such as 'university courses <u>and that sort of thing</u>'; 'I've got to wash my hair <u>and everything</u>', where speakers refer obliquely to other members of categories which they assume their listeners will be able to 'fill in'. In extract (1) from an everyday conversation at a family dinner table (taken from the Limerick Corpus of Irish English, hereafter LCIE), where the participants are talking about someone who has taken a job at a local fast-food restaurant, one of the speakers throws out an ad hoc category (Barsalou 1983, 1987):

(1)
Speaker 1: And what's he going to be doing in there?
Speaker 2: I think they're training him as a trainee manager.
Speaker 1: Frying chips?
Speaker 3: You mean he's frying chips. Basically. <laughs>
Speaker 2: He says 'I'm going to do everything. <u>Fry chips and wait tables and stuff</u>'.
Speaker 1: . . . there's no way he'll be able for that like <laughs>

The category that speaker 2 creates did not derive from any prefabricated lexical chunk before he spoke 'fry chips and wait tables <u>and stuff</u>'. Yet the speaker needed this category in this situation and he had it within his resources to create it. He did so in the knowledge that his interlocutors would know what it meant and cognitively that they would be able to fill in the set he has referred to within their shared cultural frame of reference. In the (Irish) context in which the category was projected the set refers to the range of possible activities one could be asked to undertake while working in a fast-food outlet, such as cook chips and burgers, serve customers, sweep floors, clean tables, but not paint walls, design advertising, do bookkeeping or sing to the customers. The set has a finite range, the limits of which are understood within the socio-cultural context, and for the speaker to have listed every possible item in the set would have been at best pedantic and at worst absurd. Jucker *et al.* (2003) point out that such vague categories ask the hearer to construct the relevant components of the set which they evoke and promote the active cooperation of the listener. Some more examples of the VCMs under scrutiny in this chapter are given here (taken from the CANCSOC corpus; see below):

(2)
[Speaker is talking about various people's jobs]
And my husband travelled for his father, selling <u>and that sort of thing</u>.

(3)
Speaker 1: He was interested in keeping bees.
Speaker 2: Oh yes, yes, bees and chickens <u>and all the rest of it</u>.

(4)
She frames pictures <u>and so on</u> and she doesn't have much free time.

The rationale behind this chapter is that in order to use VCMs successfully, speakers must have expectations about what their co-participants know, and that such expectations are negotiated within social space, in the sense expounded by Vygotsky (1978), for whom social relationships, language use, thought and cultural activity share the same creative space (see 'A Vygotskian perspective' below). Within a socially defined group, VCMs become a tool for creating shortcuts.

In this chapter we use three spoken corpora, two subcorpora of the predominantly British English CANCODE[1] corpus, and the Limerick Corpus of Irish English (LCIE), to explore VCMs in contexts where the participants have different degrees of shared knowledge and intimacy. We explore how the shared knowledge required on the part of the participants in order to interpret VCMs has a common core of socio-culturally ratified 'understandings' in each specific context and how the range of domains of reference of these categories is relative to the assumed depth of shared knowledge of the participants and their social relationships.

VCMs are most typically, but not exclusively, found in clause-final positions and often consist of a conjunction and a noun phrase (for example, 'and/or that sort of thing'). In the literature, they go by different terms such as: 'general extenders' (Overstreet and Yule 1997a, 1997b); 'generalized list completers' (Jefferson 1990); 'tags' (Ward and Birner 1992); 'terminal tags' (Dines 1980; Macaulay 1991); 'extension particles' (Dubois 1993); 'vague category identifiers' (Channell 1994; Jucker *et al.* 2003); and vague category markers (O'Keeffe 2003). In this chapter we adhere to O'Keeffe's terminology.

O'Keeffe (2003) refers to VCMs as recognizable chunks of language that function in an expedient way as linguistic triggers employed by speakers and decoded by co-participants who draw on their store of shared knowledge. In a corpus-based study of an Irish radio phone-in (whose data are called upon in the present chapter) O'Keeffe argues that the meanings of vague categories are socio-culturally grounded and are co-constructed within a social group that has a shared socio-historic reality. This is consistent with Overstreet and Yule (1997b), who point out that the process of establishing categories is locally contingent in discourse.

In another corpus-based study McCarthy *et al.* (2005) compared VCMs and their referents in three corpora, the 5-million-word CAN-CODE corpus, LCIE, a 1-million word corpus of Irish casual conversation, and the Limerick and Belfast Corpus of Spoken Academic Discourse (LIBEL), a 1-million-word corpus of academic discourse collected on the island of Ireland. They noted differences in VCMs in the academic data compared with the casual conversation corpora (LCIE and CANCODE). For example, 'et cetera', widely used in the academic context, was rare in the conversational ones; additionally, the academic context showed VCMs functioning to hedge factual assertions more than in conversation. O'Keeffe (2006) further compared these findings with a sample of VCMs from a corpus of media discourse and found that the forms used in political interviews most resembled those in the academic discourse from LIBEL. She also noted, like McCarthy *et al.* (2005), that the more institutionalized data contained fewer instances of vague categories. McCarthy *et al.* (2005) also found the participants in a university small group setting drew on shared knowledge and, influenced by the work of Vygotskian applied linguists (see also 'A Vygotskian perspective' below), they suggested that vague categorization was a means of the creation and maintenance of 'shared space' within this classroom setting, and a significant site for learning opportunities and concept-formation.

Such studies seem to point to the use of VCMs as purposeful, creative and highly interactive. In this chapter we hope to reinforce those views and to examine in greater detail how speakers in different contextual domains make reference to collective phenomena and experiences in ways their interlocutors can decode and share within particular contexts, and thus enter into that social space where language and thought co-exist and push into new conceptual frontiers.

A Vygotskian perspective

Value category markers are, above all, highly interactive: they invite the interlocutor to enter a conceptual space with the speaker where phenomena perceived as sharing characteristics are bundled together in acts of meaning-making. Those phenomena are 'projected' as shared experience; there is never any guarantee that two or more minds are conceptualizing the full range of identical phenomena. Such creative activity within the shared space enables new acts of cognition, whether these are instrumental in crystallizing new stances, opinions, judgements or simply different personal perspectives on people and things in the social and cultural environment. Of relevance here is Vygotsky's notion that social interaction plays a fundamental role in the development of cognition. Speaking of child development, Vygotsky (1978, p. 57) asserted:

> Every function in the child's cultural development appears twice: first, on the social level, and later, on the individual level; first, between people (interpsychological) and then inside the child (intrapsychological). This applies equally to voluntary attention, to logical memory, and to the formation of concepts. All the higher functions originate as actual relationships between individuals.

Much of what Vygotsky says concerning the child's social experience is relevant to our present concerns. Even more relevant is the child's proclivity to categorize. It is an uncontroversial observation that a child naturally sorts things into categories which share common attributes, a process which, in its initial stages, may produce categories which the adult perception would dismiss (for example, calling a sheep a 'dog' because it has four legs and a fluffy coat). Such attempts at basic categorization Vygotsky refers to as 'diffuse complexes' (1962, ch. 4). Diffuse complexes enable generalities to be made based on concrete experience by perceiving similarities among phenomena, however unstable such perceived similarities may be.

VCMs capture the fluidity and instability of the diffuse complex, the preconceptual phase where the language user attempts to make meaning from diverse phenomena and experiences, and reaches out to his or her interlocutor in an appeal to equally diffuse and unstable shared experience. Within the social space of such negotiations, it is not just language which is creative, but thought itself, and the language user has the possibility of new understandings and new critical, ethical and moral positions (Crawford 2001), whether in the pedagogical context of the school or university, in the public media context of broadcast debates, radio phone-ins and so on, or in the private and intimate fora of casual conversation. It should not be a source of surprise, therefore, that what in the lay perception may be typically characterized as sharp, focused discourse and incisive intellectual exchange (for instance, academic discussion or broadcast debate) should in fact be frequently characterized by the same kinds of vague references to non-institutionalized and only partially formulated categories of external phenomena and human experience as occur in casual conversation, as we hope to show in this chapter. Vague categories are far from vague in the negative sense of uninformative or sloppily constructed; they are at the creative forefront of language use and the collaborative making of meaning.

Data and methodology: CANCSOC as benchmark

This chapter bases its initial, wide-ranging analyses on a 1-million-word subcorpus of the CANCODE spoken corpus. The sub-corpus consists only of a sample of socializing and intimate conversations, and excludes professional (such as workplace conversations), transactional (for example, service encounters) and pedagogical (for instance, the university classroom) conversations. This last group are addressed separately in this chapter (the CANCAD corpus, see below). We refer to this socializing sub-corpus as CANCSOC.

The investigation began with an analysis of 'chunks' in the CANCSOC corpus. The analytical software used (*Wordsmith Tools*: Scott 1999) is capable of automatically retrieving recurrent strings of words and generating frequency lists for their occurrence. In this chapter we focus on those items from the first 500 (or the whole list where this is less than 500; see below) of the automatically generated rank-order frequency lists for CANCSOC which display the potential to act as VCMs.

Rank-order frequency lists of 2-, 3-, 4-, 5- and 6-word sequences were generated. The lists were then combed for all items occurring 10 times or more which could potentially act as VCMs. These were then checked against concordances to see if they were in fact used in this way. For the longer lists (the 2-, 3- and 4-word ones), only the first 500 items were considered, and only items which formed complete 'chunks' (that is to say, which displayed syntactic and semantic/pragmatic integrity; see below) were extracted. The resultant VCM chunks are presented in rank order of frequency in Table 8.1.

Many recurrent strings, although frequent, do not qualify as potential VCM chunks as they do not display syntactic or semantic/pragmatic integrity, for example, 'that sort of', 'and stuff like'. These are often incomplete segments of longer strings which do possess wholeness ('that sort of thing', 'and stuff like that'). However, some strings can be both whole in themselves and form part of longer strings, for instance, 'and that', which functions as a VCM in CANCSOC (for example, 'The fans you get in Spain are all these fancy ones with lace <u>and that</u>'), but which is also part of the longer chunk '<u>and that</u> [kind/sort] of thing'. The total frequency counts were therefore performed by subtracting and listing

Table 8.1 Value category markers in CANCSOC

VCMs	Total
and/or [something/anything/everything] (like that)	1024
(and/or) (X) stuff (like that/X)	620
and (all) (of) that	270
(and/or) thing(s) (like that/X)	579
(all) [this/that/these/those] [kind(s)/sort(s)/type(s)] of X	219
(or) whatever	90
and so on (and so forth)	60
et cetera (et cetera)	30
Xs like that	25
and all the rest of it	12
(and) this that and the other	11
Total	2940

Round brackets indicate lexical items that may co-occur. Items within square brackets are alternative but mutually exclusive (for instance, 'that [kind/sort/type]' of X implies 'that kind or sort or type of X').

separately the totals for shorter, integrated items where they also occurred as part of longer items.

Items were demarked according to their syntactic headwords: for example, items with 'kind/sort/type' as headword ('all these <u>kinds</u> of things', 'that <u>sort</u> of thing') were listed separately from items with 'thing(s)' as headword ('<u>things</u> like that', 'and <u>things</u>'). The limited scope of the CANCSOC count, focusing only on high-frequency items, does not take into account items which may operate as VCMs but which are simply not sufficiently evidenced. For example, one utterance which clearly contains a VCM is 'I was sitting with Jim <u>and that lot</u>', where a high degree of shared knowledge is presupposed (who the members of Jim's surrounding group were). However, 'and that lot' only occurs as a VCM 7 times, falling below the CANCSOC cut-off point of 10 occurrences. This issue is even more acute in the case of the two smaller, specialized corpora used for comparison (CANCAD and *Liveline;* see below). For those corpora, the CANCSOC VCMs were checked and, in addition, the two corpora were read line by line and all other VCMs, even those occurring only once, were manually added. These manually added VCMS were then back-checked in CANCSOC and any occurrences were added to the CANCSOC total.

CANCSOC and types of VCM reference

CANCSOC is a corpus of informal conversations among friends and intimates, so it is not surprising that CANCSOC VCMs encode a high degree of projected shared knowledge, often knowledge which is shared widely within the British and Irish speech communities. This means that in many cases, any member of those communities (or indeed people beyond the communities) can successfully 'fill in' the category members. However, in many cases, the categories are opaque, to the extent that category members are obscure or can be speculated upon only by the non-participant observer-analyst. A range of examples ranked from transparent to opaque serve to illustrate this (Table 8.2).

The VCM examples in Table 8.2 are all based round noun phrases, but VCMs may also refer to categories of states, actions and events:

(5)   I wasn't expecting to be sort of <u>judged and criticized and things</u>.
(6)   It was really good, it was <u>sunny and everything</u>, not at all cold.
(7)   I'll be super fit, not <u>out of breath or anything</u>.

Table 8.2 Examples of value category markers in CANCSOC

CANCSOC example	Comments
'She appreciates quietness and peace and she loves <u>flowers and that sort of thing</u>.'	Easily interpretable by most people anywhere in the world.
'We'll meet up and go to Leeds for the day because there's <u>a new Marks and er a new Debenhams and stuff like that</u>.'	Less easily interpretable; one needs to know that *Marks* and *Debenhams* are large departments store chains; most British/Irish people know this.
'So like God speaks to us through the prophets as well now doesn't he. <u>Likes of Tony Ling and that</u>.'	Interpretable only by those people with knowledge of *Tony Ling* as a religious figure within a minority Christian sect.
[speech at a family birthday party] 'Four generations here today and that's important. And Mrs Wheeler and my dad are of the first generation. And then there's old ones <u>like Bobby and Paul and so on</u>.'	Only interpretable by the family members and others at the social gathering who know the family.

Two comparative corpora: *Liveline* And CANCAD

We now turn to look at smaller amounts of contextually situated data. The results from CANCSOC will form a baseline against which these other data can be compared. Here we use two small corpora. The first is a 55,000 word sub-corpus of LCIE, consisting of data from an Irish radio phone-in show called *Liveline* broadcast every weekday on *Radio Telefís Éireann* (RTÉ). The programme has been running for twenty years and has an audience of over 365,000,[2] almost 10 per cent of the Irish population. These data were taken from a sample of programmes in 1998, comprising 44 phone calls from a total of five programmes. Topics of calls to the show include the following miscellany: female facial hair problems, tattoos, the peace process in Northern Ireland, how ears were pierced in the old days, warnings about the decline of fidelity and moral decay in general, and the growing trend of litigation in Irish society, among others (see O'Keeffe 2003).

The second small corpus, CANCAD (Cambridge and Nottingham Corpus of Academic English) is composed of 7 university seminars taken from the pedagogical section of the 5-million-word CANCODE corpus. There were a range of speaker styles and approaches evident in the seminars: in 2 the tutor held the floor for a considerable portion of the time, in 4 the tutor led a whole-class discussion throughout the session, and in one the tutor left the room during the discussion. In 4 out of the 7 seminars, participants were ready to talk about literature texts they had prepared for the class and in the other 3 handouts were given out at the start of the class containing textual extracts.

Liveline and CANCAD: analysis

Liveline and CANCAD were searched for all the VCMs found in CANCSOC; this search yielded the results shown in Table 8.3.

A comparison of the three data sets gives the following distribution, normalized to occurrences per million words, as can be seen in Table 8.4.

Even though the CANCSOC figure is only based on the first 500 items of the longer lists it exceeds that of the two smaller corpora, though the radio data are closer to CANCSOC than CANCAD is. From these initial results, we propose that the closer the speaker relationship within the participation framework (after Goffman 1981), the greater the shared space that they can exploit. The conversations in CANCSOC involve close friends and family members and have the highest number of VCMs. The radio phone-in data, as O'Keeffe (2002, 2003, 2006) has argued, involve the creation of a pseudo-intimacy within a stable

Table 8.3   Value category markers in *Liveline* and CANCAD

VCMs	CANCAD	Liveline
(all) [this/that/these/those] [kind(s)/sort(s)/type(s)] of X	7	17
(and) this that and the other	0	3
(or) whatever	6	10
and (all) (of) that	2	3
and all the rest of it	0	0
and so on (and so forth)	16	12
([and/or]) [something/anything/everything] (like that)	8	10
([and/or]) (X) stuff (like [that/X])	18	7
([and/or]) thing(s) (like [that/X])	43	46
et cetera (et cetera)	2	6
Xs like [this/that]	0	21
Total	102	135

Table 8.4 Value category markers in CANCSOC, *Liveline* and CANCAD

Corpus	VCMs	Per million
CANCSOC	2940	2940
Liveline	135	2454
CANCAD	102	1873

participation framework. Presenters, callers and audience are attempting to create a pseudo-conversational context. Overall, *Liveline* is much more like friendly conversation than formal radio debate (see O'Keeffe 2006 for a comparison of media genres).

The academic data contains fewer VCMs than the radio phone-in data. The academic data also draw on shared knowledge, but the knowledge assumed within this participation framework is mostly specific to academic disciplines and academic discourse communities (Swales 1990). Swales's notion of discourse communities includes common goals and participatory mechanisms, the use of specific genres of communication, a high level of shared expertise and specialized terminology. All of these feed into the types of VCMs found in CANCAD.

In addition to the search for those VCMs of high frequency in CANCSOC, *Liveline* and CANCAD were searched manually for all occurrences of VCMs. This rendered the following additional items (Table 8.5). In order to achieve consistency, the additional VCMs were then back-checked in CANCSOC, for which the figures also appear in Table 8.5:

Table 8.5 Additional value category markers in *Liveline* and CANCAD

VCM	*Liveline*	CANCAD	CANCSOC
Or that	2	0	2
For the X that's in it[3]	1	0	0
Or some other one of X	1	0	0
Or any of X	1	0	0
And so forth	2	1	1
Total	7	1	3

Table 8.6 Revised totals for value category markers in
CANCSOC, *Liveline* and CANCAD

Corpus	VCMs	Per million
CANCSOC	2943	2943
Liveline	142	2582
CANCAD	103	1873

Table 8.4 now needs to be slightly adjusted to take these figures into
account. The broad picture is little affected, except to bring *Liveline* even
closer to CANCSOC (Table 8.6).

Examples of these VCMs in action include:

(8) The doctor came down and said to her 'Oh it's just a wee bit of
like diarrhoea <u>or that</u>.' (CANCSOC)

(9) [a mother talking about her baby's symptoms of meningitis] . . .
his neck was sore if you had tried to move his head <u>or that</u>
(*Liveline*)

(10) [caller is complaining about lack of political debate on a consti-
tutional amendment required as part of the Northern Ireland
peace process in 1998. 'Bertie' refers to the Irish 'Taoiseach'
(Prime Minister) at the time, Bertie Ahern, 'and any of them'
refers to all politicians in the Republic of Ireland and Northern
Ireland]
I'd like *Bertie or any of them* get on and address what we're voting on on Friday which is the amendments to our constitu-
tional articles two and three (*Liveline*)

As can be seen from Table 8.5, the results add very few items to the
totals in Table 8.4, and the picture remains largely unchanged (except
to bring *Liveline* even closer to CANCSOC). This suggests that the most
frequent VCMs in CANCSOC are also widespread in *Liveline* and CAN-
CAD, though differently distributed. Both smaller corpora, then, have
features in common with banal, everyday, casual conversation.
However, as we saw in the case of CANCSOC, the category memberships
signalled by VCMs can range from universally transparent to quite
opaque. We therefore now turn to an analysis of the domains and types
of references projected by the VCMs in *Liveline* and CANCAD, in an
attempt to see whether and how they reflect an appeal to the shared
space of their co-participants, how exclusive such appeals are (in terms

of interpretability by outside observers) and what their specific functions are in the contexts in which they occur.

Reference domains of VCMs in *Liveline* and CANCAD

All of the VCMs in the *Liveline* and CANCAD corpora were examined in terms of their projected referents. Broadly, the referents may be divided into 'local', 'societal' and 'global'. 'Local' is defined as interpretable by a specific group of participants and those who share relatively exclusive social and cultural frames of knowledge, for example, a family, a group of friends, a class of students and their teacher discussing their academic subject. 'Societal' is defined as interpretable by all members of a speech community or socio-political entity who share a common culture and history, for instance, English-speakers, the population of Ireland, people from a particular city or region. 'Global' is defined as interpretable by most mature, experienced human beings throughout the world. The results for the two corpora are shown in Figure 8.1.

The largest shared domain of reference in the *Liveline* data was at the 'societal' level and when this domain was further broken down, three subcategories were identified, as shown in Figure 8.2. When the largest of these, 'general' societal knowledge, is further broken down, we find the subcategories listed in Table 8.7.

The largest domain of shared space in the Irish radio data, not surprisingly, is at a general societal level. The radio phone-in callers, presenter

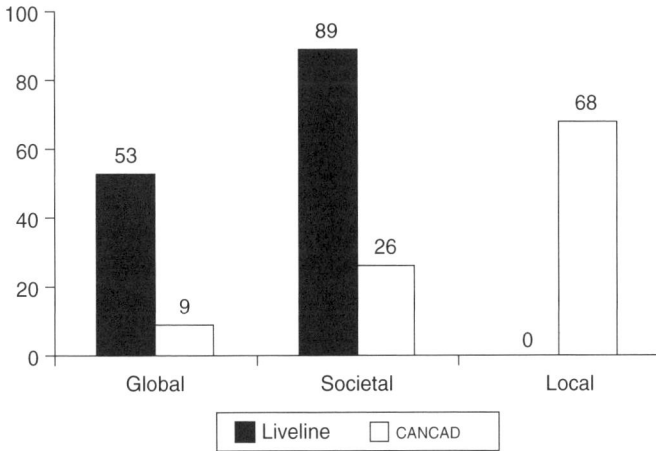

Figure 8.1   *Liveline* and CANCAD reference domains

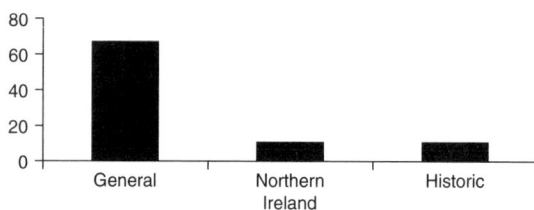

Figure 8.2   Societal domains in *Liveline*

Table 8.7   Categories within the general Irish reference domain

Category	Example	Example utterances
Social practices and attitudes	The perception of who goes to an Irish boarding school[4]	' . . . of a lot of people who go to boarding schools are from unhappy families there is that kind of element . . . '
Social responsibilities and realities	Negative social realities that come with the Celtic tiger economy	'I think there's a certain anonymity about it . . . if we understood the real difficulties that people have in breaking out of this situations of hardship and so on'
Work and financial practices	Car rental companies in Ireland	' . . . car hire firms such as Dan Ryan,[5] Budget, Avis, people like that'
Social types	Irish criminals and social undesirables	'I think there's a lot of undesirables, criminals and people like that'

and audience occupy this shared space and they know that they can draw on it to refer to things that will be understood, and as potential sites for new meaning-making. In contrast to CANSOC, outside observers (that is, Irish listeners to the radio programme) will not normally encounter opaque references at this general societal level. However, a listener from outside Irish society will frequently encounter opacity, as illustrated by the examples in Table 8.8.

What one group of language users shares as its commonage is what keeps them together, like a centripetal force, while, paradoxically, this commonage can keep others away, like a centrifugal force.

The VCMs in CANCAD were classified according to reference domain and four categories which could be understood with broad societal

Table 8.8 Examples of societal value category markers in *Liveline* likely to be opaque to listeners outside Irish society

Example	Comment
'Didn't get *a* <u>Gaeltacht grant or anything like that</u>?'	A 'Gaeltacht' is an area where Gaelic is spoken. These areas get special government grants for, for example, the setting up of enterprises in the zone.
'And the Secretariat at <u>Maryfield and all that</u>?'	The Maryfield Secretariat was a joint civil service set up by the British and Irish governments under the Anglo-Irish Agreement in1985.

Table 8.9 Breakdown of societal value category markers in CANCAD by domain

Category	Example	Example utterances
Language, culture and gender	Matching items that couples have or wear	'the fact that er a woman is assumed to have a smaller car than a man <u>and so on and so forth</u>'
Media, TV and music	Content of a film that would make it appeal to schedule writers	'They probably saw it had some nudity in it <u>or something</u>'
Transport and services	Evidence of poorly funded privatized railways in the UK	'The train I came across on from Birmingham to Nottingham was the most crappy train. And it was marked on the outside. The seats were dirty and ripped. And the floor was dirty. <u>And everything</u>'
University life	Activities that people expect to happen in university seminars	'Well it's just different people <u>same stuff</u>'

knowledge were identified (Table 8.9). Of these, 'language culture and gender' encompassed two-thirds of all the societal VCMs, which mainly occurred as part of explanations or exemplification of points under discussion. The other three categories show more similarities with the kinds of categories of societal VCMs in the *Liveline* corpus. In this case, the VCMs tend to feature in more relational episodes, of the kind that often occur at the beginning of classes or in breaks or transitions during the class.

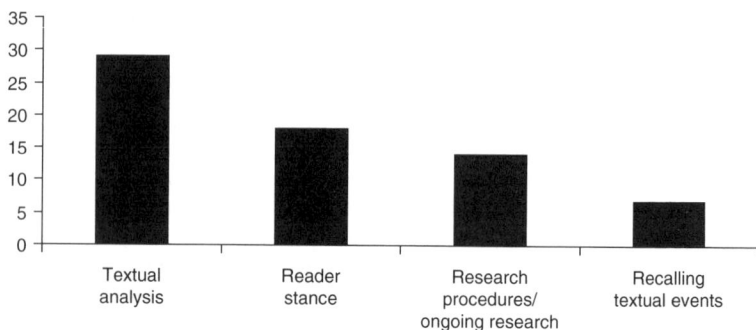

Figure 8.3   Local reference domains in CANCAD

By far the largest area of common reference found in the use of VCMs in the CANCAD data was at the 'local' level, that is to say, references to shared disciplinary knowledge and practices. Figure 8.3 gives a breakdown of this 'local' reference domain. Here we see that the immediate classroom context is the locus of the greatest amount of exploitation of shared space. The classroom material, its content and interpretation, the shared endeavour of academic activity such as understanding a text, and academic activities such as research, appear to be where the participants of a classroom can assume the greatest level of given and shared knowledge which can be drawn on as a shared resource in the creation of ad hoc categories. In example (11), which occurs at the opening stages of a postgraduate seminar on poetic language, the tutor is encouraging the students to forget the more formal kinds of analysis they may have done and instead react intuitively to the text.

(11)

Tutor: So instead of being like a machine and just thinking right I'll do a discourse analysis then I'll do a pragmatic analysis then I'll do a syntactic analysis <u>and so on</u> all the way down. There's no need to do all that because you can go straight for your gut reaction er first time around.

(CANCAD)

In this next example from an undergraduate sociolinguistics seminar, the student and the tutor are co-creating an understanding of an extract from a sociolinguistics textbook.

(12)
Student: A lot of insurance companies now do <u>things like erm clean out your car and get it fixed and stuff like that</u>. Don't they?
Tutor: Right.
Student: So it's not that weird.
Tutor: So it's not totally weird. Yeah. It's not as weird as the police and the washing machine.
Student: No.
Tutor: Yeah. Right. Because if it so = th = There's a like a semantic field with things tha = <u>to do with houses burning down and insuring yourself against fires and all of that</u>.
(CANCAD)

This example emphasizes the collaborative nature of vague category projection. In example (13), the students are struggling to find extracts from the novel *Mrs Dalloway* which exemplify a list of themes given to them by their tutor.

(13)
Student 1: But I wasn't sure if I'd got the wrong end of the stick.
Student 2: Yeah. I was reading a bit in the introduction. It's like oh yeah she was questioning her <u>sexuality and stuff</u>. Yeah.
Student 1: Yeah. I think she was.
Student 2: But then after that little bit.
Student 1: The trouble is does femin – Does femininity have anything to do with sexuality?
Student 2: Yeah.
(CANCAD)

Student 2 refers to 'sexuality and stuff', and three turns later Student 2 questions whether this category can include femininity, a topic that she had raised earlier in the seminar, thus moving the discussion on to a new phase. Jucker *et al.* (2003) found that explicit identification of a potential member of a vague set by another speaker helped maintain bonds between participants in casual conversation, but here in this academic discourse we can see that it also helps speakers refine academic argument and explore new conceptual territory. In the tutor's final turn he uses a VCM which is similar in construction to the one used by the student five turns previously, but containing the term 'semantic field'. In this way he can be seen to be signalling that her contribution is valid by ratifying it within the domain of textual analysis as accepted within the academic discourse community.

The data comparisons have shown differences in the realizations and distribution of VCMs across the three data sets. The analysis has underlined the view that VCMs are highly context-sensitive and reflect the assumed domains of shared knowledge within the three contexts under examination here (informal casual conversation among friends and intimates, radio phone-in and university classes). The conversational VCMs range wide, from those of universal reference to those referring to people and things known only to intimate groups. The Irish radio phone-in data show a great preference for general issues and those of relevance to the national 'community' to which the programme is broadcast, enabling the exchange of views against the background of a socio-political commonage. The academic data are characterized by VCMs which refer to local preoccupations within specific academic disciplines and are concerned with constructing disciplinary understandings and knowledge.

VCMs and language teaching

As regards language teaching, a number of pertinent observations may be made:

1. Utilitarian models of language based on transactional premises such as information transfer and information gaps (for example, stronger versions of communicative language teaching) run the risk of stifling the cognitive and linguistic development which is facilitated by a more creative, open-ended approach to language learning. Creativity in all its aspects, not just the more conventional, aesthetic notion of creativity, should be central to language development (Carter and McCarthy 2004). VCMs do 'transfer information', but in quite a different way from the more traditional notion of filling an 'information gap'. Activities in the classroom should be designed to provide space for vagueness and not always seek precision.

2. The lexical realizations of vague categories are, as this chapter has argued, highly patterned and eminently 'learnable'; they are chunks, and fit in well with the lexical approach to language teaching. However, as we have attempted to show, they are also context-sensitive and must always be explored and decoded in context.

3. This chapter has demonstrated that vague categories operate at different levels of assumed shared knowledge: some knowledge can be assumed to be shared by all mature, aware human beings; other knowledge is more locally constrained and culture-bound. Clearly, language teaching has to take the problems posed by restricted refer-

ences into account, and some teachers may decide initially to eschew the more circumscribed contexts as a distraction from the vocabulary-learning task, and focus on more universal references. But teachers at higher levels may see restricted contexts as windows on culture and as a site of investigation and potential bridging across cultures, the locus of the third place between the target culture and one's own starting-point as a learner (Kramsch 1993).

4. VCMs and their domains of reference are a clear example where corpus insights have an important role to play in informing language-teaching materials. As with many high-frequency phenomena in spoken language, intuition, whether that of the native speaker or the non-native expert user, is likely to be less than adequate to the task of teasing out the commonest expressions, simply because of the real-time, online nature of face-to-face interaction. Language teaching can only benefit positively from the ability of the computer to see large-scale patterns in corpora collected across a range of contexts and users.

Future research

Several directions for future research emerge from the present study:

1. Spoken corpora need not focus exclusively on the speech of native speakers; comparisons between native-speaker VCM usage and that by non-native expert users will undoubtedly prove equally fruitful, whether in terms of presence or absence of particular lexical types (Prodromou 2005), or in the possible realizations of the interpersonal functions of vague markers by other strategic means.

2. Learner corpora (especially those coded for errors) are likely to reveal interesting features concerning the successful (or otherwise) acquisition and use of typical VCMs. One frequent phenomenon many second-language teachers will be familiar with is lack of concord in expressions such as 'all these kind of things', which are often marked down by teachers and examiners. It remains to be demonstrated, however, that native speakers do not routinely do the same thing, and casual observation of the CANCODE corpus suggest that native-speaker examples such as 'the property was being kept clean and tidy and all *those kind* of things' are by no means rare.

3. Research into processing, involving protocols and similar methods, may reveal much about how learners or non-native users (or any group of outsiders) process and decode the referents of

VCMs. Here corpus observations and more psycholinguistically oriented research can fruitfully contribute to each other (for example see Spöttl and McCarthy 2004 on formulaic sequences).
4. Corpus-based cross-linguistic comparisons of VCMs are needed, especially for less-researched languages, both in terms of syntax and semantics and pragmatics. Models based on high-attention languages such as English tend to dominate; research examining other languages in their own right can serve to ratify or challenge English-dominated models. The same applies to varieties within languages such as English, where certain varieties tend to have dominated, though in the case of British and Irish English, the balance is swinging into greater equilibrium. This chapter hopes to make a contribution to that effort.

Notes

1. CANCODE stands for 'Cambridge and Nottingham Corpus of Discourse in English'. The corpus was developed at the University of Nottingham, and funded by Cambridge University Press, with whom sole copyright resides. CANCODE forms part of the larger Cambridge International Corpus. The corpus conversations were recorded in a wide variety of mostly informal settings across the islands of Britain and Ireland, then transcribed and stored in computer-readable form. Details of the corpus and its design may be found in McCarthy (1998).
2. Source: JNLR/MRBI radio figures released February 2003, quoted in Oliver (2003).
3. *For the X that's in it* is a dialectal form found in Irish English but not familiar to most British English-speakers. It is a direct translation from Gaelic, and marks a vague category relating to special occasions and the activities and behaviours which are associated with them. For example, on someone's birthday *we're having a get-together for the day that's in it,* or on the millennium year, *there were lots of celebrations for the year that was in it.*
4. Irish secondary schools are non-fee-paying, but there are still some which have a boarding facility for which fees are paid and students stay at the school during the week, or for longer periods.
5. An Irish car hire company.

References

W.L. Barsalou, 'Ad Hoc Categories', *Memory and Cognition,* 11 (1983) 211–77.
W.L. Barsalou, 'The Instability of Graded Structure: Implications for the Nature of Concepts', in U. Neisser (ed.), *Concepts and Conceptual Development: Ecological and Intellectual Bases of Categorization* (Cambridge University Press, 1987).
R.A. Carter and M.J. McCarthy, 'Talking, Creating: Interactional Language, Creativity and Context', *Applied Linguistics,* 25/1 (2004) 62–88.
R.A. Carter and M.J. McCarthy, *The Cambridge Grammar of English* (Cambridge University Press, 2006).

J. Channell, *Vague Language* (Oxford University Press, 1994).

P.D. Crawford, 'Educating for Moral Ability: Reflections on Moral Development Based on Vygotsky's Theory of Concept Formation', *Journal of Moral Education*, 30/2 (2001) 113–29.

J. Cutting, *Analysing the Language of Discourse Communities* (Oxford: Elsevier Science, 2000).

E. Dines, 'Variation in Discourse–and Stuff like that', *Language in Society*, 9 (1980) 13–31.

S. Dubois, 'Extension Particles, etc.', *Language Variation and Change*, 4 (1993) 179–203.

E. Goffman, *Forms of Talk* (Philadelphia, PA: University of Pennsylvania, 1981).

G. Jefferson, 'List Construction as a Task and Resource', in G. Psathas (ed.), *Interaction Competence* (Lanham, MD: University Press of America, 1990).

A.H. Jucker, S.W. Smith and T. Lüdge, 'Interactive Aspects Of Vagueness in Conversation', *Journal of Pragmatics*, 35/12 (2003) 1737–69.

C. Kramsch, *Context and Culture in Language Teaching* (Oxford University Press, 1993).

R.K.S. Macaulay, *Locating Dialect in Discourse: The Language of Honest Men and Bonnie Lasses in Ayr* (New York: Oxford University Press, 1991).

M.J. McCarthy, A. O'Keeffe and S. Walsh, ' "Post-colonialism, Multi-Culturalism, Structuralism, Feminism, Post-Modernism and so on and so forth"–Vague Language in Academic Discourse, a Comparative Analysis of Form, Function and CONTEXT', Presented at AAACL/ICAME Conference, University of Michigan, Ann Arbor (2005).

A. O'Keeffe, 'Exploring Indices of National Identity in a Corpus of Radio Phone-In Data from Irish Radio', in A. Sánchez-Macarro (ed.), *Windows on the World: Media Discourse in English* (University of Valencia Press, 2002).

A. O'Keeffe, ' "Like the Wise Virgins and All that Jazz"–Using a Corpus To Examine Vague Categerisation and Shared Knowledge', in U. Connor and T.A. Upton (eds), *Applied Corpus Linguistics: A Multidimensional Perspective* (Amsterdam: Rodopi, 2004).

A. O'Keeffe, *Investigating Media Discourse* (London: Routledge, 2006).

M. Overstreet and G. Yule, 'On Being Explicit and Stuff in Contemporary American English', *Journal of English Linguistics*, 25/3 (1997a) 250–8.

M. Overstreet and G.Yule, 'Locally Contingent Categorization in DISCOURSE', *Discourse Processes*, 23 (1997b) 83–97.

L. Prodromou, ' "You See, It's Sort of Tricky for the L2 User": The Puzzle of Idiomaticity in English as a Lingua Franca', unpublished PhD dissertation, University of Nottingham (2005).

M. Scott, *Wordsmith Tools*, Version 3 (corpus analytical software suite), (Oxford University Press, 1999).

C. Spöttl and M.J. McCarthy, 'Comparing the Knowledge of Formulaic Sequences Across L1, L2, L3 and L4', in N. Schmitt (ed.), *Formulaic Sequences* (Amsterdam: Benjamins, 2004).

J. Swales, *Genre Analysis: English in Academic and Research Settings* (New York: Cambridge University Press, 1990).

L.S. Vygotsky, *Thought and Language* (Cambridge, MA: MIT Press, 1962).

L.S. Vygotsky, *Mind in Society* (Cambridge, MA: Harvard University Press, (1978).

G. Ward and B. Birner, 'The Semantics and Pragmatics of "and Everything" ', *Journal of Pragmatics*, 19/3 (1992), 205–14.

Part IV
Cross-Cultural Vagueness

9
The Use of Vague Language Across Spoken Genres in an Intercultural Hong Kong Corpus

Winnie Cheng

Introduction

This chapter examines the use of vague language (VL) across different spoken genres in intercultural contexts. It analyses representative samples of the academic, business, conversational and public subcorpora in the Hong Kong Corpus of Spoken English (HKCSE), which is made up of Hong Kong Chinese and primarily native English-speakers. Its aim is to find out how the use of VL compares across spoken genres and between the two sets of speakers. The chapter then compares the findings with what school textbooks in Hong Kong say about VL in order to suggest recommendations to textbook writers, teacher educators and teachers for change and improvement.

Realizations of VL and its functions have been discussed in the literature. For instance, Crystal and Davy (1975, pp. 112–14) identify types of lexical VL, which are a mixture of 'precision and imprecision', on a spectrum from items which express 'total VL' like 'thing', 'whatsit' and 'so on', to examples such as 'I've got some tomatoes, beans and things', and the use of the suffix '-ish' in colloquial English. Dubois (1987, p. 531) describes the use of hedges such as 'close to', 'about', 'around', 'on the order of' and 'something like', with numbers in biomedical slide talks as 'imprecise' numerical expressions, suggesting that speakers and writers employ these expressions to express uncertainty in relation to one's own or somebody else's findings and to 'diminish precision'. Wierzbicka (1986, p. 597) calls 'just', 'at least', 'only', 'merely' and 'at the most' 'approximatives'. Channell (1994) describes three categories of VL, as follows:

1. Vague additives to numbers: a word or phrase is added to a precise figure to signal a vague reading ('about', 'around', 'round', 'approximately').

2. VL by choice of vague words or phrases ('and things', 'or something', 'and such', 'or anything', 'thing', 'thingy', 'whatsisname', 'whatnot').
3. VL by scalar implicature ('most', 'many', 'some', 'few', 'often', 'sometimes', 'occasionally', 'seldom').

Categories 2 and 3 differ in Channell's typology in that the meanings of the VL items in category 3 are understood by the hearer/reader in relation to a range of terms ranked relative to one another in meaning.

Research on VL has looked at discourse types, such as English plays (Graves and Hodge 1947), advertising (Leech 1964; Myers 1994), biomedical slide talks (Dubois 1987), academic writing on economics (Channell 1990), a group task that requires coordinated actions among the members (Erev *et al.* 1991), occupational standards (Drave 1995), ESL writing by Chinese students (Allison 1995), patents (Myers 1995), and telephone conversations (Urbanová 1999). Larger-scale studies (such as Kennedy 1987; Channell 1985, 1994) draw their examples from both speech and writing across a number of genres.

Cheng and Warren (2001) examine the use of VL in intercultural conversation in Hong Kong, and have found that on the whole, Hong Kong Chinese (HKC) employ VL in ways very similar to their native-English-speaker interlocutors (NES). They find that both groups of speakers are able to consciously manipulate the resources of VL to perform a variety of functions in social interaction, such as to achieve solidarity, to cover up linguistic and knowledge deficiencies, to show that they know the rules of information quantity in different speech situations and also to protect one's face and that of others.

This chapter takes the position that VL consists of a closed set of identifiable items that can be interpreted based on the particular context in which they occur, and that VL signals to the hearer that the utterance, or part of it, is not to be interpreted precisely. Thus, while its meaning in a discourse is subject to negotiation by the participants, VL does not achieve full specificity and so does not shed its status as VL as a result of the joint negotiation process (Cheng and Warren 2001, p. 82). For the purposes of identifying VL items, this chapter adopts Channell's (1994) VL typology described above.

What the textbooks in Hong Kong say about VL

An examination of the 15 textbooks currently endorsed by the Education and Manpower Bureau of the Hong Kong Government for use in Hong Kong's upper secondary schools shows that only 3 make any mention of VL usage, in the form of either general guidelines or actual examples. The guidelines provided by Esser (1999a, p. 7) are 'Be specific. Don't make vague or unclear suggestions, e.g., "some departments", "some people" '. The guidelines given by the same author in another textbook (Esser 1999b, p. 39) are:

> Student A: I think there are some organizations in Hong Kong which help students with emotional problems. (Note: Student A raises a good point . . . but he fails to give concrete examples of these organizations. He uses a vague term: some.)

Esser (1999a) warns against the use of VL, although the exemplification of what constitutes VL, 'some' + noun, is extremely limited, and in Esser (1999b, p. 39) VL is described disparagingly as failing to provide 'concrete examples', and it is again the use of 'some' which is being discouraged.

The only other textbook to mention VL use, Free Press (2002, p. 44–67), advocates the teaching of VL, but only presents two forms, 'sort of' and 'kind of' (or three forms, if one includes a brief footnote recommending 'and so on', saying that 'etcetera is not normally a spoken form'). In actual speech we use the phrases 'sort of' and 'kind of':

- The printer uses some kind of edible ink.
- It's sort of a crazy idea.
- They use some sort of stuff you can eat – like rice paper.
- It's suitable for all kinds of parties and occasions.

The survey of textbooks shows that VL use receives scant and cursory coverage in only three textbooks, and that the three textbooks that do mention VL use offer contradictory advice to the reader. Two of the textbooks suggest that VL should be avoided, while the third appears to advocate its use as being representative of 'actual speech' (Free Press 2002). The combined effect of the three sends a mixed message to students and teachers. The textbook material will be discussed later when the findings from the four spoken subcorpora are examined and discussed.

Data

The data in this study, totalling 920,000 words, consist of 230,000 words from each of the academic, business, conversational and public subcorpora of the HKCSE. The four subcorpora each contain half a million words and are considered to represent the main overarching spoken genres found in the Hong Kong context: academic discourse (such as lectures, seminars, supervisions, student presentations, telephone interviews), business discourse (such as meetings, service encounters, workplace presentations, job and placement interviews, informal office talk), conversation (naturally occurring conversations in restaurants, pubs, cafés, homes, and so on.) and public discourse (such as public speeches, forum discussions, radio and television broadcasts, press briefings). The participants in the HKCSE are made up of HKC (first language Cantonese) and primarily NES, with some speakers of languages other than Cantonese and English. All of the participants were monitored in terms of place of birth, age, gender, occupation, educational background, time spent living or studying overseas (for the HKC) and mother tongue (See Cheng, Greaves and Warren 2005, for more details of the HKCSE).

In total, the data comprise 920,000 words with a spread of 72.7 per cent and 27.3 per cent across HKC and NES respectively, because the proportions of HKC and NES participating in the study vary, which reflects the reality of the Hong Kong context. In two-party conversation, the spread is very even (51.4 per cent HKC and 48.6 per cent NES). In business contexts in Hong Kong, the majority (74.8 per cent) of the participants are HKC. This rises to 80.3 per cent in the academic context, as in Hong Kong the medium of instruction at university is English and so there is often the situation in which HKC are talking English with HKC, which would never happen in informal social contexts. Lastly, the participants in spoken public discourse are overwhelmingly HKC (87.1 per cent), which underlines the widespread use of English as the medium of communication in the media, public administration and political spheres. When comparing the findings between HKC and NES, the relative proportions of the talk spoken by the two sets of speakers are taken into account by referring to the frequency of particular vague items per 10,000 words spoken. In this way, the proportional usage of VL by HKC and NES can be compared.

Most frequently occurring vague items across four spoken genres

With the help of ConcGram©,[1] an overall word frequency list was generated for each of the subcorpora, and then the top 10 vague items, based on Channel's (1994) typology of VL, were identified (Table 9.1).

Table 9.1 Top 10 most frequent vague items in HKCSE, in each sub-corpus, and by speaker set (per 10,000 words)

Overall HKCSE Total HKC/NES	Academic Total HKC/NES	Business Total HKC/NES	Conversation Total HKC/NES	Public Total HKC/NES
'very' 37.4 35.5/42.6	'about' 35.9 40.2/18.3	'very' 46.3 45.7/47.8	'very' 42.4 46.9/35.6	'very' 35.7 36.9/27.6
'about' 32.3 32.9/30.9	'very' 25.4 21.2/42.6	'about' 34.1 33.7/35.2	'about' 33.0 37.2/27.0	'more' 26.7 28.2/16.5
'some' 24.6 24.3/25.24	'some' 24.3 24.5/23.4	'more' 23.5 23.3/24.2	'some' 29.5 34.4/23.1	'about' 26.5 27.4/20.6
'more' 22.7 24/19.2	'more' 20.5 19.4/24.9	'some' 23.0 24.3/19.2	'more' 20.1 22.7/16.6	'some' 21.5 22.0/18.2
'much' 13.8 13.8/13.7	'something' 9.9 8.8/14.6	'much' 13.9 13.6/14.8	'something' 16.5 18.6/13.6	'many' 14.7 15.5/9.1
'something' 10.4 9.2/13.8	'many' 8.7 7.5/13.2	'something' 11.4 11.0/12.6	'much' 14.0 14.7/12.7	'much' 13.5 14.0/10.4
'many' 9.7 11.7/4.27	'most' 8.2 8.1/8.4	'things' 9.9 9.6/11.4	'quite' 14.0 15.0/12.3	'most' 10.2 10.6/7.4
'quite' 8.8 8.6/9.33	'much' 7.6 5.9/14.6	'kind (of)' 9.3 10.1/7.0	'lot' 13.4 16.2/9.9	'few' 5.2 5.2/5.1
'things' 8.4 7.2/11.7	'things' 7.1 5.2/14.8	'bit' 8.4 9.0/6.7	'things' 11.3 12.3/9.8	'kind (of)' 4.6 4.9/2.4
'most' 7.6 8.3/5.9	'kind (of)' 7.0 7.7/4.2	'many' 7.4 7.6/6.7	'bit' 7.9 6.2/9.3	'quite' 4.3 4.4/4.0
Total 175.8 175.5/176.6	Total 154.5 148.5/179.0	Total 187.2 187.7/185.6	Total 202.3 224.2/169.9	Total 163.4 169.1/124.7

Altogether, 14 vague items were found across the 4 subcorpora: 10 items in 'VL by scalar implicature' ('very', 'more', 'some', 'much' 'many', 'quite', 'most', 'lot', 'few', 'bit'), 3 items in 'VL by choice of vague words or phrases' ('something', 'things', 'kind of'), and 1 item in 'vague additives to numbers' ('about') (Channell 1994).

In Table 9.1, each cell describes the total number of instances of a vague item per 10,000 words, and underneath this figure are the totals for HKC and NES respectively per 10,000 words. The first aim of the study is to find out the extent to which VL use is genre-specific. As shown in Table 9.1, the spoken genre in which VL is used most often is conversation (202.3 per 10,000 words), followed by business (187.2), public (163.4) and lastly academic (154.5) discourse. This finding supports the observations that VL is especially prevalent in conversations (Crystal and Davy, 1975, p. 111). In conversations, interlocutors are generally satisfied with vague expressions, such as vague amounts and propositions of persons, ideas, and objects, because they fit in with the purposes of interaction which are primarily 'interactional' rather than 'transactional' (Brown and Yule 1983, pp. 1–4). However, in other discourse types, such as academic and public discourse, more precision may be required or expected and so the frequency of VL use drops. This observation is confirmed by McCarthy (1991, pp. 142–3) who states that VL is less commonly found in academic lectures compared to more informal spoken discourse. Table 9.1 also shows that the 10 most frequently occurring vague items overall are not always evenly distributed across genres. First, while 'very', 'about', 'some' and 'more' are the 4 most common vague items overall and in all of the 4 subcorpora, only conversation has the same top 4 in the same rank order. Second, 'quite' is not found in the top 10 in the academic and business discourse; 'most' is not found in business discourse and conversation; and 'something' and 'things' are not found in the public discourse. Third, some vague items are found in the top 10 in some subcorpora but not in the overall corpus, for example, 'kind (of)' is found in academic, business and public discourse, 'bit' (as in 'a bit' or 'a bit of') in business and conversation, 'lot' (as in 'a lot' or 'a lot of') in conversation, and 'few' in the public discourse. Finally, there are differences in frequency of occurrence even for vague items that occur in all of the genres. For example, there are almost twice as many instances of 'many' in public discourse (14.7) compared with business discourse (7.4). While 'some' occurs with a very similar frequency across all the genres, 'much' is 2 times as likely to occur in the other 3 genres (ranging from 13.5 to 14.0) compared with academic discourse (7.6), and 'quite' is more than 3 times more common in conversation (14.0) than in public discourse (4.3). Despite these differences, the overall similarity and the similarity among the top 4 vague items across the genres are remarkable.

The second aim the chapter is to find out to what extent VL use is speaker-specific. The most interesting finding is that the 2 sets of speakers in the HKCSE use almost the same number of vague items per 10,000 words both across the top 10 vague items: HKC (175.5) and NES (176.6), and in the business discourse: HKC (187.7) and NES (185.6). However, this is not the case in the other 3 genres. In academic discourse, HKC and NES respectively use 148.5 and 179.0 vague items per 10,000 words. Two interesting vague items in academic discourse are 'about' and 'very'. HKC use 'about' much more frequently than NES (40.2 as opposed to 18.3) and NES use 'very' much more frequently than HKC (42.6 as opposed to 21.2), and these will be examined in more detail below. In conversation, with the exception of the tenth item, 'bit', HKC use the top 9 forms between 30 and 40 per cent more frequently than NES. In the public discourse, HKC exceed NES in all of the 10 items. The findings therefore show that HKC and NES have differing frequencies of use for certain of the vague items within the same genre. Further studies would need to explore whether there exist cultural preferences for using certain vague items in certain domains of use by the 2 groups of speakers or whether NES are using a wider repertoire of VL than the HKC which reduces the dependency on the more commonly used forms. Given that one of the roles of VL is to hedge, maybe HKC prefer to hedge more than the NES or the NES use a wider variety of hedges which would not appear in the top 10 list.

Analysis of 'very', 'about' and 'something'

To corroborate the quantitative findings discussed above, qualitative analysis of the use of VL by the two sets of speakers was conducted. Three vague items ('very', 'about' and 'something') which represent the most frequently occurring examples of each of Channel's (1994) three functions of VL use in the data are examined and their respective usage compared across the four subcorpora and the two sets of speakers. 'Very' is the most frequent form of VL by scalar implicature ('very' is also the most frequent form of VL overall); 'about' is the most frequently occurring example of a vague additive used in combination with a number; and 'something' is the most common instance of VL by choice of vague words. With respect to 'very', Channell (1994, p. 110) is of the view that 'very', among with other members in the scale ('a bit', 'somewhat', 'quite', 'very', 'extremely'), when used with adjectives, might be argued not to be vague while other scales of implicature are vague. However, this chapter argues that all items constituting scalar implicature are vague and only understood within an assumed shared understanding of approximate parameters in a particular context. This chapter, therefore, argues that 'very' in, for example, 'very differently', is vague as its meaning is unspecified, or underspecified, in this context.

Extract 1 illustrates an instance of vague use of 'very' used by speaker B (a HKC male):

Extract 1
1B   um at this point I want you to er divide into small groups
2   (.) so as to have a discussion on this derivation because in
3   after this diagram I want you you to derive something so
4   you can have a group discussion on it okay
5   (pause)
6B   but first of all let us just er digest this diagram okay
7   because this diagram is <u>very important</u> it is the um the
8   first step for us to determine the lambda that means the
9   the value er of the displacement in the transverse
10   direction and in the longitudinal direction

In this example of the vague item 'very', a lecturer is giving a lecture to engineering students and he asks them to break out into groups for a discussion. Before they begin their discussion, he asks them to 'digest this diagram' (line 6) because it is 'very important' (line 7). The vague status of 'very important' is underlined by the need for him to then explain at length why the diagram needs digesting (lines 7–10) and hence why it is 'very important'. Without the explanation the students would be unable to determine the meaning of 'very important' in this context.

Extract 2 shows 'about' used as a vague item by speaker A (HKC female) and B (NES male):

Extract 2
1   A   . . . he moved into the flat er in the end of last year
2   B   right
3   A   I moved into it er after I get married
4   B   yea so he's lived in it <u>about a year</u>
5   A   <u>not about a year</u> I think er oh yea
6   B   mm
7   A   nearly
8   B   yea so . . .

In this example of the vague use of 'about', two friends are discussing speaker A's living arrangements before and after her marriage. On line 1 she says that her husband moved into the flat 'at the end of last year' (before the marriage). On line 4, speaker B says 'so he's lived there about a year' and on line 5 speaker A disagrees and then, after hesitating, agrees, but adds 'nearly' on line 7. Although 'about' is a vague additive with numbers (here 'a' equates with 'one' on lines 4 and 5), speaker A is not entirely happy with this usage ('about' includes the meanings 'less than' or 'more than') and she seems to prefer another vague additive – 'nearly' – which excludes 'more than'. This is a good example of speakers communicating effectively with VL, but also demonstrates that VL is open to negotiation in context.

Extract 3 shows 'something' used as a vague item:

Extract 3
1 A oh ((laugh))
2 B did I order dessert (.) no
3 A no
4 B okay I just got this [oh I didn't know whether you ordered that thing for me
5 A .... [oh man
5 B thing for me
6 A I didn't
7 B okay
8 A I would not order <u>something</u> for you that you didn't know
9 B well I thought I thought that I ordered it

Two friends are discussing the arrival of a dessert to their table in a restaurant. The waiter has given the dessert to speaker B but he is sure that he hadn't ordered dessert (line 2). He wonders whether speaker A ordered it for him and she assures him that she 'would not order something for you that you didn't know' (line 8). Although she could be referring to ordering anything anywhere for her friend, in this context her use of the vague item 'something' is interpreted in this context as food in restaurants, as can be seen by speaker B's response on line 9.

Vague and non-vague uses of 'very'

The lexical item 'very' can be used in both vague and non-vague ways, but the vague usage predominates across all of the genres and speakers (see Table 9.2).

The non-vague use of 'very' is low across the board, but there is a difference nonetheless from one genre to another. Business discourse has the highest non-vague usage (2.7 per 10,000 words) with its use being evenly spread across the two sets of speakers, and public the lowest (1.2). Examples of non-vague use of 'very' are mostly found in such phrases as 'the very best', 'the very fact that ...' and 'at the very beginning ...'

Table 9.2 Frequencies of vague and non-vague usage of 'very' (per 10,000 words)

Speaker	Academic vague/ non-vague	Business vague/ non-vague	Conversation vague/ non-vague	Public vague/ non-vague	HKCSE vague/ non-vague
HKC	19.8/1.35	43.0/2.79	45.76/1.18	35.8/1.1	35.3/1.63
NES	40.16/2.42	45.2/2.58	33.96/1.7	25.6/2.02	44.0/2.1
Total	23.9/1.6	43.5/2.7	40.9/1.5	34.5/1.2	35.7/1.8

which function to emphasize a superlative adjective or adverb or to specify a position or point in time.

Examination of all the instances of 'very' in the data shows that the two most frequent meanings are vague, namely to give emphasis to an adjective or adverb, and the use of 'not very', also used with an adjective or adverb, to say that something is not at all true, or that it is true only to a small degree. The frequency of the vague use of 'very' varies markedly across the four genres. Business discourse has the most per 10,000 words (43.5), followed by conversation (40.9), public (34.5), and lastly academic (23.8). In other words, in more formal genres such as academic and public discourse, the use of 'very' to emphasize or intensify is less frequent or this function is realized differently. When the two sets of speakers are compared, they use 'very' as a vague item similarly in business discourse. In academic discourse, NES make much more use of 'very' than HKC (40.2 as opposed to 19.8), whereas in both conversation and public discourse, HKC use the vague 'very' more often. When used in a vague manner, 'very' functions as an adverb or adjective and is spoken in combination with another adverb or adjective, or in combination with a noun. Table 9.3 lists the top ten items that combine with 'very' in the data studied.

The items with which 'very' combines tend to vary across different genres along with the frequencies of these combinations. In conversation, for instance, speakers make greater use of the combinations 'very much' (1.6), 'very strong(ly)' (2.2), 'very nice(ly)' (1.9) and 'very difficult' (1.4) more than in any other discourse type. In business discourse, 'very good' (4.6), 'very very' (3.3) and 'very different(ly)' (0.96) occur more frequently than elsewhere in the data. In common with conversation, business discourse has more instances of 'very good' (4.6 in business; 4.4 in conversation), and, with public discourse, more examples of 'very important(ly)' (1.9 in business; 2.6 in public) with public discourse having the most. Public discourse has similar frequencies of 'very much' compared with conversation and business discourse (1.3, 1.6, 1.3, respectively), and

Table 9.3 Ten most frequent patterns of 'very' + adverb or adjective (per 10,000 words)

'very' + pattern	Academic, total HKC/NES	Business, total HKC/NES	Conversation, total HKC/NES	Public, total HKC/NES	Overall HKCSE, total HKC/NES
'very' + 'good'	1.2 0.9/2.6	4.6 4.5/5.0	4.4 3.5/5.3	1.7 1.6/1.7	3.0 2.5/4.3
'very' + 'very'	1.9 0.4/7.9	3.3 3.5/2.8	2.1 1.1/3.0	1.5 1.4/2.0	2.2 1.6/3.7
'very' + 'important(ly)'	1.3 0.8/3.1	1.9 1.6/2.9	0.6 0.3/0.8	2.6 2.7/2.0	1.6 1.5/1.8
'very' + 'much'	0.96 0.6/2.4	1.3 1.1/1.9	1.6 1.9/1.3	1.3 1.3/1.3	1.3 1.2/1.6
'very' + 'strong(ly)'	0.04 0/0.2	0.78 0.9/0.5	2.2 2.2/2.0	0.56 0.5/0.7	0.9 0.8/1.2
'very' + 'nice(ly)'	0.17 0.2/0.2	1.0 0.9/1.2	1.9 1.4/2.4	0.08 0.05/0.3	0.8 0.5/1.5
'very' + 'difficult'	0.58 0.1/2.6	0.5 0.4/0.7	1.4 1.8/1.0	0.5 0.6/0	0.76 0.6/1.1
'very' + 'well'	0.13 0.1/0.2	0.9 0.8/1.4	0.9 0.9/0.8	1.04 1.1/0.7	0.75 0.7/0.8
'very' + 'high(ly)'	0.87 0.9/0.7	0.3 0.2/0.5	0.35 0.4/0.3	0.66 0.7/0.7	0.55 0.6/0.4
'very' + 'different(ly)'	0.04 0/0.2	0.96 1.0/0.9	0.47 0.3/0.6	0.35 0.3/0.3	0.45 0.4/0.6

a similar frequency of use of 'very well' as in the business discourse. Academic discourse has more examples of 'very high' (0.87), but lowest occurrence of five patterns: 'very good', 'very much', 'very strong(ly)', 'very well' and 'very different(ly)'. These findings underscore the importance of genre not only in terms of overall frequencies but also in terms of the likely collocates for vague items such as 'very'.

In addition to the genre-based similarities and differences, there are also similarities and differences between the HKC and NES. Generally speaking, NES use 'very' in the above combinations more often than HKC. This is particularly true in one genre – academic – where it is possibly a result of the role in the discourse played by the NES participants (that is, teacher or supervisor) which results in the higher usage

(0.9, HKC; 2.6, NES). Also, certain combinations, 'very good' (2.5, HKC; 4.3, NES), 'very very' (1.6, HKC; 3.7, NES) and 'very nice(ly)' (0.5, HKC; 1.5, NES) are used proportionately much more by NES in their talk. This underscoring or emphasizing by speakers by means of 'very' may be a cultural preference on the part of NES relative to their HKC interlocutors, or this function may simply be realized differently by HKC, and would be interesting to investigate further.

The non-vague use of 'very' is confined to two main categories, the first of which is to specify an extreme position or point in time, as exemplified in the list below:

. . . make one conclusion at the very end . . .
. . . opt to do a Q&A at the very end . . .
. . . from the very beginning . . .
. . . start at the very bottom . . .

This form of non-vague use is most common in academic discourse (35 out of 36 non-vague instances) and business discourse (58 out of 63 non-vague instances), but less common in conversation (25 out of 34) and relatively uncommon in public discourse (10 out of 28).

The second non-vague use of 'very' is to emphasize the seriousness or importance of what is being said, as exemplified in this list:

. . . the one China principle was the very foundation . . .
. . . the very fabric of Hong Kong society . . .
. . . is the very nature of our society . . .
. . . just for the very reasons that you've given . . .
. . . by the every fact that you do that . . .

Examples are found in public discourse more than the other three discourse types, probably because many of the speakers are politicians or government officials. Also, we saw earlier that the pattern 'very important(ly)' is most frequent in public discourse. While the numbers are small, NES appear to make use of this category of non-vague 'very' more frequently than the HKC.

Vague and non-vague uses of 'about'

According to *Cobuild* (1995, p. 4), there are 10 possible meanings for 'about', and of these only the 6th and 10th meanings on the list are vague: when 'about' is used in front of a number ('about 10 people') and when 'about' is used to indicate that something is going to take place

Table 9.4   Frequencies of vague versus non-vague usage of 'about' (per 10,000 words)

Speaker	Academic vague/ non-vague	Business vague/ non-vague	Conversation vague/ non-vague	Public vague/ non-vague	HKCSE vague/ non-vague
HKC	2.0/38.2	4.8/28.9	6.3/30.9	5.7/21.6	4.6/29.9
NES	4.6/13.7	4.7/30.5	5.2/21.8	3.7/16.9	4.8/21.8
Total	2.5/33.3	4.8/29.3	5.9/27.0	5.5/21.0	4.7/27.7

soon but the exact time in unspecified ('I think he's about to go'). The most common non-vague uses of 'about' are when it functions as a preposition to introduce a person, entity or activity, or in metadiscourse to say what the next topic will be ('he told me about his job', 'I know a lot about anxiety', 'I'd like to talk about').

Table 9.4 compares the frequencies of occurrence of 'about' with vague meanings to that with non-vague meanings.

Unlike the other two items ('very' and 'something') studied, 'about' has a vague meaning only in a minority (4.7 vague; 27.7 non-vague) of instances overall. Its use as a vague item appears to be influenced by the genre, as it ranges from 2.5 in academic, 4.8 in business, 5.5 in public and 5.9 in conversation. Thus, while 'about' occurs most frequently in the academic discourse, it occurs in its vague form least frequently in the academic genre, and is almost three times more frequent in conversation.

With the exception of academic discourse, it is HKC who use 'about' as a vague item more frequently, with the highest usage in conversation (6.3). A possible explanation for the higher usage by HKC could be a cultural preference for hedging which is coupled with a preference for indirectness generally (Cheng 2003) and may also account for the less frequent use of the booster 'very' discussed earlier.

Four patterns of association with 'about' being used with a vague meaning have been identified in this study. They are 'about' + number, 'about' + 'a'/'an'/'the' in front of a quantity or period of time, 'about' + 'the same'/the most', and 'about' + period of time (Table 9.5).

The most common pattern is 'about' followed by a number (4.0) both for all genres and for both sets of speakers. However, the frequencies are uneven, with conversation (5.0) and public discourse (4.9) having similar frequencies with business discourse (3.9) not far behind, but academic discourse (2.3) having far fewer. In fact, academic discourse has the lowest frequencies for all of the patterns.

Table 9.5 Frequencies of patterns associated with 'about' (per 10,000 words)

Pattern associated with 'about'	Academic, total HKC/NES	Business, total HKC/NES	Conversation, total HKC/NES	Public, total HKC/NES	HKCSE, total HKC/NES
'about' + number	2.3 1.7/4.4	3.9 4.1/3.6	5.0 5.7/4.2	4.9 5.2/3.4	4.0 4.1/4.0
'about' + 'the same/ 'the most'	0.08 0.05/0.2	0.08 0.1/0	0.22 0.2/0.3	0.17 0.2/0	0.14 0.3/0.2
'about' + 'a'/ 'an'/'the' + quantity/ period of time	0.08 0.1/0	0.3 0.3/0.3	0.56 0.4/0.7	0.17 0.1/0.3	0.28 0.2/0.4
'about' + period of time	0.08 0.1/0	0.4 0.3/0.7	0.08 0.08/0.08	0.17 0.2/0	0.19 0.2/0.2

Conversation has the highest frequency of use for all patterns except for 'about' + period of time (0.08), for which business discourse has the highest frequency (0.4). In the academic discourse, NES make proportional greater use of this vague form (4.4) which may be due to their role as teacher or supervisor and the greater need to hedge the presentation of information in this role. Further investigation is needed to determine whether other vague forms are being used in genres such as academic discourse to perform the same functions as those discussed here. Here are some examples of the first pattern, 'about' + number:

> . . . about 18 dollars . . .
> . . . about 53 billion US dollars . . .
> . . . about two weeks . . .

In the second pattern, 'about' + 'a'/'an'/'the' + quantity/period of time, 'a'/'an' is equivalent to one, and so while it is not a number, it effectively substitutes 'one':

> . . . about a spoonful of sugar . . .
> . . . about an hour . . .
> . . . about a week . . .
> . . . about a year . . .

The third pattern is 'about' + 'the same'/'the most':

> . . . did you join about the same time . . .
> . . . I don't think you'll earn more I think you'll earn about the same . . . '
> . . . probably 6 per cent; 5 percent is about the most you can do with the civil servants . . .

The fourth pattern is 'about' + a period of time, such as a month or a year, rather than a numeral. In the third of the list below, '1986' is treated as a period of time rather than a number in the same way as 'about March April'. Likewise, the fourth shows a combination of 'about' followed by 'the' in 'about the third week'.

> . . . about March April . . .
> . . . about May June . . .
> . . . about 1986 or 85 . . .
> . . . about the third week . . .

Regarding non-vague use of 'about', the proportionately higher use in academic discourse can in part be explained by the fact that, generally speaking, the academic discourse, compared with other discourse types, contains more metalanguage, with the speakers informing the hearers what they intend to talk about. This phenomenon is less common in the other three subcorpora. Table 9.6 shows the frequency of occurrence of the four most common metadiscoursal patterns across the four genres, namely 'talk^2 + about', 'say + about', 'tell + about' and 'mention + about'.

All four patterns of non-vague use of 'about' occur most often in the academic discourse. By far the most common pattern is 'talk + about,' which occurs 11.3 times per 10,000 words in academic discourse, and between 4.9–6.8 in the other three genres. These findings confirm the genre-specific nature of metadiscourse and account for the higher occurrence of 'about' in academic discourse compared with the other genres (Table 9.6).

Frequencies of use of 'something'

In *Cobuild* (1995, p. 1590), all the 8 meanings for 'something' listed are vague. The present chapter finds that the 2 most frequent meanings of 'something' are to refer vaguely to an object, situation, event or

Table 9.6 Frequencies of non-vague, metalanguage patterns of 'about' in academic discourse

VERB + 'about'	Academic, total HKC/NES	Business, total HKC/NES	Conversation, total HKC/NES	Public, total HKC/NES	HKCSE, total HKC/NES
'talk' + 'about'	11.3 10.1/16.1	6.74 6.2/8.5	4.9 4.4/5.2	6.8 6.4/9.8	7.4 7.1/8.5
'say' + 'about'	0.7 0.6/1.1	0.2 0.2/0.2	0.2 0.3/0.1	0.3 0.2/03	0.3 0.3/0.3
'tell' + 'about'	0.7 0.7/0.7	0	0.04 0.1/0	0	0.2 0.2/0.1
'mention' + 'about'	0.5 0.6/0.7	0.4 0.3/0.5	0.2 0.1/0.3	0.3 0.3/0	8.3 0.3/0.4
Total	13.0 11.9/18.5	7.3 6.7/9.1	5.3 4.8/5.5	7.3 6.9/10.1	8.3 7.9/9.3

notion ('every time he does something good'); and to indicate that the description or amount that the speaker is supplying is inexact ('around 10 10 something'). The last two of the eight meanings listed in the dictionary, which are common in the data studied here, occur when 'something' is used in the phrases 'or something' and 'something like'. No table is given to show the distribution of vague versus non-vague uses of 'something' because all of the instances in the data are vague. In Table 9.7 the most frequent patterns of usage associated with 'something' are described.

The most frequent patterns associated with 'something' occur to both the left and right of 'something' (as compared with 'very' and 'about,' where the patterns of association are to the right). An examination of the proportional distribution of the instances of 'something' in the data shows that this vague term is used much more frequently by NES than by HKC (13.8 as opposed to 9.2; see Table 9.1). The difference in usage between HKC and NES is most pronounced for three patterns: 'something' + 'like' (1.7, HKC; 2.5, NES), 'something' + 'else' (0.28, HKC; 0.5, NES) and 'or' + 'something' (0.8, HKC; 1.9, NES). The difference between the two sets of speakers is greatest for these three patterns in the conversations. Possible explanations for this difference that requires further study are that HKC are more formal in their language use and so avoid patterns associated with 'something' in favour of other forms, and

Table 9.7 Ten most frequent patterns associated with 'something'

'something' pattern	Academic, total HKC/NES	Business, total HKC/NES	Conversation, total HKC/NES	Public, total HKC/NES	HKCSE, total HKC/NES
'something' + 'like'	1.7 1.7/2.0	2.1 1.9/2.8	2.8 2.3/3.1	0.2 0.2/0.3	1.7 1.4/2.5
'is' + 'something'	1.5 1.4/2.2	2.1 2.0/2.4	1.4 1.1/1.6	0.9 0.9/1.0	1.5 1.3/1.9
'or' + 'something'	0.3 0.3/0.4	1.0 0.9/1.2	3.0 2.5/2.2	0.1 0.1/0	1.1 0.8/1.9
'something' + 'that'	0.7 0.7/0.9	1.6 1.6/1.4	0.5 0.5/0.5	0.6 0.5/1.0	0.9 0.9/0.8
'do' + 'something'	0.8 0.9/0.7	0.9 0.8/1.0	0.7 0.6/0.8	0.4 0.4/0.7	0.7 0.7/0.8
'something' + 'about'	0.6 0.5/1.1	0.5 0.5/0.5	0.3 0.4/0.2	0.2 0.2/0	0.4 0.4/0.4
'say' + 'something'	0.3 0.3/0.2	0.5 0.5/0.3	0.7 0.6/0.8	0.1 0.1/0	0.4 0.36/0.5
'something' + 'to'	0.3 0.4/0.2	0.3 0.3/0.3	0.6 0.7/0.6	0.3 0.2/0.3	0.4 0.37/0.44
'something' + 'else'	0.5 0.4/0.9	0.5 0.4/0.9	0.03 0.3/0.3	0.04 0.05/0	0.4 0.28/0.5
'something' + 'you'	0.3 0.2/0.4	0.3 0.2/0.5	0.7 0.8/0.5	0.08 0.1/0	0.3 0.28/0.44

that the difference could be a product of formal school teaching which does not cover patterns such as these.

Marked differences between the four genres are observed in the frequency of use of 'something' (see Table 9.1). Conversation (16.5) has the most instances, then business (11.4), academic (9.9) and last public (3.9), and so conversationalists are more than four times more likely to use this vague term ('something') than those engaged in public discourse. Indeed, 'something' is ranked fourteenth for public discourse. Differences in the frequencies of the patterns of association are also observed across the four genres. Conversation has the highest occurrence of 'something' + 'like' and 'or' + 'something', business has the most 'is' + 'something' and 'something' + 'that', and academic has the most instances of 'something' + 'about'.

Comparison of findings with Hong Kong textbooks

In the HKCSE examined, the frequency of occurrence of vague items is 175.8 per 10,000 words. The top ten vague items – 'very', 'about', 'some', 'more', 'much', 'something', 'many', 'quite', 'things' and 'most' – are found in all of the academic, business, conversational and public domains of interaction and by both HKC and NES, despite varying frequencies of use. The findings show that VL use is given too little and inadequate coverage, if any, in the textbooks. The advice against the use of VL (Esser 1999a, p. 7) is mistaken, as the present chapter has clearly demonstrated VL use in real-life communication in a range of contexts of use and interaction. In addition to that, the examples of VL given in the textbooks are far too limited for the students to master effectively this very important pragmatic use of language to meet their communication needs. The view that VL impairs communication needs to be replaced with the view that it facilitates communication when used appropriately in context.

Implications for language learning and teaching

This chapter has shown that when the most frequent forms of VL are studied across four different spoken genres (academic, business, conversational and public discourse), while there are similarities in the forms of VL most frequently found, there are differences in frequency of occurrence which are products of the respective genre conventions, with the greatest use in conversation. When HKC and NES are compared, there is no difference found in the overall frequency of use, but discernible differences are found across genres. Analysis of the patterns associated with 'very', 'about' and 'something' has also lent support to the genre-specific, rather than speaker-specific, tendencies of VL use. The conclusion is therefore that discourse type, rather than speaker group, seems to be the major determinant of both the forms of VL employed by the speakers and the frequencies with which these forms occur. Conversation and business discourse have tended to have the higher number of instances of the forms of VL studied, possible reasons being the communicative purposes and formality of the discourse types. There remains the possibility that VL may be achieved with other, less frequent forms in more formal discourse events, such as academic and public discourse, rather than that they are less vague. Further studies therefore need to explore further the possible reasons for different VL uses to determine the connections between speakers and the genres in which they are operating.

While the present chapter has only examined the top ten most frequently occurring vague items found in 920,000 words of the HKCSE, it has revealed a big gap in both the teaching guidelines and examples in the Hong Kong textbooks surveyed. It has indicated a need to improve what is taught in the textbooks to better reflect real world language use when exemplifying VL and, if space is limited, the most frequently occurring vague items should feature prominently in the textbooks. As shown in this chapter, the four most common items are 'very', 'about', 'some' and 'more'. The comparison between the corpus data and school textbooks has also raised a few very interesting questions. Can an assumption be made that the HKC-speakers, similar to the current student generation, did not learn to use VL from school textbooks; and if the assumption is confirmed, by what means did they learn to use the vague items in terms of the range and frequencies, in ways similar to those of NES? In teaching VL, the question to ask is not whether an expression is vague, but 'For whom is it vague? Vague as opposed to what other expression? To what end is it vague?' (Myers 1996, p. 13).

Hong Kong textbooks are not alone in ignoring the learning and teaching of VL. The mantra of business English textbooks – be simple, clear and precise – only serves to perpetuate the negative image of VL use. Meanwhile, in the real world, VL's role in hedging, boosting and sustaining relationships through asserting shared understandings, the maintenance of face, and communicating informality and formality by means of VL choices, is indispensable and a key strategic resource for speakers and writers. Textbooks need to both include VL and indicate the ways in which its use is context-specific. Examples of real world communication where VL is highlighted and discussed would be valuable for learners. Classroom activities in which learners have to describe or respond to unfamiliar scenarios or objects facilitate VL use. One simple activity is to ask students in groups to describe objects they do not know the name of while concealing the object from the group. Such activities encourage students to build up the confidence to be able to communicate by means of VL and also demonstrate the value of doing so. Having established VL's practical value, students' awareness can then be further developed to hone their sensitivity to its use in specific contexts.

Implications for research

Future studies of VL would need to examine it qualitatively, situated in context in order to evaluate successful communication in terms of both the wider and the immediate context of interaction, including the cultural meaning of the genre, as well as the distance, status and power relations of the participants have to be taken into account. In addition to that, examining an even wide range of text types, with varying degrees of formality in the discourse and communication purposes, would increase the extent to which the conclusions drawn from the research can be generalized. This chapter has demonstrated that across frequently occurring VL items there are genre- and speaker-based similarities and differences. Future studies can pursue these issues further within the framework employed here.

Finally, further research can examine whether more formal genres have developed distinct forms of VL which have been overlooked by concentrating on more frequently occurring VL. Work on VL to date has tended to focus on the more obvious and indisputable VL forms of the likes of 'things', 'stuff' and 'something' so typical of conversationalists, but what of academics who speak equally vaguely at times of 'points' and 'items', and politicians who speak of unspecified 'issues' and 'factors'? There is clearly scope for more studies that examine the links between genre, speaker and VL use.

Acknowledgements

The work described in this chapter was substantially supported by grants from the Research Grants Council of the Hong Kong Special Administrative Region (Project no. B-Q714). Thanks are due to Chris Greaves for his innovative ConGram© search engine.

Notes

1. ConcGram© is designed and written by Chris Greaves, Senior Project Fellow, English Department, The Hong Kong Polytechnic University. It is a search engine primarily devised for those working in corpus linguistics and related fields.
2. Forms including *talks, talking* and *talked* are included, and this applies to other verbs *say, tell* and *mention*.

References

D. Allison, 'Why "Often" isn't "Always"', in *Language Awareness in Language Education* (Department of Curriculum Studies, University of Hong Kong, 1995).

J. Channell, 'Vagueness as a Conversational Strategy', *Nottingham Linguistic Circular*, 14 (1985) 3–24.

J. Channell, 'Precise and Vague Quantities in Academic Writing', in *The Writing Scholar: Studies in the Language and Conventions of Academic Discourse* (Newbury Park, CA: Sage, 1990).

J. Channell, *Vague Language* (Oxford: Oxford University Press, 1994).

W. Cheng, *Intercultural Conversation* (Amsterdam: Benjamins, 2003).

W. Cheng, C. Greaves and M. Warren, 'The Creation of a Prosodically Transcribed Intercultural Corpus: The Hong Kong Corpus of Spoken English (Prosodic)', *ICAME Journal,* 29 (2005) 5–26.

W. Cheng and M. Warren, 'The Use of Vague Language in Intercultural Conversations in Hong Kong', *English World-Wide,* 22/1 (2001) 81–104.

Collins Cobuild English Language Dictionary (London: HarperCollins, 1995).

D. Crystal and D. Davy, *Advanced Conversational English* (London: Longman, 1975).

N. Drave, *The Pragmatics of VL: A Corpus-Based Study of VL in National Vocational Qualifications,* unpublished master's dissertation, University of Birmingham (1995).

B. Dubois, '"Something on the Order of Around Forty to Forty-Four": Imprecise Numerical Expressions in Biomedical Slide Talks', *Language in Society,* 16 (1987) 527–41.

I. Erev, T.S. Wallsten and M.M. Neal, 'Vagueness, Ambiguity, and the Cost of Mutual Understanding', *Psychological Science,* 2 (1991) 321–4.

D. Esser, *Teach and Practice: AS-level Oral English for Form 6* (Hong Kong: Pilot, 1999a).

D. Esser, *Teach and Practice: AS-level Oral English for Form 7* (Hong Kong: Pilot, 1999b).

Free Press, *The Use of English Oral Handbook* (Hong Kong: Free Press, 2002).

H. Graves and A. Hodge, *The Reader Over Your Shoulder: A Handbook for Writers of English Prose* (London: Cape, 1947).

G. Kennedy, 'Quantification and the Use of English: A Case Study of One Aspect of the Learner's Task', *Applied Linguistics,* 8/3 (1987) 264–86.

G. Leech, *English in Advertising* (London: Longman, 1964).

G. Myers, *Words in Ads* (London: Arnold, 1994).

G. Myers, 'From Discovery to Invention: The Writing and Rewriting of Two Patents', *Social Studies of Science,* 25 (1995) 57–105.

G. Myers, 'Strategic Vagueness in Academic Writing', in *Academic Writing: Intercultural and Textual Issues* (Amsterdam: John Benjamins, 1996).

L. Urbanová, 'On Vagueness in Authentic English Conversation', *Anglica,* 25/5 (1999) 99–107.

A. Wierzbicka, 'Precision in Vagueness: The Semantics of English 'Approximatives', *Journal of Pragmatics,* 10/5 (1986) 597–613.

10
{ / [Oh] Not a < ^ Lot > }: Discourse Intonation and Vague Language

Martin Warren

Introduction

Vague language (VL) is defined variously in the literature. VL has been referred to by scholars as 'fuzziness, vague language, generality, ambiguity and even ambivalence' (He 2000, p. 7), as 'vague language' (Channell 1994) and 'vague expressions' (Carter and McCarthy 1997), while others talk of 'imprecision' or 'imprecise language use' (Crystal and Davy 1975, pp. 112–14; Dubois 1987). Stubbs (1996, p. 202) places 'vague language and lack of commitment' in opposition to 'certainty and commitment'; VL is equated with uncertainty. VL, as described by Cheng and Warren (2003, pp. 394–5), covers a closed set of identifiable items which are inherently imprecise, and which the participants interpret based on an understanding of what the speaker is indicating: that what is said is not to be interpreted precisely. In other words, VL can be interpreted without recourse to judgements based on the particular context in which they occur. They argue that given that the precise meaning cannot be retrieved by the hearer, the successful use of VL requires the participants in the discourse to have a shared understanding of the relative status of a particular set of vague items. For the purposes of this study, in line with Cheng and Warren (2003), VL refers to language which has an inherently unspecified, or underspecified, meaning in the context in which it occurs.

It is generally recognized that the employment of VL is more widespread in spoken discourse than in written (Biber *et al.* 1999, p. 1045), although the use of VL varies across spoken genres (Cheng, Chapter 9 this volume). One reason for this is that in spoken discourse, participants are more likely to share a context than in written discourse, and they usually have the possibility of supplementing verbal communication with non-verbal communication. Another reason is the difference in expectations relating to precision: informal spoken genres demand less precision than formal written ones (see 'expectation-driven understanding', Cook 1989, p. 71). These fundamental differences between face-to-face spoken communication and written communication have implications for the interpretation of VL and also form part of the explanation for VL's wider use in spoken discourse.

Another resource available to speakers is discourse intonation (Brazil 1985, 1997), which they employ to add communicative value to what they say. This study explores the contribution that speakers' discourse intonation makes to the interpretations of VL. The relationship between VL use and speakers' choices of intonation has received relatively little attention (one exception is Channell 1994) and so this study breaks new ground in the study of the interrelationship between VL use and discourse intonation.

Discourse intonation

The discourse intonation system as described by Brazil (1995, 1997) and others (Coulthard and Brazil 1981; Coulthard and Montgomery 1981; Sinclair and Brazil 1982; Hewings 1990) is concerned primarily with the function and communicative value of intonation in English. It needs to be remembered however that discourse intonation is not the sole conveyor of discourse meaning. In this chapter, analysis of the communicative role of discourse intonation serves as an additional and not as the sole means of understanding how forms of VL function in context.

As pointed out in a study by Chun (2002, pp. 15–45), discourse intonation offers a description of intonation different from the grammatical (Chomsky and Halle 1968; Liberman and Prince 1977; Pierrehumbert 1980; Pierrehumbert and Hirschberg 1990) and the attitudinal (O'Connor and Arnold 1973; Crystal 1975; Cruttenden 1997). The grammatical description suggests that there are tones which are typically chosen with particular syntactic structures, such as rise tone with yes/no questions, and fall tone with wh- questions, statements and commands, and that even when the conventional structure is not employed, the meanings conventionally associated with them will also be spoken with these same tones. The attitudinal description ascribes to tones a set of meanings depending on the function of the utterance. The rise tone, for example, is described as having the attitudinal meaning of 'reassuring' with wh- questions (Cruttenden 1997, p. 99) and 'non-committal' or 'grumbling' with declaratives (Cruttenden 1997, p. 97). Importantly, the discourse description of intonation suggests that there are a set of choices available to speakers which are not formulated with reference to grammar and which have no fixed attitudinal meanings – they are situation-specific.

In Brazil's (1997) description of discourse intonation, speakers can select from 13 intonation choices in 4 systems: prominence, tone, key and termination; see Table 10.1, adapted from Hewings and Cauldwell (in Brazil 1997, p. vii).

The 13 intonation choices in discourse intonation are motivated by real-time, situation-specific decisions by speakers to add extra layers of meaning to words as they are spoken. All of the choices occur within the boundaries of a tone unit. In discourse intonation, a tone unit is taken to mean a stretch of speech with one tonic segment, comprising at least one tonic syllable, but which may extend from an onset (first prominent syllable) to the tonic (final prominent syllable) (Hewings 1990, p. 136). Each of the independent systems is a source of 'local meaning' (Brazil 1997, p. xi), which represents moment-by-moment judgements made by speakers based on their assessment of the current state of understanding operating between the participants. Each of the 4 systems and their respective choices are briefly described below.

Prominence

Brazil (1997, pp. 23–5) states that prominence is used as a means of distinguishing those words which are situationally informative. Prominence is not assigned on the basis of grammar or word-accent/stress; it is a choice made by the speaker in context. For Brazil, speakers have available to them two paradigms: existential and general (ibid. p. 23). The existential paradigm is the set of possibilities a speaker can choose from in a given situation. The general paradigm is the set of possibilities that is inherent in the language system.

Table 10.1 Discourse intonation systems and choices

System	Choice
Prominence	Prominent/non-prominent syllables
Tone	Rise-fall, fall, rise, fall-rise, level
Key	High, mid, low
Termination	High, mid, low

Speaker decisions within the prominence system are made on the basis of the speaker considering the status of individual words (ibid. p. 39). The other three systems in discourse intonation (tone, key and termination) are not attributes of individual words but of the tonic segment, that section of the tone unit that falls between the first prominent syllable and the last.

Tone

In discourse intonation, there are five tones that speakers may choose from. Four of these are used to distinguish between information that is common ground (referring tones, that is, fall-rise and rise), and information that is new (proclaiming tones, that is, rise-fall and fall). The fifth tone is a level tone, which is associated with tone units which precede an encoding pause or otherwise truncated tone units (ibid. p. 140). It is also chosen either for rhetorical effect (ibid. p. 170) or when the speaker does not intend to proclaim or refer and, in so doing, disengages from the immediate interactive context: the speaker says something as if it is already known, in the sense of a precoded, well-established and highly practised procedure (ibid. pp. 36, 136).

Key and termination

Brazil (1997, p. 40–66) states that a speaker has a choice when it comes to the relative pitch, or key, at the start of each tone unit. Key choices are relative to the preceding tone unit and are chosen from a three-tier system: high, mid and low. The choice of key is made on the first prominent syllable of the tonic segment and Brazil claims that each key adds meaning to what is said. High key has a contrastive value, mid key has an additive value and low key carries the sense of 'self evident' (Brazil 1985, p. 84).

Lastly, Brazil (1997) states that the speaker chooses pitch level again at the end of the tonic segment on the tonic syllable (that is, the last prominent syllable in the tone unit which is underlined in the transcripts), and Brazil terms this system 'termination' (p. 11).

The local meaning of termination can be summarized using three broad scenarios. In the case of yes/no questions, high termination means that adjudication is invited from the hearer, while mid termination seeks concurrence (Brazil 1997, pp. 54–5). In wh-type questions, high termination means that 'an improbable answer is expected' and mid termination is a 'straightforward request for information' (ibid. p. 56); in declaratives, high termination denotes 'this will surprise you' and mid termination 'this will not surprise you' (ibid. p. 58). Low termination closes a pitch sequence and, importantly, represents the close of some 'discrete part of the discourse' (Brazil 1995, p. 246).

Given the extensive role of discourse intonation in contributing to situation-specific meaning, it is interesting to examine some of the ways discourse intonation aids participants in spoken discourse to both convey and interpret VL in context.

The data

The data set used in this study is the Hong Kong Corpus of Spoken English (prosodic). The HKCSE (prosodic) is a 1-million-word corpus made up of naturally occurring discourse primarily between Hong Kong Chinese and native speakers of English. All of the HKCSE (prosodic) has been both orthographically and prosodically transcribed based on the four systems (that is, prominence, tone, key and termination) of discourse intonation (see Cheng *et al.* 2005 for a more detailed description of the contents of the corpus). This prosodically transcribed corpus is a representative cross-section drawn equally from the four subcorpora of the 2-million-word Hong Kong Corpus of Spoken English (HKCSE). As explained in Chapter 9 of this volume, the four subcorpora of the HKCSE each comprise half a million words of academic discourse (lectures, seminars, supervisions, presentations), business discourse (meetings, interviews, service encounters, presentations, informal office talk), conversation (social discourses collected in homes, restaurants, cafés and cars) and public discourse (public speeches, public forums, radio and televisions discussions). It is important to note that the HKCSE is not a 'learner' corpus (Granger 1998). The Hong Kong Chinese speakers are all functioning competently in their roles through the medium of English and their English constitutes a good example of International (or World) English (Brutt-Griffler 2002; Melchers and Shaw 2003) which has been for some time the main variety of English (Graddol 1999).[*]

Discourse intonation and VL

This study examines five manifestations of the role of intonation in adding situation-specific meaning to a speaker's use of VL. The five manifestations are vague tagging, alternative 'or', approximative use of numerals, premodification of vague determiners, and repeated vague form.

---

[*] See transcription conventions at the end of the chapter.

Vague tagging

Channell (1994, pp. 136–40) discusses what she terms 'intonation and tagging'. In examples such as 'what about things like when you read sentences or something' (ibid. p. 137), Channell argues, the ambiguity is reconciled by the speaker's intonation. If 'read sentences or something' is said in one tone unit, the speaker effectively delimits the exemplar and the tag, and removes the ambiguity so that the hearer understands that it is the verb phrase 'read sentences' that is tagged (ibid. p. 137).

In the data, there are 21 instances of speakers using the vague tag 'or something', and 16 instances 'or something like' (4), 'or something like that' (9), 'or something like this' (2), and 'or something of that nature' (1). Instances of these vague tags are shown in Example 1.

Example 1
Vague tags: 'or something', 'or something like', 'or something like that', 'or something like this' and 'or something of that nature':

1 > } A2: ** { \ [MUST] be a TEST on < MONday > or something } a: * { / a [TEST] on < ^ MONday > } A2: ** ((i
2 > } { ∨ or [SWAM] to the river < BANK > } { ? or < SOMEthing > } a: { \ i do not [KNOW] the < DE * tails > }
3 < PHRASE > from } { \ [CANtonese] < ^ Opera > or something } { = i don't < _ reMEMber > } b: { / < ^ REALly >
4 < DID > e- } { ∨ [DIDn't] you have a < MEnu > or something like } { = < SO > you can } { = < YOU > can } { =
5 so [THAT] they can HAVE a new < MARket > } { \ or something like < *THAT* > } { = i think < ^ THIS > } { \ in <
6 > seat } { = it's in [SEventeen] < H > } { = or something < LIKE > this } a: { = < ER > } { = [SEventeen]
7 ? er a } { ∨ a [FAshion] < deSIGner > } { ∨ or something of [THAT] < NAture > } ((laugh)) a: { ∨ when <

In Example 1, it is possible to identify two general patterns associated with vague tagging. First, when speakers use the tag 'or something' (21 instances), with the exception given in line 2, 'or something' is always spoken in the same tone unit as the item that it is tagged with, and this enables the hearer to set parameters on what might be included in 'or something'. So, for example, in line 1, '{ \ [MUST] be a TEST on < MONday > or something }' is said in one single-tone unit, meaning that the hearer would understand it to tag Monday and so relates to other possible test days.

The exception to this pattern (shown in line 2) is discussed in Example 2 below.

Example 2
1 B: { \ < Okay > } { ∨ so the [Others] got < BACK > } { ∨ in the < BOAT > }
2 { ∨ or [SWAM] to the river < BANK > } { ? or < SOMEthing > }
3 A:{ \ i do not [KNOW] the < DEtails > }

Two friends are discussing a boating accident in which a boat was overturned and the occupants were thrown into the water. Speaker B in lines 1–2 is speculating about what happened to the people after they were thrown into the water and he lists two possibilities before ending with 'or something'. If the speaker had included 'or something' in the same tone unit as 'or swam to the river bank', the hearer would have understood it to have included all of the other potential places the people might have swum to, but with this choice of tone unit boundaries the hearer would understand it to include all of the possible things that people in such a predicament might do. Thus the discourse intonation choices made by the speakers in relation to 'or something' fit with the observations of Channell (1994).

The second pattern, not mentioned by Channell (1994), is that 'or something like', 'or something like this', 'or something like that', 'or something of that nature' typically occur in a separate tone unit to the item that they tag (11 out of 16 instances). The reason why this pattern is typical (line 4 illustrates that these tags are sometimes spoken in the same tone unit as the tagged item) is that they lack the same potential for ambiguity as 'or something' by having a component that specifically refers back to what is tagged (that is, 'like', 'like that', 'like this' and 'of that nature').

It is also worth noting that all but two of the instances of 'or something' are non-prominent, but in the entire 1-million-word corpus, 65.7 per cent (490 out of 746) of the instances of 'something' are made prominent by speakers. It can therefore be concluded that this vague tag is almost always perceived by speakers to be not situationally informative. In the case of the vague tags that included a component that specifically refers back to what is tagged, then, typically, either 'that' or 'like' is usually considered by speakers to be situationally informative and selected to be prominent (13 out of 16 instances).

Alternative 'or'

The second of the two examples of the interplay between intonation and VL described by Channell (1994, pp. 54–5) is based on a study by Crystal (1969, pp. 263–73) and is related to the use of 'or' in the presentation of alternatives (see Crystal's example, 'would you like gin or whisky or tea?'). Crystal claims that each alternative is normally uttered in a separate tone unit and that the final item in the list is said with rise tone if the extent of the list is unspecified (that is, vague) and with fall tone if the alternatives represent the limit available. Two examples from the data studied are given below to illustrate the role of discourse intonation in such potentially ambiguous contexts.

Example 3

1 . . . [\ it's [RAIning] < outSIDE >] [\ i'll [BUY] you < LUNCH >] [\
2 [WHAT] would you < LIKE >] [= < HOTdog >] [\ or < HAMBURger >]

In Example 3, the speaker limits the list of options for lunch to just 'hot-dog' and 'hamburger' by choosing fall tone on 'hamburger', and so the use of alternative 'or' is not vague here.

Example 4

```
1 B: { ∨ like a < SCRIPT > writer } * { = [ OR ] < OR > } { = < OR > }
2 a:                    ** { \ < YEA > }
3 { \ < YEA > } { / or a < JOURnalist > } { / or an [ Editor ] or <
4 SOMEthing > like that }
```

In Example 4, the full enumeration of the list provided by speaker B in lines 3–4 is made vague by the speaker choosing rise tone in the last tone unit. Brazil (1997, pp. 88–93) terms this the 'continuative use' of the rise tone. The VL of the list is further confirmed by the speaker ending with 'or something like that'.

In the data studied, it was found that the pattern of intonation differs at times from that described by Channell and Crystal. A number of the alternative questions in the data are from service encounters and job interviews in which the service providers and interviewers ask routine, precoded and highly practised alternative questions, and, as Brazil (1997, pp. 36, 136) predicts, the speakers frequently choose level tone when asking these questions. Some typical examples of these kinds of questions are given here.

Example 5

5a
{ = [YOU] like to pay by < CREdit > card } { = *or* by < CASH > }

5b
{ = < SIR > } { = you pay < CASH > or } { = < CREdit > card }

5c
{ = so would you < LIKE > to have } { = < WINdow > seat or } { = [JUST] by the < AISLE > }

5d
{ / would you [LIKE] to have one way < TICket> } { = or < ROUND > trip }

5e
{ \ < Okay > } { \ [THAT'S] < IT > } { = [^ reGARding] < ALL > this } { = < STUFF > } { = do you have < ^ Any > } (.) { ∨ < PROblem > } { = or < QUEStion > }

The speakers in Examples 5a–5e choose level tone rather than rise or fall tone in these often repeated questions involving the use of alternative 'or'. It can be assumed that this choice presents no problems for the hearer, assuming that the hearer is equally familiar with the context of interaction. The hearers will understand these to be clearly delimited in the context and not exemplars from a longer list of alternatives, and so the use of the level tone is another means of communicating to the hearer that the enumerated items are non-vague rather than vague. It is interesting to note that while Brazil (1997) identified this particular use of the level tone in British English, it is found that it also holds for the Hong Kong Chinese speakers in these examples.

Approximative use of numerals

An important feature of discourse intonation is that the choices within the system are not determined by attitude or grammar but are made by speakers within the specific context of interaction. However, despite this important corollary, it is still possible to observe patterns of recurrent discourse intonation choices because, while every context of interaction is unique, speaker behaviour is to some extent predictable in certain contexts, though by no means guaranteed or predetermined. An example of such an observable pattern in relation to the use of prominence is illustrated and discussed below.

Speakers frequently use 'or' in combination with cardinal numbers to represent a vague approximation. In Example 6, we can see speakers using the vague approximatives 'two or three' and 'one or two'. These phrases are not to be interpreted as presenting alternatives (see the vague use of 'or' to present alternatives earlier in this chapter), but here are understood by the hearer to represent approximations within a range of the numbers stated. Thus 'two or three' has the sense of being in the range of these two numbers and equates to other vague terms such as 'few' and 'several'. Similarly, 'one or two', according to Quirk *et al.* (1985, p. 963), is to be understood as having the vague meaning of 'a small number'. Example 6 contains examples of 'one or two' (8 instances in total) and 'two or three' (13 instances in total).

Example 6

1 { \ or < ^ aNOther > } { = or to < DROP > } { = [ONE] or two < Items > } { \ from your [PROduct] < ^
2 = [LINE] < BAlanCING > } { = and [PERhaps] one or two Other < _ TOpics > } { \/ < oKAY > } { \ {
3] it's BEST TO < ER > } { = may be [WORK] in ONE outLET or < TWO > } * { \ for the < MOST > } { = a
4 uHUH > } a3: { = they < COST > me er } B: { = [TWO] or three < ^ HUNdred > } a1: * { \ < NO > } a3:
5 t [^ IF] the number should < GO > up to } { \ [TWO] or three < ^ THOUsand > } { = < _ THAT > } { = t

The choice of prominence by the speakers for these vague approximatives follows a fairly predictable pattern (see lines 1, 4 and 5), which is that the first numeral is prominent (20 out of 21 instances), 'or' is always non-prominent and the second numeral is non-prominent (16 out of 21 instances). This general pattern fits with Brazil's (1997, p. 23) observation that when an item is predicted by a prior item, speakers will choose to make the predicted item non-prominent. In commonplace vague approximatives such as these, once a speaker utters 'two or' and 'one or', the next numeral is non-selective in Brazil's sense of prominence selection, and is therefore not perceived by the speaker to be situationally informative, unlike the first numeral that is spoken. Given that discourse intonation choices are context-dependent, it is to be expected that the HKCSE (prosodic) also contains instances when this general pattern is not observed, and these are discussed below.

A second pattern is observed (4 times) in which both numerals are prominent and 'or' is, again, non-prominent (see line 3). In this both context the speaker can be seen to be effectively capping the range at 'two' by saying 'for the most' after the approximative. The speaker has choosen to make 'two' prominent because it is situationally informative in this context. Based on this evidence, we might presume that the other instances of the same intonation pattern are understood as limiting the top of the range because of the marked choice of prominence on the second numeral.

A third pattern, with only one instance in line 2, is observed, and that is neither of the numerals is prominent. This is probably because these numerals are preceded by the adverbial 'perhaps' which modifies the status of the approximative, indicating that 'perhaps' is perceived by the speaker to be more situationally informative in this context than the approximative itself (the role of premodification of various kinds is looked at in more detail below).

In addition to prominence, the approximative use of numerals is examined in relation to tone units. In the case of an utterance such as 'would you like one or two lumps of sugar', Channell (1994, pp. 54–5) and Crystal (1969, p. 268) argue that if the meaning is approximative, rather than specific, then 'one' or 'two' will co-occur in the same tone unit. Conversely, when the numbers are uttered in separate tone units, they are not interpreted vaguely, as illustrated in Example 7.

Example 7

1 { \ < _ YEA > } { = [THANK] you for < THAT > } { \ < QUEStion > }
2 { / < ^ GENErally > } { \ it [dePENDS] on HOW many < SUITS > } { \
3 you < NEED > to have } { \ for < WORK > } (.) { \ for [^ MOST] people i <
4 THINK > } { \ < THREE > } { \ will be < eNOUGH > } { \/ < YOU > know }
5 { \ [^ NORmally] unLESS you HAVE to go OUT and see a lot of CLIENTS
6 then < oKAY > you can have } { = < FIVE > or } { \ [SIX] < ^ PIECE > }

In Example 7, the speaker has been asked for advice regarding formal work attire and, at the end of the utterance, says 'five or six' with each number spoken in a separate tone unit. This discourse intonation choice has the communicative effect of meaning literally 'five or six' rather than meaning a range of possibilities based on these numbers.

Premodification of vague determiners

Another example of a recurrent discourse intonation pattern is the premodification of a vague determiner. Premodification of vague determiners refers to a determiner modified by an adverbial. Both the determiners and the adverbials are members of different sets of scalar implicature (Levinson, 1983, pp. 133–6) which are inherently vague in meaning and which require a shared understanding between the speaker and hearer in order to interpret their vague meanings in context. The use of prominence will be examined. Example 8 shows examples taken from the 37 instances of these particular commonly used vague expressions in the corpus which are comprised of a determiner, 'a lot (of)', 'a bit of' and '(a) few', which has been modified by an adverbial, 'quite' and 'very'.

Example 8

1 ? they are < conFRONted > with } { /\ [*QUITE*] *a lot of* < DIFficulties > } { (.) } { = < ONCE > } { \ < ON
2 { = < SO > } { = < THERE > was er } { \ [*QUITE*] *a LOT of* < ^ FOcus > } { \ on < Areas > } { = of language
3 ou } { = < YOU > } { \ you're [ASking] *quite a lot* from < ^ HER > } B: [/ [OH] not a < ^ LOT > } {
4 \ < ^ taiWAN > visitors } { \ spend * [*QUITE*] *a bit of* < MOney > } { = < ON > } { \ < SHOPping > } { \ as
5 i should < SAY > } { { / < toDAY > } { \ [*QUITE*] *a few* < THOUGHTS > } { \ [WENT] through my < MIND > }
6 } { only a < COUple > you know } { \/ [*VEry*] < *FEW* > } { / [VEry] low < resPONSE > you know } { = i
7 be GOOD for social < staBIlity > } { \ [*VEry*] *few* GOvernment < offIcials > } { \ would be [SO] < F
8 { \ ** but you [HAVE] *very* < *FEW* > } { ? < VEry > few mistakes } { ? [beLIEVE] in
9 me in big < COMpanies > } { = [VEry] *very few* people < UNderstand > } { { ? and } { \ [HAVE]

A strong pattern of discourse intonation choices was found among the speakers. In 30 out of 37 instances of these forms of vague expression, the adverbial premodifying the determiner is said with prominence and the determiner is non-prominent (this pattern is illustrated in lines 1, 4, 5 and 7). This suggests that speakers typically perceive the premodifier, and not the determiner, to be situationally informative in such contexts of interaction. There are exceptions to this general pattern of intonation with these vague phrases. On three occasions (see, for example, lines 2 and 6), speakers select prominence on both the premodifier and the determiner, which serves to make both situationally informative. Conversely, on two occasions (see, for example, line 3) speakers choose to make the premodifier and the determiner non-prominent, which has the opposite communicative effect in those contexts of interaction. Interestingly, in lines 6 and 8, we find speakers first selecting a less typical choice of discourse intonation, but in both cases the speakers then appear to self-correct and the subsequent choice of prominence fits with the general pattern for vague expressions of this kind. Finally, in line 9, we observe a different configuration which arguably confirms the most common selection of prominence found here. The speaker says 'very

very few' with prominence on the first 'very', and non-prominence on the second 'very' and 'few', suggesting that it is the first component in these kinds of phrases which tends to be made prominent by speakers.

Repeated VL use

The last manifestation of the role of intonation in adding situation-specific meaning to a speaker's use of VL discussed in this chapter is the choice of prominence or non-prominence in relation to the repeated use of vague items. Example 9 shows the repeated use of 'a lot' and Example 10 'things'.

Example 9

1 b: { = < SO > } { \ < ^ WELL > } { = she is [ACtually] < enJOYIng > }
2   { \ a < ^ LOT > }
3 B: { \ < MM > }
4 b: { \ but < ^ NOW > } { ? you } { / < YOU > came } { = < AND > erm } { = 5 you } { = < YOU > } { \ you're [ASking] *quite a lot* from < ^ HER > }
6 B: { / [OH] not *a* < ^ LOT > } { = but i [THINK] we've upSET < HER > }

In Example 9 two friends are discussing speaker's B's poor relationship with a third party. In lines 1 and 2, speaker b says that the woman concerned was enjoying life 'a lot' with prominence and high key and termination on 'lot'. Speaker b then contrasts this state of affairs with the current situation by saying that now speaker B is 'asking quite a lot from her', and 'quite a lot' is non-prominent with prominence and high termination on 'her' (line 5). Speaker B concedes that he has upset the woman but disagrees that he is asking a lot from her, and he selects prominence and high termination on 'lot' (line 6) to add communicative value to this message. In this short extract, the speakers can be seen to adjusting their choice of intonation, that is, prominence and high key and termination, in relation to the vague form 'a lot' to add additional layers of meaning to the message.

Example 10

1 and [THEN] i think FOR < THE > } { \ < ^ reMAINder > } { \ of
2 [THAT] < CLASS > } { ? [^ MOST] of < WHAT > you } { / < COvered > } 3 { = [WAS] conCERNED < WITH > } { = [proDUCtion] PLANning and <
4 conTROL > } { \ [IN] the very BROAD < SENSE > } { \/ [beCAUSE] it
5 LOOKED at *things* LIKE < FORECASting > } { \/ or it [SHOULD] have
6 looked at *THINGS* LIKE < foreCASting > }

In Example 10, the male Hong Kong Chinese speaker, a lecturer, is beginning a new topic and is relating it to another class taken by the students to do with 'production planning and control'. In lines 4–5 the lecturer states that the new topic is related to the previous class in a broad sense because that class has 'looked at things like forecasting' and he says 'things' without prominence because it is the exemplar which he makes situationally more informative. Later, in lines 5–6, the speaker seems to go back on the prior assumption and casts doubt on what the other class did cover by saying 'or it should have looked at things like forecasting'. This time 'things' is made prominent as the contents covered in the other class are now queried. Again, we can see how a speaker's differing choice of discourse intonation can serve to add additional meaning to vague items in context.

Conclusions and implications

In this study, the additional role of discourse intonation in adding situation-specific meaning to VL has been examined. It has been shown that a speaker's choice of intonation can serve to disambiguate VL use or add additional layers of meaning to vague items based on the speaker's perceptions of the context including the perceived shared knowledge between the participants. While discourse intonation choices are situation-specific, and are neither predetermined nor guaranteed, it has been shown that patterns of discourse intonation can be described, and thus to some extent predicted in contexts of VL use.

Learning and teaching implications

The implications of this study are twofold. First, it has underlined the importance and prevalence of VL in spoken discourse and learning and teaching materials need to explicitly include VL (see Cheng, Chapter 9 this volume). Second, it illustrates the role played by discourse intonation in aiding both speakers and hearers in situation-specific contexts of VL use and hence the need to place greater emphasis on discourse intonation in learning and teaching materials. The learning and teaching of discourse intonation has yet to find its way into mainstream English language learning and teaching materials (Chun 2002, p. 199), but where it has been introduced (Cauldwell 2002), examples drawn from real instances of language use can serve as models for learners to discuss and replicate.

Corpora such as the HKCSE (prosodic) examined in this chapter could well serve as the basis for learning and teaching materials and offer learners the opportunity for both the quantitative and qualitative study of discourse intonation in real world contexts. Corpora are able to provide useful models for what is said and how across a wide range of discourse types and these real-life examples could usefully replace what little is covered on intonation in most EFL/ESL textbooks, which tends to be based on the intuitive notions of the authors.

The study of discourse intonation should become a staple part of English learning and teaching, especially to intermediate and advanced students. This study has shown that discourse intonation consists of a set of choices that have to be clearly explained to learners. Activities which raise awareness of the choices available and the effects those choices have on local meaning would serve as a good introduction. Once the systems are introduced, learners could engage in sensitization listening exercises (Chun 2002, p. 202), controlled imitation activities, practice activities, or rehearsed role-plays which then lead on to less controlled activities that could be recorded and later discussed. For example, Bradford (1988) encourages learners to experiment with intonation choices and to discuss their effect on the meaning potential of utterances. Such activities supported with real-life examples taken from a corpus would be a useful addition for the language learner. All of the examples illustrated in this chapter have the potential to be adapted and used in the classroom. If discourse intonation becomes part of the curriculum then, when VL is taught, the discourse intonation employed by the speakers would become an integral part of the learning process.

Research implications

More studies are needed to uncover the full extent of these and other patterns of discourse intonation in order to better understand how participants in naturally occurring discourse communicate so effectively when employing VL. When only an orthographic transcription of spoken discourse is available to the researcher, an important ingredient in the meaning-making process is missing. This chapter has attempted to extend our understanding of the communicative synergy between VL and discourse intonation that enables speakers to communicate successfully in situation-specific contexts, and how it enables hearers to interpret what is being communicated. Future studies can usefully explore the complete range of VL available to speakers and so more completely describe the interrelationship between VL and discourse intonation. Such studies are likely to uncover more patterns of discourse intonation use of the kind described in this chapter and would further our understanding of how discourse intonation functions in situation-specific contexts to add meaning to VL.

Acknowledgements

The work described in this chapter was substantially supported by grants from the Research Grants Council of the Hong Kong Special

Administrative Region (Project no. B-Q714). Thanks are due to Chris Greaves who designed and implemented the search engine, iConc©, specifically to interrogate the HKCSE (prosodic).

Transcription conventions

Tone unit:	{ . . . }
Prominence:	UPPER-CASE LETTERS
Tone:	fall rise – ∨, rise – /, fall – \, rise fall – ∧, level – =
Key:	high – [^]
	mid – [ ]
	low – [_]
Termination:	high – < ^ >
	mid – < >
	low – < _ >
Unclassifiable	?
Overlapping talk	* (commencement of overlap – current speaker)
	** (commencement of overlap – interrupter)

References

D. Biber, S. Johansson, G. Leech, S. Conrad and E. Finegan, *Longman Grammar of Spoken and Written English* (London: Pearson Education, 1999).

B. Bradford, *Intonation in Context* (Cambridge University Press, 1988).

D. Brazil, *The Communicative Value of Intonation* (Birmingham: English Language Research, 1985).

D. Brazil, *A Grammar of Speech* (Oxford University Press, 1995).

D. Brazil, *The Communicative Role of Intonation in English* (Cambridge University Press, 1997).

J. Brutt-Griffler, *World English: A Study of its Development* (Clevedon: Multilingual Matters, 2002).

R. Carter and M. McCarthy, *Exploring Spoken English* (Cambridge University Press, 1997).

R.T. Cauldwell, *Streaming Speech: Listening and Pronunciation for Advanced Learners of English* (Birmingham: Speechinaction, 2002).

J. Channell, *Vague Language* (Oxford University Press, 1994).

W. Cheng and M. Warren, 'Indirectness, Inexplicitness and Vagueness Made Clearer', *Pragmatics*, 13/3 (2003) 381–400.

W. Cheng, C. Greaves and M. Warren, 'The Creation of a Prosodically Transcribed Intercultural Corpus: The Hong Kong Corpus of Spoken English (Prosodic)', *ICAME Journal*, 29 (2005) 5–26.

N. Chomsky and M. Halle, *The Sound Pattern of English* (New York: Harper, 1968).

D.M. Chun, *Discourse Intonation in L2: From Theory and Research to Practice*, (Amsterdam: Benjamins, 2002).

G. Cook, *Discourse* (Oxford University Press, 1989).

M. Coulthard and D. Brazil, 'The Place of Intonation in the Description of Interaction', in *Analyzing Discourse: Text and Talk* (Washington, DC: Georgetown University Press, 1981).

M. Coulthard and M. Montgomery (eds), *Studies in Discourse Analysis* (London: Longman, 1981).

A. Cruttenden, A. *Intonation,* 2nd edn (Cambridge University Press, 1997).

D. Crystal, *Prosodic Systems and Intonation in English* (Cambridge University Press, 1969).

D. Crystal, *The English Tone of Voice* (London: Arnold, 1975).

D. Crystal and D. Davy, *Advanced Conversational English* (London: Longman, 1975).

B. Dubois, '"Something on the Order of Around Forty to Forty-four": Imprecise Numerical Expressions in Biomedical Slide Talks', *Language in Society,* 16 (1987) 527–41.

D. Graddol, 'The Decline of the Native Speaker', *Aila Review,* 13 (1999) 57–68.

S. Granger (ed.), *Learner English on Computer* (London: Longman, 1998).

Z.R. He, 'A Further Study of Pragmatic Vagueness', *Journal of Foreign Languages,* 125/1 (2000) 7–13.

M. Hewings, *Papers in Discourse Intonation* (Birmingham: English Language Research, 1990).

M. Hewings and R.T. Cauldwell, 'Forward'. In *The Communicative Role of Intonation in English* (Cambridge University Press, 1997).

S.C. Levinson, *Pragmatics* (Cambridge University Press, 1983).

M. Liberman and A. Prince, 'On Stress and Linguistic Rhythm', *Linguistic Inquiry,* 8 (1977) 249–336.

G. Melchers and P. Shaw, *World Englishes: An Introduction* (London: Arnold, 2003).

J.O'Connor and G. Arnold, *Intonation of Colloquial English: A Practical Handbook,* 2nd edn (London: Longman, 1973).

J.B. Pierrehumbert, *The Phonology and Phonetics of English Intonation,* unpublished doctoral dissertation (MIT, Cambridge, MA, 1980).

J.B. Pierrehumbert and J. Hirschberg, 'The Meaning of Intonational Contours in the Interpretation of Discourse', in P. Cohen, J. Morgan and M. Pollack (eds), *Intentions in Communication* (Cambridge, MA: MIT Press, 1990).

R. Quirk, S. Greenbaum, G. Leech and J. Svartvik, *A Comprehensive Grammar of the English Language* (London: Longman, 1985).

J. Sinclair and D. Brazil, *Teacher Talk* (Oxford University Press, 1982).

M. Stubbs, *Text and Corpus Analysis. Computer-Assisted Studies of Language and Culture* (Oxford: Basil Blackwell, 1996).

11
'Und Tralala': Vagueness and General Extenders in German and New Zealand English

Agnes Terraschke and Janet Holmes

Introduction[1]

Vague language (VL), as Crystal and Davy (1975, p. 111) point out, 'is one of the most important features in the vocabulary of informal conversation', since a lack of precision and intellectual control 'helps create a relaxed conversational atmosphere and establish interpersonal rapport' (p. 112). In other words, expressions such as 'and that kind of thing', which signal referential imprecision, simultaneously serve important affective functions. Different languages have different socio-pragmatic norms and conventions for the appropriate deployment of vagueness, with obvious consequences for second-language learners. Hence identifying areas of socio-pragmatic contrast where L1 transfer may cause problems for second-language learners may assist in reducing instances of cross-cultural misunderstanding.

This study analyses native and non-native use of general extenders, a specific set of linguistic forms for expressing vagueness. The particular focus of the analysis is the discursive functions of general extenders in three data sets: (1) dyads comprising native speakers of New Zealand English (NSNZE), (2) dyads comprising native speakers of German (NSG), and (3) dyads comprising German non-native speakers of English (GNNSE) with native speakers of New Zealand English. We also consider the implications of the differences identified for second-language learning and teaching, and identify a number of potential areas of further research. We begin with a review of the literature, a definition of the term 'general extender', and a description of the corpus.

General extenders: previous research

The term 'general extender' (henceforth GE) was introduced by Overstreet (1999) to refer to a set of pragmatic devices that are generally assumed to express epistemic modality, and that typically include a vague noun such as 'thing', for example English 'and things like that', 'or something', and German 'und solche Sachen', 'oder so was'.

Pragmatic devices almost always comprise a semantically elusive set of forms. It is nearly impossible to pinpoint an exact meaning for these linguistic items, since they can take on different connotations depending on the context. They can be omitted without substantially changing the content, but they nonetheless contribute to the understanding of the utterance in context (Brinton 1996, pp. 33–4). In other words, their meanings are contextually dependent and, as such, pragmatic devices can serve a multitude of purposes, and often more than one at the same time (Erman 1987; Holmes 1990, 1995; Brinton 1996). Broadly speaking, there is agreement that pragmatic devices characteristically express at least two distinct types of meaning, namely referential meaning and affective meaning (Holmes 1982, 1986, 1988). At a more detailed level, however, with the emergence of growing academic interest in pragmatic devices, a wide range of more specific functions has been identified, including those of verbal fillers (Edmondson 1981), turn-taking devices (Schiffrin 1987) and devices for the creation of discourse coherence (Lenk 1996), together with markers of uncertainty (Lakoff 1975) and of interpersonal politeness (Overstreet 1999).

GEs are no exceptions to this characterization of the complexity of pragmatic devices. Thus, Dines's (1980) investigation of GEs in Australian English focused on their referential, intratextual use. Dines (1980, p. 22) maintains that 'in every case their function is to *cue the listener to interpret the preceding element as an illustrative example of some more general case*' (italics in original). This function of category implication has dominated research on GEs for many years (Ward and Birner 1993; Channell 1994). But GEs have affective functions too.

Overstreet (1999) highlights the interpersonal functions of GEs, drawing on Grice's maxims or 'principles of cooperation' (1975) and Brown and Levinson's 'politeness principle' (1987) to argue her case. Focusing on GEs in American English, Overstreet collected a corpus of ten hours of talk, including personal face-to-face interactions and telephone interactions between familiars.

In relation to their referential function, Overstreet (1999, p. 126) maintains that adjunctive markers function as hedges on the 'maxim of quantity': they allow the speaker to indicate that more could be said, without actually having to say it. Disjunctive extenders, by contrast, function as hedges on the maxim of quality: they mark what has been said as possibly inaccurate (Overstreet 1999, p. 112). As such, both extenders function as markers of imprecision, and can be used to express the referential meaning of epistemic modality.

But imprecision or vagueness can also serve as a strategy for conveying affective or interpersonal meaning. By being vague, the speaker suggests that what has been omitted need not be made explicit–it is shared knowledge. Since a vague utterance conveys the implication that more could be said, the speaker treats the hearer as someone who understands the implication. This assumption of common ground reduces social distance and contributes to the construction of interpersonal solidarity. Hence, GEs work as positive politeness devices since they invite solidarity (Overstreet 1999, p. 104). In addition, GEs may express negative politeness since they may hedge face-threatening discursive moves such as directives or suggestions, where 'a speaker is in danger of imposing his or her wants on the hearer' (Overstreet 1999, p. 105).

Very little research has been done on the functions of GEs in German. Some researchers mentioned them in passing while discussing a larger group of particles. Schwitalla (1997), for example, groups the German GEs 'oder so' and 'und solche Sachen' under two headings: 'Heckenausdrücke' (hedges) and 'Etceteraformeln' (extenders). Schwitalla focuses only on the referential meanings of German GEs, as expressions of epistemic modality and the abbreviation of lists. Both of these groups are treated as subsets of what he terms 'lexikalische Gliederungssignale' or lexical discourse signals.

In a more recent study, Overstreet (2005) takes a closer look at German GEs and compares their forms and functions to English extenders. Her study reveals that even though German and English extenders are very similar with regard to form and function, there are also some noticeable differences. Thus, generally speaking, in both German and American English, disjunctive extenders seem to be used more often than adjunctive extenders, and in both languages extenders can be used to add emphasis (Overstreet 2005, p. 1861). Moreover, Overstreet suggests that GEs are used more frequently in English, and that English GEs have greater variability of form than German GEs (ibid.). In addition, she identifies a number of forms, such as 'or what' and 'oder was weiß ich (noch alles)', that do not seem to have a formal and/or functional equivalent in the other language (2005, pp. 1860–1).

General extender: a definition

While Dines's (1980) definition of GEs is based on both their form and their category-implicating functions, Overstreet (1999) includes only forms which serve interpersonal functions. This has implications for the range of forms categorized as GEs. We include reference to both form and function in our definition. For the purpose of this study, GEs are defined as 'forms which serve referentially as expressions of vagueness, and interpersonally to build rapport, and which conform to a specifiable structural pattern'.

In English this structural pattern can be described as in (A).

(A) AND/OR (PREMODIFIER) VAGUE NOUN (LIKE THAT).

In German it takes the form specified in (B).

(B) UND/ODER (PREMODIFIER) VAGUE NOUN (POSTMODIFIER)

This allows us to formulate a general structure for GEs in both English and German, as specified in (C).

(C) CONJUNCTION (PREMODIFIER) VAGUE NOUN (POSTMODIFIER)

This open formula, with the rather non-specific VAGUE NOUN segment, allows for a large number of combinations and new creations.[2] The conjunctions 'and' and 'or' provide a basis for dividing GEs into two broad categories: adjunctive ('and') and disjunctive ('or') GEs (Overstreet 1999, p. 4).

This definition accounts for all the instances of GEs in the three data sets, as illustrated by the lists of forms produced by native speakers of each language provided in Tables 11.1 and 11.2. These forms, and their frequencies in the data sets, are analysed further in Terraschke (forthcoming). It will be interesting in future research to see whether this formula can account for instances of GEs in larger data sets, and to explore whether, with appropriate ordering amendments, it applies to other languages too.

GEs express vagueness in the sense that they open up the preceding proposition to a range of less precise interpretations. As Overstreet notes, adjunctive extenders, such as 'and everything' express vagueness by indicating that the information given is not as detailed as it could be (maxim of quantity), while disjunctive extenders, such as 'or something', express vagueness by attenuating the speaker's commitment to the propositional content of the utterance (maxim of quality). Additionally, all GEs convey affective meaning since expressions of vagueness appeal to shared knowledge between the interlocutors, and thus contribute to the establishment or maintenance of solidarity.

Table 11.1   Range of English general extenders used in interactions

Adjunctive GEs	Disjunctive GEs
and stuff	or something
and everything	or whatever
and things	or something like that
and so on	or anything
and all sorts of things	or things like that
and that kind of thing	or anything like that
and things	
and all that	
and all of those	
and all this other contextual stuff	
and all that kind of rubbish	
and something	
and stuff like that	
and things like that	
and that sort of stuff	
and that kind of thing	

Table 11.2   Range of German general extenders used in interactions

Adjunctive GEs	Disjunctive GEs
und so	oder so
und so was	oder so was
und alles	oder was
und tralala	oder so ähnlich
und allem	oder keine Ahnung
und alles drum und dran	oder sonst irgendwas
und irgendwelche Sachen	oder sonst was
und lauter solche schönen Sachen	oder sonst wo
und so irgendwie	oder wie auch immer
und solche Sachen	oder was es alles gibt
und so'n Mist	oder weiss ich nicht wo
und so'n Scheiß	oder weiss ich nicht
und so'n Zeug	

In addition to these two basic meanings (referential and affective), GEs may also convey a range of additional referential and affective nuances, as we illustrate below.

The corpus

The corpus for this study comprises 20 dyadic face-to-face conversations between female students, aged between 20 and 30, all but two of whom had not met before the recording session. Ten of the participants were native speakers of German (NSG) and 10 were native speakers of New Zealand English (NSNZE). Each participant took part in two conversations, one with a fellow native speaker and one in a cross-cultural dyad. This yielded approximately 7 hours of interaction and 80,500 words of transcription. The corpus can be divided into three sections: 5 NSNZE–NSNZE interactions, 5 NSG–NSG interactions and 10 NSNZE–GNNSE interactions. All conversations took place in the same room on campus, and were recorded with a minidisc player and a video camera. The participants were asked to engage in conversation for 20 to 30 minutes. They were free to talk about anything they liked, although topic suggestions were provided. To encourage informality, the researchers were not present for the recording. We turn next to a discussion of the meanings and functions of GEs identified in these interactions.

The meanings of GEs in the usage of native speakers

As noted above, GEs are multifunctional pragmatic devices, expressing a wide variety of meanings, ranging from predominantly referential functions, as indicators of imprecision or vagueness for instance, through to affective and interpersonal functions, establishing rapport and reducing social distance.[3] Because GEs work on so many different levels simultaneously, it is virtually impossible to specify the entire range of functions they may serve, since these vary slightly and often subtly from point to point in a conversation. However, knowledge of the wider discourse situation, together with attention to additional pragmatic devices, discourse strategies and phonological cues, can generally help in identifying the potential meanings of a particular extender in a specific context. In this section we illustrate some of the functions or discursive meanings conveyed by GEs in our data set.

Referential meanings of GEs

In this study, GEs are defined as forms whose referential function is to convey imprecision or vagueness, but which also express affective meaning, establishing rapport by appealing to the interlocutors' shared knowledge. These two basic functions characterize both the NZE and the German GEs.

Focusing first on the referential meanings conveyed by GEs, we identify two broad categories depending on whether the GE relates to a specific lexical item or to a proposition. Lexically oriented GEs function as hedges on particular lexical items, indicating that the speaker's choice of a specific item is for some reason imprecise: conveying the speaker's degree of (un)certainty with regard to the accuracy of a number, for example, or the speaker's qualifications about the precision of a specific lexical item, or indicating that the focus lexical item is just one illustration of a larger class of potentially relevant items. The second broad category constitutes GEs which convey the speaker's degree of (un)certainty about the validity of a proposition. Thus, GEs may function as hedges on the truth conditions of propositions. We illustrate these categories from our data set.

Lexical hedges

Example 1 illustrates a GE functioning as a lexical hedge on a number, conveying approximation.

> Example 1*
> F: so were your were your parents living there for a bit?
> C: yeah for uh about uh + six years *or* <u>something</u> they lived they lived there

Carol is talking about where her parents lived before she was born, so it is not surprising that she is not completely confident about exact details. She uses the extender 'or something' to indicate that the time period of six years is not necessarily precise but rather a rough approximation.

Example 2 illustrates a lexical hedge 'oder so ähnlich' expressing the speaker's uncertainty about the precision of the specific lexical item 'Stickmen'. By using the GE, Frauke indicates that she is not completely sure of the name of the movie.

---

* See transcription conventions at the end of the chapter.

Example 2
F: ja ich hab neulich gesehen ich glaub Stickmen *oder so ähnlich*
F: *the other day I watched I think Stickmen <u>or something like that</u>*

The interpretation of the general extender 'oder so ähnlich' as a lexical
hedge is supported by the co-occurrence of the pragmatic device 'ich
glaube'.

Example 3 illustrates a GE which functions as a lexical hedge signalling that the focus lexical item is just one example of a class, implying that more items could be provided. Overstreet (2005) identifies this
referential function of GEs, noting that such hedges orient to Grice's
maxim of quantity. The GE suggests that more relevant agricultural
products could be listed, and that 'good grass and sheep' are just representative examples of a larger class.

Example 3
V: and apparently [university name] ranked but they only rank
    because they grow good grass and sheep <u>and things</u> and they are
    the only university in New Zealand that do that

Example 4 illustrates a German GE used in the same way: that is as a
lexical hedge signalling that the focus lexical item is just one example
of a larger class. Stephanie recounts her reasons for travelling to New
Zealand for postgraduate studies, and points out that, because of an
agreement between Germany and New Zealand, it is cheaper for
German students to attend university in New Zealand than in the
United States of America.

Example 4
S: ja genau und deswegen hab ich das jetzt einfach dann mal//weil
    das\ ja erschwinglicher jetzt ist als wenn du in den usa <u>oder so</u>
    machst
S: *that's right and that's why I because it's cheaper to do it here than in*
    the States <u>or something</u>

The general extender 'oder so' indicates that in addition to the USA
there are other English-speaking countries that are more expensive than
New Zealand. Incidentally, this example also nicely illustrates the con-
current interpersonal or affective function of GEs, since it appeals to

assumed shared background knowledge, presupposing that the addressee knows that other countries could be mentioned in this context. This point is elaborated below.

Propositional hedge

Propositional hedges convey the speaker's degree of (un)certainty about the validity of a proposition. Example 5 illustrates a GE functioning as a hedge on the proposition 'it's something about the *Rainbow Warrior*'. Carol and Felicity are talking about the fact that tertiary education in France is free for New Zealanders.

Example 5
F: maybe it's something about the Rainbow Warrior *or something* [small chuckle]

The *Rainbow Warrior* was a Greenpeace ship which was illegally blown up and sunk in a New Zealand harbour by French secret service agents, killing a crew member, and causing a major diplomatic furore. Felicity's use of 'or something' here suggests 'something of similar political significance'. However, the context and tone of voice indicate that Felicity's implicit suggestion (that the political crisis surrounding the illegal sinking of the *Rainbow Warrior* might account for this preferential treatment) is made in jest. The GE 'or something' reinforces this non-serious key by expressing vagueness and imprecision, and indicating that she does not mean to be taken too literally.

These examples illustrate that even the referential meanings of GEs function as complex hedges, expressing vagueness in relation to concepts at different levels. And while we have distinguished different types of referential hedges, it should be noted that the distinctions are not always clear-cut. Overlapping meanings are typical of authentic interpersonal discourse. Even the distinction between lexical and propositional meaning is not always easy to draw. (See Example 10 below.) Furthermore, in addition to hedging referential aspects of talk, such as quantity and quality, GEs typically also appeal at some level to the interlocutors' shared knowledge, thus serving affective functions too. So, for example, Felicity does not explain what she means by the item '*Rainbow Warrior*'. She does not recount the details of the international political incident, but rather assumes that Carol shares her cultural, national and historical knowledge of the event, and will therefore understand the socio-cultural reference. Such assumptions of shared knowledge reduce social distance and create interpersonal rapport. In the next section we focus more explicitly on such meanings.

Affective meanings of GEs

The analysis in the previous section suggested that GEs which express some degree of referential uncertainty simultaneously convey affective meanings. In this section, we illustrate some of the affective meanings which may be conveyed by GEs, selecting examples where the affective functions are particularly prominent. We focus on two broad categories: first, GEs used to actively construct rapport, and second GEs used to attenuate negatively affective discursive moves, that is contributing to rapport indirectly by ameliorating a face-threatening act (Spencer-Oatey 2000).

Constructing rapport

Probably the most pervasive interpersonal or affective meaning of GEs is their contribution to the creation and maintenance of rapport through their appeal to shared knowledge and assumed common experience. Example 6 illustrates how the GE 'and stuff' may function in this way. A series of unfortunate circumstances forced Vivienne to quit her degree. Her main reason for returning to study was to avoid feeling she had spent a lot of time and money with nothing to show for it.

> Example 6
> V: mhm but I wanted something for my money↑ you know I already had three years now so
> L: mhm
> V: two and a half
> L: hence the cross-crediting //to get a\ degree
> V: /yeah// just so that I can have something to . to show for so many years at university
> L: yeah and just the investment of money <u>and stuff</u> as well
> V: mhm it is eh like to have that huge student loan is one thing but then to have nothing

Referentially, the GE 'and stuff' functions here as a lexical hedge, indicating that Lauren understands that the focus lexical item 'money' is just one example of what has been invested. Affectively, this GE can be interpreted as an indication that Lauren is on the same wavelength as Vivienne. She picks up Vivienne's reference to what she has invested and signals that she understands her position.

Examples 7 and 8 provide parallel examples from German. In Example 7, Ute criticizes the university system in New Zealand, saying that it is too much like school. German universities, she says, expect students to work much more independently, and some German students perceive the school-like New Zealand system as an imposition on their freedom.

Example 7
U: ja ich find das irgendwie das system find ich doch schon sehr verschult mit hausaufgaben teilweise <u>und so'n Mist</u>
U: *I think the system is very much like school with homework <u>and shit like that</u>*

The affective rapport-creation function of the GE 'und so'n Mist' is foregrounded by the inclusion of the inoffensive expletive ('mist' literally means 'manure').

In Example 8, Ute complains about the stress and the workload of her university courses. She is taking four courses, which is a heavy load.

Example 8
U: ich weiss echt nich wo mir der kopf steht irgendwie mit den ganzen blöden assignments und essays und examinations <u>und tralala</u> + weisst und irgendwie kann ich jetzt noch nicht mal sagen okay ej leute ich pack's nich ich will wenigstens drei kurse ordentlich abschliessen
U: *I really have so much to do these with all those stupid assignments and essays and examinations <u>and tralala</u> you know and I can't even say listen guys I can't do this I just want to do well in three courses*

Ute lists three substantial demands of her in-course assessments and then adds the creative (but semantically transparent) extender 'und tralala'. By abbreviating the list of things she has to do in this way, Ute appeals to Lisa's knowledge of the university system, and the stress involved in coping with it all. The implication that the list could go on and on, and that the workload is even larger, functions as an appeal for Lisa's understanding. Moreover, the use of a marked, pointedly informal, non-standard form, 'und tralala', attenuates the force of the complaint, jokingly trivializing the workload, and thus softening the force of the complaining discursive move.

Attenuating negative discursive moves

A second interesting affective meaning expressed by GEs is their function as hedges on the force of negatively affective discursive moves, such as criticism and disagreement. Example 9 is a case in point. Katja claims that New Zealanders are usually nice on an interpersonal level, but that she cannot develop a deeper relationship with them since they seem to have conservative, and in Katja's view, outdated, beliefs and ideologies.

Example 9
K: du kannst einfach . ich find's super nett hier mit leuten rumzugehen weil's einfach so es gibt so'n level an freundlichkeit der einfach . irgendwie da ist und es ist immer nett mit einen <u>und so</u>. aber so richtig . also ich hab schon gemerkt das sie teilweise sehr veraltet waren in ihren einstellungen <u>und so</u>
K: I think it's really nice to hang out with people because there is always a level of friendliness that's just it's always nice with them <u>*and stuff*</u> but I noticed that they are very conservative in their attitudes and beliefs <u>*and stuff*</u>

This is a particularly interesting example since the two instances of 'und so' have very similar referential functions, namely propositional functions relating to general friendliness and conservativeness, but somewhat different affective functions in that the first builds rapport while the second attenuates a criticism.

In addition to these more general politeness functions, GEs may also express a wide range of more subtle and complex affective meanings. Owing to space constraints, we here discuss just one example, but it is representative of a host of others where the precise meaning of the GE is complex, as well as very context-dependent. The focus in Example 10 is Barbara's use of the GE 'or whatever'.

Example 10
B: good old Don Brash em + I think he's trying to appeal to kind of lower socio-economic Pakeha who feel like they've been disempowered <u>or whatever</u>

In this context, the GE can be interpreted as conveying the general referential meaning of vagueness or imprecision. The referential focus appears to be the lexical item 'disempowered', although this is an example where the distinction between lexical and propositional hedge is not very clear-cut, since the proposition appears relatively semantically empty apart from this specific lexical item.

Affectively, the GE can be interpreted as appealing to shared knowledge, that is 'or whatever' indicates that the speaker assumes that the addressee can construct the relevant kinds of meanings which have been left unspecified. But it also seems possible to interpret the GE in this context as conveying additional components of affective meaning. As Overstreet (1999, p. 123) points out, the lexeme 'whatever' has 'a dismissive quality', signalling that the details are not important in the context. This dismissive component of meaning seems relevant to the interpretation of 'or whatever' in Example 10. It is also possible that 'or whatever' functions in this example to suggest that the speaker considers the word 'disempowered' to be a rather pretentious lexical choice, given the informality of the conversational context. One could go even further and suggest that the GE 'or whatever' suggests that Barbara is distancing herself from the kind of Pakeha she is talking about. All in all then, this example illustrates some of the complexities that may be conveyed by GEs in specific contexts, and some of the challenges that face both native and non-native speakers in interpreting their potential meanings.

While this preliminary analysis of the different functions of GEs is far from exhaustive, the results nevertheless indicate that in both German and NZE these forms function like GEs in American English. Our analysis indicates that between New Zealand native speakers of English and between German native speakers, GEs express both referential and affective meanings. They function to convey vagueness or imprecision as well as to construct and develop rapport. More-specific referential functions include those of hedges on numbers and specific lexical items, expressing approximation or signalling that more examples could be provided, as well as hedges on the truth conditions of propositions. Affectively, GEs appeal to the speakers' assumed shared background knowledge, thus constructing rapport and solidarity between the participants, as well as conveying a range of more subtle affective and attitudinal meanings in specific contexts. We turn next to a consideration of how these functions are expressed in cross-cultural encounters.

The meanings of GEs in the usage of non-native speakers

Very few studies have examined non-native use of pragmatic devices. In their investigation of the Hong Kong Corpus of Conversational English (HKCCE), Cheng and Warren found that Chinese non-native speakers of English used tag questions less often than their native counterparts, and they treated them as invariant tags, disobeying the rules of concord (2001, pp. 1426–7). Similar differences were found by Nikula's analysis of the non-native use of pragmatic devices in informal conversations between Finnish non-native speakers of English and native English-speakers (1996, p. 74). Her study detected a preference for speaker-oriented and thus egocentric pragmatic devices such as 'I think' and 'I mean' among Finnish NNS, while native speakers used more other-oriented, interactional devices such as 'you know'. No previous studies have focused on non-native use of GEs.

Referential meanings of GEs

Our cross-cultural data, involving conversations between NSNZEs and GNNSEs, indicates that the non-native speakers made appropriate use of English GEs at the referential end of the continuum, to express vagueness and imprecision. In Example 11, Stephanie uses the GE 'or something' to express numerical approximation, indicating that she is not too sure exactly how old she was when she came back to New Zealand to study.

Example 11
S: I came back to study like em when I was twenty-two <u>or something</u>

In Example 12, Valena, the GNNSE, is explaining to Felicity what her research in geography is all about. This example illustrates her use of the GEs 'or something' and 'something like that' as lexical hedges on the word 'erdrutsch' indicating that she is aware that it may not be the most precise choice in the context.

Example 12
V: yeah that's about debris flow hazards in the Marlborough Sounds ↑
F: em what flow?
V: debris   flow ↑   that's   like + em + oh + murenabgang ↑   in German ↑
F: mh no
V: em + //erdrutsch\ <u>or something yeah something like that</u>

Felicity has lived in Germany for a while and can speak German, hence Valena's use of a German term 'erdrutsch' in attempting to clarify the technical expression 'debris flow'. Her use of the GEs as lexical hedges here is perfectly appropriate.

There are also examples in the GNNSE corpus illustrating that the German students can use English GEs to indicate that a particular lexical item is just one instance of a more general class and that more options could be specified. Example 13 illustrates this usage by Ute, a German student, in interaction with Vivienne, a New Zealander. Both young women are studying anthropology, and Ute tries to ask Vivienne whether she is studying any other subjects besides anthropology. However, it takes her several attempts to make her question clear to Vivienne. Ute's use of the disjunctive GE 'or something' signals that religious studies is only one instance of a subject that people might typically study in conjunction with anthropology.

Example 13
U: are you studying only anthropology or also mhm // + \ some other studies
V: /oh I see\\ ++ so do you get to pick like other papers and
U: no are you only studying anthropology or also religious studies <u>or something</u>
V: oh okay
U: other stuff
V: just one major? ++ oh are you asking me oh okay sorry

Finally, Example 14 illustrates the use of a GE as a propositional hedge, indicating vagueness about the general proposition being considered. Anna confesses to Helen that she tends to buy Australian red wine, and justifies this by claiming that Australian wine is generally less expensive than New Zealand wine. However, when Helen responds 'oh too expensive?' Anna retreats from her claim using a GE to convey her vagueness about the relative costs.

Example 14
A: I would buy New Zealand red wine if I found some //which\ isn't too expensive [inhales] yeah [chuckles]
H: /mh\\ oh too expensive?
A: e- I don't know how how much the New Zealand wine is maybe it's like the Australian's just the cheapest <u>or so</u> ↑
H: oh
A: I don't know

The general extender 'or so', while technically inappropriate in form (since native speakers use 'or so' only following numbers), effectively conveys a lack of certainty in this context, indicating that Anna is not too sure that her implied proposition (that Australian wine is cheaper than New Zealand wine) can be sustained, or whether it is just that she has not yet found any affordable New Zealand red wine.

This brief analysis of the non-native use of English GEs in their predominantly referential functions of expressing vagueness or imprecision indicates that at least some GNNSEs do use GEs both as lexical hedges and as propositional hedges. These GNNSEs use GEs to express similar meanings in English and in German, and they use them in similar ways to NSNZEs. The next step is a detailed quantitative analysis to investigate whether all GNNSEs use the various referential functions appropriately, and whether they use them in similar proportions to native speakers (Terraschke in progress).

Affective meanings of GEs

Like native speakers of both German and English, GNNSEs also use GEs to express a range of affective meanings, including establishing rapport and reducing the degree of face threat of negatively affective discursive moves.

In Example 15, Maggie shares with Stephanie, a German student, the fact that she is pleased she has returned to university study following an injury which stopped her from becoming a professional musician. Stephanie responds with suggestions for further courses Maggie might consider. The GE 'or something' expresses referential vagueness in that the film, theatre and drama courses mentioned represent just a small selection of what Maggie could get involved in. The GE also does affective work, contributing to the construction of rapport and reducing social distance.

Example 15
M: I'm so glad I came back to uni . 'cos I wanted it to sort of take my mind off it and that's worked and that's good and it's great to have a different focus //because\ before I was working and feeling depressed about not being able to play . and now I'm like just going in a different direction that's good
S: /yeah\\
S: oh definitely //and then\ it's a good choice for languages.
M: /yeah\\ [chuckles]

S: if you're artistic yeah . you should maybe consider taking some film classes or theatre or drama <u>or something</u> come along whenever you feel like it I mean it's really just a very neat department ↑

It could also be argued that Stephanie uses the GE to soften the potentially face-threatening act of making a suggestion to Maggie. Stephanie's suggestion to get back into arts subjects by taking some film or drama classes could be perceived as inappropriate or pushy. The GE, spoken with a falling intonation, decreases the illocutionary force of the offer. This interpretation is supported by the co-occurrence of the hedge 'maybe', the non-specific invitation 'come along whenever you feel like it', the use of the pragmatic particle 'I mean', and finally the high rising terminal intonation, another pragmatic device which has been identified as expressing solidarity (Britain 1998, p. 232).

Example 16 provides another example where a German participant uses a GE interactively to construct rapport, in this case appealing to the understanding of her addressee on a sensitive topic. Lisa, the German student, is describing to Barbara, the New Zealander, a difficult living situation that Lisa found herself in.

Example 16
B: were you having problems with the first one?
L: yeah like she was em a single mum and she always had her daughter on the weekends . and she used to be an alcoholic <u>and stuff</u> and she like really got attached to me like as if I was her best friend <u>or something</u> ↑
B: oh no
L: and then she got like really jealous of my boyfriend and like wouldn't let me see him any more <u>and stuff</u> ↑ and that was just //just weird yeah

The two instances of the adjunctive GE 'and stuff' suggest that more could be said to describe the situation, but that Lisa chooses not to get into further details. The disjunctive extender 'or something' suggests that the simile of best friend is approximate, that is she is indicating the kind of relationship rather than being precise. Affectively, the GEs serve as affective appeals to Barbara's solidarity and understanding on this sensitive topic. Such an interpretation is supported by the use of high rising terminals on two of the GEs. The GEs can be interpreted as indicating that Lisa does not want to talk extensively or in detail about her former host mother. Furthermore, it is possible to interpret the GEs as contributing affectively to the softening of a negatively affective discursive move of complaint or criticism.

This attenuating or softening function of negatively affective discursive moves is also apparent in Example 17. Claudia and Eve are talking about being stressed out by study, and how to cope with the stress.

Example 17
C: I've noticed like when I first when I first started my midwifery degree I did a . you know study sup- . you know a seminar on how to study ↑
E: mhm +
C: and I tried to do all those things and I went [sighs]
E: mhm
C: and I was all worried and stressed out <u>and</u> //<u>stuff</u>\
E: /oh\\

Claudia, the GNNSE, describes how she used to be worried about doing all the things she was told to do to help study. The general extender 'and stuff' intensifies the message that she was experiencing considerable stress, and appeals to Eve's understanding. This short excerpt illustrates nicely how a GE may contribute to the joint construction of rapport, since Eve's supportive minimal responses 'mhm' and 'oh', provide further evidence of this process.

Finally, in Example 18, the GE 'and so on' can be interpreted as an appeal by the GNNSE to common knowledge and the interlocutor's understanding. Ute and Vivienne are talking about tuition fees and Ute says that in Germany she has to pay money for student activities and other things.

Example 18
V: oh my goodness
U: and for some for some student activity //stuff\
V: /yup [laughs]\\
U: <u>and so on</u> and yeah so I paid //only eighty
V: /mine were\\ about five thousand

The words 'for some student activity stuff and so on' were expressed with some degree of hesitation, suggesting that Ute does not really know exactly what she had to pay for. Since Vivienne has never been to a German university, and therefore could not be expected to know what else might be on the list, the GE can here be interpreted as an appeal to Vivienne's general knowledge of what universities might claim money for, to fill in the blanks. Again Vivienne's responses suggest the interchange is effectively contributing to the construction of rapport.

Our analysis of these examples indicate that overall these GNNSE appear to use English GEs in conversation with native speakers for a variety of interpersonal functions that are comparable to their range of functions in both German and NZE conversations. Obviously the results of this small study must be treated with caution, but they have usefully established some of the parameters and the groundwork for further more detailed quantitative research comparing native and non-native speaker patterns in the use of GEs.

Applications

Cross-cultural pragmatic research of the kind reported in this chapter has the potential to make a valuable contribution to our understanding of the difficulties faced by non-native speakers of English in the acquisition of pragmatic devices such as general extenders. Our analysis suggests that such studies can usefully indicate areas where native-speaker and non-native-speaker norms overlap, thus encouraging learners by identifying areas of potentially positive language transfer, as well as warning them of areas where negative transfer is a risk.

There are many ways of exploring the results of such studies for the benefit of learners of English as a second language. One specific example of an approach we have found valuable is the use of authentic materials as a basis for interpretation and discussion, followed by role-play. This approach can provide an invaluable starting-point in raising awareness of the importance of socio-pragmatic aspects of interpersonal interaction (Newton 2004; Riddiford and Joe 2005). We first present language learners with transcribed exchanges from authentic interactions between native speakers, such as those in our pragmatic particles data set. We then ask the learners to suggest possible interpretations of what is going on in the interactions, with the option of focusing specific attention on certain features, such as GEs. We follow up with suggestions in worksheets which guide learners to notice certain features of the spoken exchange. The next step involves learners in practising the focus features in role-play situations devised to provide opportunities for their use. Knowing how to avoid being too precise is a very useful skill for a second-language learner. This approach has proved very successful, and has potential for expansion to a wide range of socio-pragmatic features.

Further research

There are many further research questions that would merit exploration. Perhaps most interesting is an analysis of the range and relative frequencies of forms used as GEs by native vs. non-native speakers of English (see Terraschke forthcoming). A related area is an exploration of the extent to which the GE general structure formula provided in this chapter can account for instances of GEs in larger data sets, and it will also be interesting to see whether, with appropriate ordering amendments, it can perhaps be extended to apply to other languages.

Further research on GEs is also clearly required to establish the extent to which our suggestions concerning the range of referential and affective meanings associated with GEs in each language can be generalized beyond this exploratory sample, as well as the areas of overlap and potential transfer between languages.

Another potentially very valuable area for further research involves comparing the different contexts where VL is appropriate, or even required: In what kinds of situation is it appropriate to be vague as opposed to precise? For example, compare a casual chat with giving evidence in a law court. And is it the case that GEs occur more often in particular kinds of speech acts or discourse moves?

From a sociolinguistic perspective, it would be interesting to explore the interaction of social variables such as gender, age and social background with the frequency and range of GEs used by speakers in different languages, where again the potential for cross-cultural contrast and misinterpretation is obvious. Finally, it would also be worth while, paralleling Channell's (1994) research for English, to ask native speakers of German to rate the level of certainty or vagueness expressed by specific GEs; in other words, do different GEs express different degrees of uncertainty?

Conclusion

This chapter provides the first comparison of native speaker norms in the use of GEs with the usage of GEs by non-native speakers of English in cross-cultural conversations. Having identified a general formula for the structure of GEs in both languages, namely CONJUNCTION (PREMODIFIER) VAGUE NOUN (POSTMODIFIER), we provided lists of the range of forms instantiating this formula produced by native speakers in our data set of dyadic conversations, comprising 80,500 words.

Our analysis of the function of these GEs indicated that both the New Zealand students and the German students, whether speaking English and German, used GEs to express a similar range of meanings, including both referential and interpersonal meanings. In terms of their referential meaning, German students in both languages and New Zealanders speaking English used GEs to express vagueness, and to hedge on the precision of lexical items and the validity of propositions. Affectively, all groups also used GEs as interpersonal devices, appealing to shared knowledge and understanding between the interlocutors, constructing rapport and reducing social distance.

We have indicated some ways the results of the analysis described in this chapter could be applied for the benefit of second-language learners, referring in particular to the value of authentic materials in developing sensitivity to complex socio-pragmatic meanings. Finally, we have suggested some directions for further research–ways in which the analysis in this chapter could be extended to throw additional light on the range, frequency, socio-pragmatic complexity and social distribution of GE structures in different languages.

Transcription conventions

All names are pseudonyms.

[university name]	Used when real name is being withheld
[laughs]	Paralinguistic features in square brackets
[drawls]	
.	Pause of less than a second
+	Pause of up to one second
++	Two-second pause
..../ ...... \ ...	Simultaneous speech
..../ ...... \	
?	Question intonation
↑	High rising terminal on declarative
publicat-	Incomplete or cut-off utterance

Notes

1. We express our appreciation to Laurie Bauer who has contributed generously to the discussion of the material in this chapter, and provided valuable comments on a draft. We also thank the students who contributed the wonderful conversations which form the basis of the analysis.
2. We have used the word VAGUE NOUN for what SIL label a *proform* defined as 'a word, substituting for other words, phrases, clauses, or sentences, whose meaning is recoverable from the linguistic or extra-linguistic context' (Loos 2004).

3. GEs also serve as discourse markers, signalling a transition-relevant point (TRP), or the potential end of a speaker's turn. This is not discussed further in this chapter.

References

L.J. Brinton, *Pragmatic Markers in English: Grammaticalization and Discourse Functions* (Berlin: de Gruyter, 1996).

D. Britain, 'Linguistic Change in the Intonation: The Use of High-Rising Terminals in New Zealand English', in *The Sociolinguistic Reader. Volume 1: Multilingualism and Variation* (London: Arnold, 1998).

P. Brown and S. Levinson, *Politeness: Some Universals on Language Use* (Cambridge University Press, 1987).

J. Channell, *Vague Language* (Oxford University Press, 1994).

W. Cheng and M. Warren, ' "She Knows More About Hong Kong Than You Do Isn't It": Tags in Hong Kong Conversational English', *Journal of Pragmatics,* 33 (2001) 1419–39.

D. Crystal and D. Davy, *Advanced Conversational English* (London: Longman, 1975).

E.R. Dines, 'Variation in Discourse–"and Stuff Like That"', *Language in Society, 9* (1980) 13–31.

W. Edmondson, *Spoken Discourse: A Model for Analysis* (London: Longman, 1981).

B. Erman, *Pragmatic Expressions in English: A Study of You Know, You See and I Mean in Face-to-Face Conversation* (Stockholm: Almqvist & Wiksell, 1987).

P.H. Grice, 'Logic and Conversation', *Syntax and Semantics,* 3 (1975).

J. Holmes, 'The Functions of Tag Questions', *English Language Research Journal,* 3 (1982) 40–65.

J. Holmes, 'Functions of *You Know* in Women's and Men's Speech', *Language in Society,* 15 (1986) 1–22.

J. Holmes, '*Sort of* in New Zealand Women's and Men's Speech', *Studia Linguistica,* 42 (1988) 85–121.

J. Holmes, 'Hedges and Boosters in Women's and Men's Speech', *Language and Communication,* 10 (1990) 185–205.

J. Holmes, *Women, Men and Politeness* (London: Longman, 1995).

R. Lakoff, *Language and Woman's Place* (New York: Harper Colphon, 1975).

U. Lenk, *Marking Discourse Coherence: Functions of Discourse Markers in Spoken English* (Tübingen: Narr, 1996).

E.E. Loos, (ed.), *SIL International–Glossary of Linguistic Terms* (2004). http://www.sil.org/linguistics/GlossaryOfLinguisticTerms/ (accessed 19 September 2005).

J. Newton, 'Face-Threatening Talk on the Factory Floor: Using Authentic Workplace Interactions in Language Teaching', *Prospect,* 19 (2004) 47–64.

T. Nikula, *Pragmatic Force Modifiers,* (University of Jyväskylä, 1996).

M. Overstreet, *Whales, Candlelight, and Stuff Like That: General Extenders in English Discourse* (Oxford University Press, 1999).

M. Overstreet, 'And Stuff *Und so:* Investigating Pragmatic Expressions in English and German', *Journal of Pragmatics,* 37 (2005) 1845–64.

N. Riddiford and Angela Joe, 'Using Authentic Data in a Workplace Communication Programme', *New Zealand Studies in Applied Linguistics*, 11/2 (2005) 103–10.

D. Schiffrin, *Discourse Markers* (Cambridge University Press, 1987).

J. Schwitalla, *Gesprochenes Deutsch: Eine Einführung* (Berlin: Schmidt, 1997).

H. Spencer-Oatey, 'Rapport Management: A Framework for Analysis', in *Culturally Speaking. Managing Rapport Through Talk Across Cultures* (London: Continuum, 2000).

A. Terraschke, 'Comparing the Structure of General Extenders in New Zealand English and German' (forthcoming).

A. Terraschke, 'Pragmatic Particles in New Zealand English and German', PhD. Victoria University of Wellington, in progress.

G. Ward and B. Birner, 'The Semantics and Pragmatics of *and Everything*', *Journal of Pragmatics*, 19/3 (1992) 205–14.

Part V
Conclusion

12
'Doing More Stuff – Where's It Going?': Exploring Vague Language Further

Joan Cutting

Chapter overview

In this chapter, I describe my model of VL and focus on the social dimensions, discussing my studies on the influence of the function, depth of relationship and gender. Next, I point to several areas that still require investigation, my aim being to inspire others to research, and I also summarize suggestions made by contributors in this volume. The chapter then explores, in depth, applications of findings about VL. I outline ideas that abound in the literature, add my own ideas *vis-à-vis* TEFL, and again I summarize suggestions made by contributors to the volume.

Social dimensions of vague language

My model of vague language

I first developed my model of VL from a study of the in-group code used by an academic discourse community of applied linguistics students in the University of Edinburgh (Cutting 2000). This was a longitudinal study looking at changes over a year. My model consists of lexical, grammatical, clausal and utterance-level features which are heavily context-dependent, and whose meaning is clear only to speakers who share the background context.

The lexical features are metonymical proper nouns, superordinate nouns and general nouns and verbs. My choice of metonymical proper nouns was influenced by Brown and Levinson (1987), who include jargon and local terminology in their description of in-group codes, and Swales (1990, p. 32), who mentions technical terms as part of his definition of the academic discourse community code. In my model, metonymical proper nouns refer not to the person or entity named but to an unnamed entity. Thus 'How's <u>your Chomsky</u>?' refers not to the man himself but to a 'project on Chomsky', and the question 'Are you going to <u>stylistics</u>?' asks not about the field but about the stylistics lecture, just as 'Has anybody done their <u>syntax</u>?' asks about preparation for the syntax workshop.

I include superordinate nouns, guided by Halliday and Hasan (1976) and by Ullman's (1962) description of generic words, such as 'bird', referring to classes of entities. My own definition of the superordinate noun, in this context, is that which refers to a specific member within a general category by using the general category label rather than indicating which of the category members it is. Thus, students say, 'How's <u>the project</u>?', '<u>the paper</u>'s due in next Friday' and 'What about <u>the article</u>?'; there are many projects, papers and articles that speakers could be referring to, but the hearers know which one it is, because they share the background knowledge.

My choice of general nouns and verbs was guided by Crystal and Davy's (1975) dummy nouns expressing total vagueness ('thing') and Channell's (1994) vague 'placeholder' words ('thingy' and 'whatsisname'). General nouns, such as 'stuff', 'event' and 'people', are on the borderline between a lexical item and the personal pronoun, just as general 'do' verbs are on the borderline between the lexical verb and the substitute (Halliday and Hasan 1976, pp. 274–81). It is this that makes them relatively empty semantically. Conversely, they are heavily laden pragmatically. The general nouns in my model are ones that are not lexically cohesive and they refer to a specific entity known by speaker and hearer (unlike many of the cases of VL mentioned in this book, in which the referent is itself vague or unknown). Examples in my data are 'So I typed <u>that thing</u> up again after you'd gone', 'I haven't given you <u>your thing</u> back' and 'I haven't got <u>the thingymajog</u>', in which there is no lexical and grammatical cohesion in the preceding co-text. The category general verb includes pro-verbs 'do' in non-anaphoric contexts, as in 'What're you <u>doing</u>?' (in which there is a very limited range of expected possible answers), and lexical 'do' verbs which could actually be substituted by a semantically transparent verb meaning the same, as in 'I haven't <u>done</u> any Chomsky' ('done' meaning 'revised'), 'You <u>do</u> Language Planning don't you?' ('do' meaning 'take the course') and 'I've <u>done</u> all the people' ('done' meaning 'made notes on'). Again, only in-group members sharing the background knowledge would have access to the exact meaning of these lexical items.

The vague features I am calling 'grammatical' are a particular type of referential ones: non-anaphoric demonstrative pronouns and adverbs, and non-anaphoric third-person personal pronouns. I am interested in pronouns and adverbs with no cohesion with another expression in the preceding text (Halliday and Hasan 1976) that point to a definite entity, place, time or state, the meaning depending critically upon mutual knowledge, beliefs and suppositions (Clark and Murphy 1982). Examples from my data are 'They sent me this,' 'You shouldn't be here. That was yesterday!' and 'He's nearly there,' all uttered out of the blue.

Finally, my model includes clausal and utterance-level features: vague clauses, clausal ellipsis and humorous conversational implicature. 'Vague clauses' are those with low semantic content, which the speaker assumes that the hearer could substitute with a more contentful clause or noun phrase with the same pragmatic meaning. An example is 'Are going to do what you thought you'd do about your project?', in which the hearer knows that 'what you thought you'd do' refers to their 'ways of teaching Taiwanese university students about English accents across the world'. In this study, I use the term 'clausal ellipsis' not to mean initial clausal ellipsis, as in 'Been doing that since a couple of years ago,' which is a marker of intimacy and informality but does not depend on shared background knowledge for its meaning. I use it to mean unfinished ends of sentences, with or without general extenders. Here, the speaker knows that the hearer could finish the utterance or substitute the extender with more contentful noun phrases. Examples are 'They had the er mental and the . . . ' and 'You're not bothering with going through Bloomfield and all those kind of things?' Finally, the humorous conversational implicature observed in my data is that in which the speaker flouts the cooperative maxims of quantity and quality (Grice 1975). In the utterances 'Well you know what he's like', 'I can imagine why you wouldn't want to' and 'I really like the teacher very much', the speaker expects the hearer to know that she is being intentionally unclear or ironic, and to appreciate the unspoken message of the in-joke.

Social function in the Edinburgh study

I began my study of the function of VL by examining my corpus of the applied linguistics students in the University of Edinburgh (Cutting 2000). Exploring the association between VL and length of relationship, I found that VL is a marker of intimacy, in that the longer the students know each other, the denser their VL features become (density expressed as a percentage of VL features out of all words).

In the Edinburgh study, VL is used mostly in moves that have an interactional function and solidarity-giving speech acts. Whereas 62 per cent of all discourse units in the 26,000-word corpus are interactional, an overwhelming 90 per cent of the discourse units containing VL are interactional. In addition, there is increase in interactional utterances over time, and this coincides with the increase in VL density. The solidarity-giving speech acts of the common room can be expressed in terms of the following social maxims: 'express a positive attitude to your interlocutors' and 'express a negative attitude to yourself and to the situation'. When utterances obeying the maxims are packed with VL, the common ground claim is strengthened. An example will illustrate this. In the following, two male students, English AM and Canadian CM, convey a negative attitude to the reading material and the lecturer for the syntax module, and use a metonymical proper noun, a general noun and non-anaphoric personal pronouns.

CM   You when you read over <u>that syntax</u> didn't it seem very simple?
CM   You know when I first looked at it I thought what's this?
CM   I'll never get <u>this stuff</u>.
AM   Do you remember when <u>he</u> came to talk about <u>it</u>?
CM   Yeah.
AM   <u>He</u> could <u>he</u> couldn't seem to explain <u>it</u> simply but (0.5 second's pause) you can.

It could be concluded that using VL is a high-involvement strategy for claiming in-group membership. However, it is probable that the function of the VL varies according to the VL feature. The lexical, the clausal and the utterance-level features (metonymical proper names, superordinates, general words, vague clauses, clausal ellipsis and humorous conversational implicature) are likely to have been chosen consciously, to assert in-group membership. The grammatical features (non-anaphoric demonstrative pronouns and adverbs, and personal pronouns) may be an unconscious reflection of in-groupness, complying with the maxim of quantity, or, equally, they may be used to exclude outsiders.

Social function in CANCODE studies

I then investigated the influence of social factors on VL (Cutting 1998, 1999), using a database of 40 randomly selected dialogues from CANCODE (the Cambridge and Nottingham Corpus of Discourse in English). Of particular interest were the effect of the depth of relationship and function on VL use, and gender differences. These studies are strictly preliminary case-studies and as yet unpublished. I describe them here in general terms, with a view to offering ideas for researchers to take up and carry forward.

The genres in my CANCODE database were six: casual conversation, service encounter, joint task, narrative, lecture/tutorial/class and interview. I tagged the VL features in each discourse unit in each genre, and my analysis showed that VL occurs in all genres, regardless of the level of formality. Thus, for example, even in a service encounter about setting up a mortgage, a formal interaction between strangers, the client uses a general verb, a general noun and a non-anaphoric third-person personal pronoun: 'but I'm <u>doing</u> a PhD and there's various <u>things they</u> want'. I then labelled the discourse units in each genre for depth of relationship and function, and divided the dialogues into three groups: female-to-female, male-to-male and mixed-sex.

My analysis of the depth of relationship and the density of VL features showed a positive correlation between them. The dialogues that contain the highest density of VL are the casual conversations between close friends. Witness the following example, with its vague clause, and general noun and verb:

A: You know when we were in the pub that time with Stuart, and John was saying to Stuart <u>what you said</u>. I told you that Stuart told Ed, didn't I?

B: I – I shouldn't have told him <u>all the stuff I did</u>, cos I told him so much.

It could be that in conversations between friends, the gossip and self-disclosure require language aimed at intentionally excluding outsiders (including the recorder).

Analysis of the function of VL revealed that the most frequent function was that of giving little importance to the referent, either to be friendly or to be critical. To take an example, when three friends talk informally as they engage in the joint task of organizing the sale of secondhand goods, they show a friendly attitude to each other by referring to each other's duties using a general verb and noun, ''Cos I'm thinking if we got that then Alison could start <u>doing her stuff</u>.' In this example, the VL minimizes the imposition of the suggestion. Similarly, when friends engage in the joint task of shopping together, they show their disgust for the prices by reducing the value of the referent: 'Seven pounds for <u>that little thing</u>?'

I come finally to gender differences in VL use. Before I discuss my findings, I should say that the literature VL and gender would seem to suggest that this is not a significant variable. Channell (1994, p. 193) surmises that 'it may be that vagueness is stereotypically associated with women, whether or not they actually use more vague expressions ' or that VL

> may be an exponent of power relations, particularly in relation to politeness. If, in turn, women are often the less powerful in mixed-sex interactions, then women will be expected to use more vague expressions.

Shalom (1997, p. 187) shows that in personal advertisements in lonelyhearts columns of magazines and newspapers, which 'resonate with ambiguity', the most stereotypical lexis being 'imbued with a vagueness', that men and women use VL.

When I compared VL of males and females in my data, taking all the dialogues together, there was indeed little difference. However, when I examined the data divided into three gender groupings (female-to-female, male-to-male and mixed-sex) differences emerged. In mixed-sex dialogues, females use double the density of VL that males do. Significantly, females in female-to-female dialogues use seven times the density of VL that males do in male-to-male dialogues. The following example is from a female-to-female casual conversation: it bears an accumulation of general nouns, a general verb, non anaphoric demonstrative pronoun and personal pronouns, and clausal ellipsis with an extender.

<F2>   Helen said that you're really bogged down with <u>things</u> as
          / well /
<F1>   / Yeah / I am. It's either I can't seem to be working and <u>doing</u>
          my / soc / <u>stuff</u> at the same time / it's/ either work or mess
          up and at the moment it's mess up.
<F2>   / Mm. / Oh really.
<F1>   So it's a bit worrying really.
<F2>   Yeah. / haven't you em / I thought you weren't involved
          with <u>that</u> any more though. / I thought /
<F1>   No I am but the end <u>it's</u> the end of term.
<F2>   The end of term. Oh that's not long.
<F1>   No. No it's just like a really big event's coming up.
<F2>   Oh really.
<F1>   There's a lot of organization <u>and stuff</u>. Yeah.
<F2>   God.

('/' indicates overlapped speech.)

The VL here coexists with an in-group term '<u>soc</u> stuff', as well as markers of solidarity and convergence: backchanelling ('Mm. Oh really'), echoing ('the end of term'), inclusive fillers/hedges ('I mean'), softeners/mitigators ('a_bit worrying really'), colloquialisms ('mess up' and 'really bogged down'), and swearing/blasphemy ('God'). This suggests that in female-to-female casual conversation, VL is itself a strong marker of solidarity and convergence.

It is evident that social studies of VL are in their infancy. In the next section, I invite students and scholars to consider what directions VL research could go in next: I offer ideas of my own and remind them what the other contributors have suggested.

Further research in social dimensions

Vague language and social groups

The models of analysis of VL could be extended to other social groups and other languages. The social factors mentioned in this book could be examined more deeply, and other factors such as regional and social differences could be explored. In this section I do not offer evidence based on systematic studies; I offer my own experiences in a series of anecdotes, and my ideas, hunches and general impressions. This chapter aims to trigger off research questions in the reader's mind.

Other student communities could be examined. Research could be carried out to find whether students, and indeed staff, in other linguistics and language departments in universities, colleges and schools around the English-speaking world speak a similar VL. The students in the Edinburgh study were British and Canadian; it would be interesting to investigate to what extent Australian, Irish, New Zealand and US students have a similar VL and social maxims. Carter (2006) observes that American English, in general, seems to contain less VL than British English. Whereas a British person, asked what time the film starts, might answer, 'I don't know, 9.15 or something', a North American is more likely to answer, '9.15'. It might be revealing to compare undergraduate and masters students with PhD students, in any subject: the PhD student community is not so tightly knit as that of students who meet and study together on a daily basis. It could be that the PhD students share the metonymical proper nouns and superordinate nouns because they belong to the specialism and the institution, but lack the non-anaphoric definite reference, clausal ellipsis and in-jokes because these depend more on shared interpersonal knowledge.

Non-academic communities of practice could be examined. Of interest would be any group of people brought together by a mutual engagement and endeavour, who jointly construct a range of values and appropriate behaviours, and whose membership is created and maintained through social practices, linguistic or behavioural, at a local rather than a global level (Eckert and McConnell-Ginet 1998; Davies 2005). For example, studies of cleaning staff, organized peace protesters, allotment-holders, football team supporters, street-gangs or regular cronies in a senior citizens' drop-in centre might produce illuminating results.

Web-based communities of practice beg analysis, and this process has been researched for a number of years now (Crystal 2001). Emails and instant messaging present a fertile ground for study, with their semi-written, semi-spoken style, minimalist spelling and grammar, and often private, highly intertextual nature. Chatrooms, by comparison, might have less VL because of the anonymity, and topic looping and intermeshing. Contributors to internet newsgroups, discussions forums and blogs may develop their own sort of VL. Bloggers who post entries frequently in interactive networks and collaborative publications of cultural, social and topical articles, could be tracked and analysed. 'Wikis', being web pages operated by communities for the purposes of collaborative writing, are even more likely to have their own VL. The same may become true of podcasting, since it is being used to distribute recordings to a known audience, for example religious, sports and academic groups.

Family and couples' language is obviously more difficult to study because the recorder trespasses on their privacy. However, the very privacy is likely to lead to a greater amount of VL, partly because of the wealth of shared interpersonal knowledge and partly because of the need to exclude the intruder. On the other hand, it would be enlightening to examine the language of long-term married couples and discover whether their VL density is indeed less, if they feel no need to avoid showing uncertainty or a lexical gap, avoid being offensive, and so on. There could be less VL because it is associated with interactional language, and many long-term married couples have less need of phatic communion to fill silences. Readers may know the joke about the woman who went to a marriage counsellor and complained, 'Our small-talk is getting smaller and smaller.' Within families, too, some members might habitually indulge in more VL than others. Readers might know family members who address each other like this:

A: Where's the er – ?
B: Oh, it's on the er –

An area of particular interest is that of VL and speakers of other languages. Initially, two research questions need to be pursued: 'How do speakers of other languages use English VL?' and 'What sort of VL exists in other languages?' Speakers of other languages might understand some parts of English VL and not others; they might want to produce some and not others. This will be determined by their cultural habits as regards explicitness, politeness, cooperative principles and speech act realizations. It would be helpful to know if non-native-speaker-of-English international students at Australian, British, Canadian, Irish, New Zealand and US universities are kept apart from native speakers of English by their inability or reluctance to speak vaguely and informally. This isolation might exist not only in seminars and workshops, but also in social gatherings outside class.

Research could be carried out to discover whether the VL model is generalizable to other languages. A brief preliminary glance at other languages shows this to be the case: French has general nouns ('truc', 'machin') and verbs ('faire'); German has general nouns ('Ding', 'Zeug' and 'Dingsbums'), extenders ('was auch immer', 'oder so') and verbs ('machen'); Japanese has general nouns ('mono', 'koto', 'yatsu' and 'iroiro'), extenders ('ka nanka') and verbs ('yasu'); Russian has general nouns ('shtukovina' and 'kak bish ego?'); and Spanish has general nouns ('cosa', 'fulano'), extenders ('y eso') and verbs ('hacer'). This merits examination, and indeed there may be VL features in other languages that do not exist in English. The social function and status of VL in other languages may differ from that of English, too, as may each language's way of asserting group membership. If parallels and equivalents could be drawn up between languages, this could help language teaching, as well as business and other relationships between countries.

Researchers could also look into studies of social and personal variation *vis-à-vis* VL. It could be that working-class people have a different VL from middle-class people, and that teenagers use VL differently from senior citizens.

Vague language to include or exclude

The question of whether VL is mainly a sign of social cohesion or principally a tool to assert power needs further investigation. In this section, I approach this question in conjunction with the concepts 'VL to include', 'VL to not include' and 'VL to exclude'.

When addressors use VL 'to include' the addressee and point implicitly to known-to-be-shared referents, this does not always mean that their aim is social cohesion. Fairclough's view that texts with power impose implicit assumptions the addressee (1989) is relevant here. An example of an interesting direction to investigate is the written and spoken discourse of advertisements: in the 1990s and 2000s it contains VL that behaves as if it aims to include, but is in fact being used to persuade consumers to buy more. Advertising employs 'do' and 'happen' and 'it' in promotional slogans to include everything, everyone and every action, and impose assumptions of relevance on all who read or hear it. Witness 'Don't shop for it, Argos it' (Argos, the catalogue shop), 'You can do it when you B&Q it' (the do-it-yourself chain), 'Move it' (Lucozade, the soft drink), 'I'm lovin' it' (McDonalds, the burger bar), 'Just do it' (Nike, the sportswear firm), 'See what you can do' (02 the mobile phone company) and 'Make it happen' (the Royal Bank of Scotland). These slogans are expressed in unspecific terms in order reach all potential consumers by making each believe that the company or bank can satisfy their individual personal needs.

VL used 'to include' abounds in humorous literature and comedy. It would be interesting to explore how VL is used to entertain and amuse. A text that springs to mind is the opening paragraph of a chapter in the children's book *Winnie The Pooh* (Milne 1994, p. 42):

> The Old Grey Donkey, Eeyore, stood by himself in a thistly corner of the Forest, his front feet well apart, his head on one side, and thought about things. Sometimes he thought sadly to himself, 'Why?' and sometimes he thought 'Wherefore?' and sometimes he thought 'Inasmuch as which?' – and sometimes he didn't quite know what he *was* thinking about.

Here, the wistful 'Why?', 'Wherefore?' and 'Inasmuch as which?' invite the reader to imagine the rest of the clause and eventually to suspect that Eeyore does not have a referent in mind, and therein lies the humour. Many stand-up comedians use VL to comic effect; those who use double entendres expect the audience to understand whole paragraphs behind expressions such as 'Say no more!' and 'You know what I mean?'

Even when it tries to include, VL does not always communicate effectively. A study of minor breakdowns in communication brought about by VL being used ineffectively is a whole area of study to itself. Sometimes speakers might wrongly assume that the hearer has the same referents in their mind. I once received a mobile-phone text message with nothing but 'It's not having one'. The message (with its intertextual non-anaphoric pronoun, general verb and non-anaphoric substitute) was incomprehensible to me, until I recalled that I had texted the sender, several days before, asking when her bar was having its opening night. I was recently at a seminar in which a friend approached my row of seats with the words: 'You guys haven't paid yet.' I replied that I and the colleagues beside me had indeed paid the fee for the seminar, and then learned that her general noun 'guys' referred to my colleagues at work, and the implied object of the verb was 'the annual membership fee for the association'.

Sometimes VL is used with the aim of 'not including', in the sense that the speaker thinks that the details are not important or that the hearer does not need to know them. I once asked a hotel waitress at a buffet table what was in the fruit pie, and she explained, 'It's got fruit on the top and <u>creamy stuff</u> in the centre'. Her choice of the general noun 'stuff' suggested that she was not sure of the contents and did not consider it important, and her informality sounded friendly. On another occasion, I was told by a catering staff member in my work canteen that there would be a delay with the food: 'The plates aren't ready. We're waiting for the chips <u>and stuff</u>'. It was unclear to me what 'and stuff' included, but she obviously felt that I did not need to know. Finally, I should mention a man who, in answer to his girlfriend's question 'What have you been up to today?' on the telephone, invariably replies 'Oh – organizing bits and pieces.' He claims that this is sometimes because it is too complicated to explain and she does not need to know the details, sometimes because he has done nothing interesting and knows that it would bore her, and sometimes because he has not been doing anything at all and would rather that she did not know. There appears to be a fine line between excluding and not including.

VL used 'to exclude' occurs when the speaker would rather that the hearer did not know the precise reference. Wodak's (1996, pp. 101–29) finding that imprecise references and pronominalizations and inexplicit intertextuality can exclude some addressees needs following up. Studies could be carried out to find how VL is used to exclude on an informal personal level, and on a formal public or political level.

Examples of VL 'to exclude' on a personal level are abundant in everyday life. As a university external examiner, I was once sitting outside a room waiting for my slot in a Board of Examiners meeting, when someone hurried out of the room and past me, with the words 'We've run into <u>a slight snag</u>!' The general noun 'snag' and mitigator 'slight' suggested that she would rather not tell me. On another occasion, I brought together two old friends, and as they caught up on the thirty years since their last meeting, one talked of a mutual acquaintance: 'She was an editor in <u>whatsit</u> road.' I became aware that compound nouns and vague adjectives could exclude and merited study. In formal public domains, VL can be used to obfuscate. Politicians in TV and radio interviews and party broadcasts often use it to evade difficult questions. In Peter Sellers's comic sketch, 'Party Political Speech' (1958), the politician uses it to avoid mentioning specific policy plans. I quote a small excerpt:

> My friends, in the light of present day developments, let me say right away that I do not regard existing conditions likely. On the contrary, I have always regarded them as subjects of the gravest responsibility, and shall ever continue to do so. / . . . / For I have no doubt whatsoever that whatever I may have said in the past or what I am saying now is the exact, literal and absolute truth as to the state of the case.

The humour of the passage lies in the exaggerated accumulation of VL. There is a plethora of general nouns ('present day <u>developments</u>', 'existing <u>conditions</u>', '<u>subjects</u> of the gravest responsibility') and vague clauses ('whatever I may have said in the past' and 'absolute truth as to the state of the case'). The VL is used to befuddle the audience, and hoodwink them into voting for the party.

Political discourse in real-life broadcasts could be analysed along the same lines. I illustrate this with an example from a BBC1 news bulletin, 2 April 2001. 2001 saw the worst outbreak of foot and mouth disease in the UK for a hundred years. The prime minister, Tony Blair, announced that he would delay the local elections until June, to concentrate on wiping out the disease.

Interviewer: Everybody watching and listening will take it from what you said that there is going to be a general election on June 7th. Is it not possible simply to confirm that?

Mr Blair: I think it's very important (0.5 second's pause) that (0.5 second's pause) we ensure that the proper process of government goes on. I mean the very reason I've announced this d – delay to the local elections is precisely so that we can carry on with the business of government, putting in place the mechanisms to eradicate the disease. Now, you know, I've no doubt there'll be lots of speculation. I'm not (0.5) er – standing here and saying to you there won't be, but it's important that the formal process is gone through in the proper way.

The vague nouns 'process', 'business' and 'way' hide whether he is talking about everyday government or plans for a general election. The ellipsis in 'saying to you there won't be' is ambiguous because it could mean 'there won't be speculation' or 'there won't be a general election'.

Further research suggested in this volume

Koester, Trappes-Lomax and Cheng recommend moving on from the research described in this volume, and extending it to different genres and text types. Koester, who examined VL in office conversations, believes that an examination of a variety of workplace genres could yield valuable insights into the genres that have a high density of VL and those that do not. She wonders whether situations where the need for speed and accuracy discourage any discursive vagueness, have VL. Trappes-Lomax, who explored VL in conference talks, believes that research into the effects of different subgenres and styles of academic speaking on use of VL would be worth while, as would a study of all tension management variables, including VL, in perceived levels of tension and consequent tactics. Cheng, who also analysed a variety of social contexts, recommends studies into VL and the distance, status and power relations of the participants. She suggests that there should be an examination of VL in a wide range of text types, with varying degrees of formality in the discourse and communication purposes.

Adolphs and Warren express a desire to broaden their studies to include other social variables and features of VL. Adolphs, who studied VL in healthcare contexts, says that further research into the effect of the physical distance between health workers and patients is needed, in order to discover whether the health worker's lack of the situational context, when speaking to patients on the phone, is the cause of the VL use. Warren, who wrote about VL and discourse intonation, recommends studies to explore the complete range of VL features available to speakers, in order to understand better the relationship between VL and discourse intonation.

Rowland, Evison, McCarthy and O'Keeffe, and Terraschke and Holmes have an interest in extending their research into the domain of other countries, examining the VL used by speakers of other languages. Rowland, who looked at VL in UK mathematics classrooms, recommends that research explore VL in mathematics classrooms in other countries, in order to know how learners give voice to their propositional attitude about mathematical conjectures, and how their linguistic and cultural constraints compare with those in his study. He suggests research into ways that VL is used in classrooms where other subjects are taught, and whether it is associated with uncertainty. Evison, McCarthy and O'Keeffe, who analysed a variety of social contexts, recommend comparisons between native-speaker vague category marker (VCM) usage and that of non-native speakers. They feel that learner corpora are likely to reveal interesting features concerning the acquisition and use of typical VCMs, and that research may reveal how learners decode the referents of VCMs. Terraschke and Holmes, who examined general extenders (GEs) used by Germans speaking English, suggest an analysis of the range and frequencies of GEs used by native as opposed to non-native speakers of English. They recommend an exploration of how GEs are structured and function in other languages, and a study of a variety of contexts, to find what in what context VL is appropriate. They suggest an exploration of social variables such as gender, age and social background.

Applications of vague language findings

We saw in the previous section that an area of particular interest is that of VL and speakers of other languages, and several contributors to the volume have recommended studies that would enhance language learning. This section looks at VL in TEFL coursebooks and teaching methodology, and examines the extent to which EFL learners can be trained to notice VL features. The section ends with a mention of applications to non-TEFL areas such as general medicine and clinical pragmatics, law and forensic linguistics.

TEFL applications

Since the mid-1990s, a limited number of applied linguistics and methodology books have begun to contain a discussion of possible teaching techniques to raise students' awareness of VL. Channell (1994) suggests that they could be asked to locate vague words in a text, explain their meaning and note the changes to the text when they substituted the vague words for more precise words. Jordan (1997) recommends exercises highlighting the correspondence between vagueness and hedging, and caution or tentativeness in academic writing, such as asking students to rewrite hedged sentences in a non-tentative way. His ideas are useful for formal higher education domains, but not for training students to speak naturally in the informal settings and thus cohere socially and be accepted in the discourse community, should they so aspire.

Carter and McCarthy's (1997) *Exploring Spoken English* is one of the rare coursebooks that trains students of linguistics to analyse naturalistic conversational data, and notice general words as in 'thing' and 'business', extenders as in 'or something', and fillers such as 'kind of'.

Carter (2006) suggests a series of exercises; I adapt his suggestions here, so that they fit the specific focus of VL. He says that students could be provided with the VL to make it possible to describe difficult entities before they have learnt the specialist vocabulary. Thus, if asked to explain how to cook dishes from their own country, students might provide sentences like, 'You add a bit of this hot red stuff and use a wooden thing to do like this.' Another exercise is to ask students to remove words from a textbook dialogue (in the sense of adding ellipsis) to make the dialogue more 'real' sounding; they could then memorize the dialogue and practice similar ones. I take as an example *Headway Intermediate* (Soars and Soars 1986, p. 18), which has this dialogue:

Man I'm dying of thirst. Would you make me a cup of tea?
Boy OK. I'll put the kettle on.
Man And could you bring some biscuits?
Boy Yes, I'll open the new packet.

Students might rephrase the dialogue, using ellipsis, and say:

Man Dying of thirst. Make me a cup of tea?
Boy OK.
Man Biscuits?
Boy Yes. The new packet.

Another exercise is to present students with two dialogues – a real conversation and a 'tidied-up' version – and ask them to underline the differences. The real conversation might contain an utterance such as the following, taken from a Cutting (2000) MSc common room student dialogue:

DM What's that? Psycholinguistics?
AF Mhm. I have difficulty getting my brain going first thing in the morning.
DM She certainly fills – fills it up, doesn't she? She's got lots of things to tell you, I'm sure.

The tidied-up version might look like this:

DM What's that <u>book</u>? <u>Is it</u> psycholinguistics?

AF <u>Yes</u>. I have difficulty getting my brain going <u>at ten to nine</u> in the morning.

DM <u>Dr Brown, the psycholinguistics lecturer</u>, certainly fills <u>the lecture</u> up, doesn't she? She's got <u>50 theoretical concepts</u> to tell you, I'm sure.

Students could then be asked to add VL to their textbook dialogues. Learners might rewrite the <u>Headway Intermediate</u> dialogue above thus:

Man I'm <u>sort of</u> dying of thirst. Would you <u>do</u> me a cup of tea, <u>or something</u>?

Boy OK. I'll put <u>the thing</u> on.

Man And could you bring <u>something to eat</u>?

Boy Yes, I'll open the new <u>whatsit</u>.

Another exercise recommended by Carter is a variant on a well-known exercise: the learners translate natural spoken language dialogue into their first language and then back, and notice the differences. Some VL elements might transfer quite easily in and out of the languages, the general noun for instance.

The scope for VL training in EFL books is endless. Controlled exercises could be devised to train students to remove content from words and leave less contentful words in their place, thereby speaking more informally. They could then be given free practice in using VL, talking in groups, perhaps guided by strips of paper containing vague words and expressions that they should try to work into the conversation.

In the belief that, were students trained to recognize VL, they might appreciate when the cause of their lack of comprehension of native speakers of English conversations is their own linguistic or cultural gaps, and when it is the VL, I carried out a study with an EAP class in the University of Sunderland (Cutting 1999). I taught the students about VL features and helped them to notice them in a sample dialogue from the Edinburgh common-room data. The students then went and recorded native-speaker-of-English students talking informally. They were trained to transcribe the dialogues, and analysed them for VL features, successfully. A questionnaire revealed that they did not understand their dialogues but realized that the VL was partly to blame. They were reassured. A significant proportion agreed that VL was a marker of intimacy.

TEFL applications in this volume

Warren, and Terraschke and Holmes commend the use of transcribed exchanges from authentic interactions between native speakers, in class. Warren feels that the real data could provide VL models for learners. Terraschke and Holmes say that learners could be asked to suggest possible interpretations of what is going on, and recommend worksheets which guide learners to notice certain features of the spoken exchange. They suggest that learners could interact in role-play situations devised to provide opportunities for VL use.

Koester, Evison, McCarthy and O'Keeffe, and Cheng believe that the main application is to use findings to sensitize learners to the importance of context, culture, and social variables and conventions. Koester says that in the teaching of business English, teachers and students should recognize that overly explicit language can be inappropriate or even rude. She says that learners should be made aware that VL can convey information about the speaker's attitude towards the interlocutor or the business at hand, and can be used strategically for politeness or solidarity. Evison, McCarthy and O'Keeffe are convinced that the lexical realizations of vague categories must always be explored and decoded in context, and that language teaching can benefit from corpora collected across a range of contexts and users. They believe that teachers at higher levels may see contexts as windows on culture and as a potential bridging across cultures. Cheng suggests that students should be taught about VL's role in sustaining relationships through asserting shared understandings, maintaining face, and communicating informality and formality. She also proposes that learners be asked to use VL to describe or respond to unfamiliar scenarios; a classroom activity could require students to describe objects they do not know the name of, while concealing the object from the group.

Sensitivity in TEFL application

It should be kept in mind that not all international students may want to sound Australian, British or Canadian. They may feel that they wish to preserve more of their own cultural identity. Carter (2006) warns that the issue about teaching spoken grammar is one bound up very much with identity, ideology and community membership, and it is a matter of how far they want to affiliate themselves with the target language. It is possible that they have different ways of expressing in-groupness in their own cultures that they will prefer to reflect. Beebe (1988, p. 63) points out that second-language learners 'may find that the reward of being fluent in the target language is not worth the cost in lost identification and solidarity with their own native language group.'

The question is whether international students want to produce VL themselves, to sound more like native speakers of English and claim ingroup membership. It could be that the solution is for books to sensitize students and help them to understand the features, without actually training them to use or produce VL themselves. The solution may be for teachers to raise awareness, in order to provide choices; that way, students can either opt in or opt out. Learners could be encouraged to keep a diary of how they feel about what they learn VL and what they want to learn, so that the teacher can monitor their affiliation with the language and their desire to use VL. It could be said, however, that if one is to follow the learning-by-doing philosophy, one could argue that only by trying to produce VL themselves can students fully internalize the forms and social functions.

Non-TEFL applications

The VL findings in this volume could be applied to education in general, workplace and public language, medicine and law. Rowland states that he would like to raise mathematics teachers' awareness of the function of VL, believing that they can be sensitized to the use of hedges by children as an indicator of propositional attitude, principally of uncertainty.

Trappes-Lomax and Cook see applications to workplace and public language. Trappes-Lomax believes that his study could help in interaction management. Cook suggests that readers of public-relations discourse can ask questions of its companies that will oblige them to abandon the VL that covers up the reality of what have they done to prevent ill-health among consumers of their products, and to address the injustices of wealth and food distribution.

Clinical pragmatics, which deals with clients with communicative disabilities because of semantic-pragmatic disorders, in part by developing their pragmatic knowledge, could benefit from being informed of the findings about VL. Hassibi and Breuer (1980) found psychotics who were unaware that hearers must share knowledge of the meaning of the words that they use, and who employed pronouns without providing the reference. Wodak (1996, pp. 145–6) found that psychotic patients spoke with 'private meanings and private language'. It is my feeling that the findings about VL could be used to demonstrate to patients with semantic-pragmatic disorders how speakers refer to entities in a vague way and yet identify them sufficiently to guarantee communication. Clients could be made to see the social function of VL, and how using it can make them more accepted as one of the group or at least one of a pair.

Adolphs, in this volume, claims that there is a need to train non-native speakers of English health professionals in the use of VL, as it is motivated by the goal of interactional convergence. She recommends the use of language samples from routine healthcare encounters, with the contextual, institutional tensions and complexities inherent in professional – patient communication. She suggests that learners be trained to look at how participants respond to each other's meaning.

The findings about VL are also relevant to forensic linguistics, the science in which linguists analyse police transcripts and tape-recordings of suspects' conversations, to determine whether they are fabricated, what the intentions of the interlocutors seems to be, and suchlike. Coulthard (1992) finds that the fabricator of interview records can make the mistake of making nominal groups and clauses 'over-explicit'. One speaker apparently gives information that he is known to know, or uses more pre-head or post-head modifiers than is necessary or relevant, as in 'Walker was carrying two white plastic carrier bags. Walker gave me one of the white plastic carrier bags.' Shuy (1993, p. 16) finds that 'vague reference' in recordings of suspects' conversations can be so vague that the interlocutors fail to understand each other; 'incomplete sentences or ambiguously uttered ones' in which third-person personal pronouns are 'the major culprit'. VL features described in this volume could be looked for in interview records: if the language was more vague than required, this could indicate that suspects might have the intention to make the communication impenetrable to any overhearer, and to have something to hide.

Cotterill, in this volume, says that hostile interactional strategies in court may lead to the mistreatment of some types of witness, in particular those with limited English who do not qualify for the services of an interpreter. She feels that lawyers, judges and jurors should be sensitive to the potential uses and abuses by all sides of VL in court. She hopes that her study will help courts to detect when there is vagueness because of witness failings in integrity and when it is because of language limitations. She feels that a discussion of these language issues could be included in a law degree.

Conclusion

This final chapter in *Vague Language Explored* has presented a model quite different from others in the book. The model contains a great number of features: metonymical proper nouns, superordinate nouns, and general nouns and verbs, non-anaphoric demonstrative and personal pronouns and adverbs, vague clauses, clausal ellipsis and humorous conversational implicature. It has suggested that this form of VL seems to be more a feature of social cohesion than a tool to assert power.

This chapter has pointed to areas that could be investigated: VL in other social groups and other languages, and the relationship between VL and various social factors. It has focused too on the applications of findings. It looked at the implications of the model for clinical pragmatics, forensic linguistics, pedagogical grammars, teaching methodology and TEFL coursebooks.

All that remains now is to take VL on in the research directions suggested above, and to apply the findings to TEFL, public relations, medicine and law. Sort of, 'end of – ', or something.

References

L.M. Beebe, 'Five Sociolinguistic Approaches to Second Language Acquisition', in L.M. Beebe (ed.), *Issues on Second Language Acquisition. Multiple Perspectives* (Rowley, MA: Newbury House, 1988).

P. Brown and S. Levinson, *Politeness: Some Universals in Language Use* (Cambridge University Press, 1978).

R. Carter, 'Spoken Grammars, Written Grammars', unpublished talk given to National Association for Teaching English and Community Languages to Adults (NATECLA), Stevenson College Edinburgh, 22 April (2006),

R. Carter and M. McCarthy, *Exploring Spoken English* (Cambridge University Press, 1997).

J. Channell, *Vague Language* (Oxford: Oxford University Press, 1994).

H. Clark and G. Murphy, 'Audience Design in Meaning and Reference', in J. LeNy and W. Kintsch (eds), *Language and Comprehension.* (Amsterdam: North Holland Publishing Company, 1982).

M. Coulthard, M., 'Forensic Discourse Analysis', in M. Coulthard (ed.), *Advances in Spoken Discourse Analysis* (London: Routledge, 1992).

D. Crystal, *Language and the Internet* (Cambridge University Press, 2001).

D. Crystal and D. Davy, *Advanced Conversational English* (London: Longman, 1975).

J. Cutting, 'Opening Lines from the Floor', *Language at Work,* 13 (Clevedon: Multilingual Matters, 1998).

J. Cutting, *Papers from Seminar of the British Association of Applied Linguistics 'The Grammar of Spoken English and EAP Teaching'*, (University of Sunderland Press, 1999).

J. Cutting, *Analysing the Language of Discourse Communities* (Oxford: Elsevier Science, 2000).

B.L. Davies, 'Communities of Practice: Legitimacy, Membership and Choice', *Leeds Working Papers in Linguistics,* 10 (2005).

P. Eckert and S. McConnell-Ginet, 'Communities of Practice: Where Language, Gender and Power All Live?', in J. Coates (ed.), *Language and Gender: A Reader* (Oxford: Blackwell, 1998).

N. Fairclough, *Language and Power* (Harlow: Longman, 1989).

H.P. Grice, 'Logic and Conversation', in P. Cole and J. Morgan (eds), *Syntax and Semantics: 9* Speech Acts, (New York: Academic Press, 1975).

M.A.K. Halliday and R. Hasan, *Cohesion in English* (London: Longman, 1976).

K. Harvey and C. Shalom (eds), *Language and Desire* (London: Routledge, 1997).

M. Hassibi and H. Breuer, *Disordered Thinking and Communication in Child.* (New York: Plenum Press, 1980).

R.R. Jordan, *English for Academic Purposes: A Guide and Resource Book for Teachers.* (New York: Cambridge University Press, 1997).

A.A. Milne, *Winnie The Pooh. The Complete Collection of Stories* (London: Methuen Children's Books, 1994).

P. Sellers, 'Party Political Speech', in *Best of Sellers,* GBR LP Parlophone PMD 1069 (1958).

C. Shalom, 'That Great Supermarket of Desire: Attributes of the Desired Other in Personal Advertisements', in K. Harvey and C. Shalom (eds), *Language And Desire* (London: Routledge, 1997).

R.W. Shuy, *Language Crimes* (Oxford: Blackwell, 1993).

J. Soars and E. Soars, *Headway Intermediate* (Oxford: Oxford University Press, 1986).

J. Swales, *Genre Analysis: English in Academic and Research Settings* (Cambridge University Press, 1990).

S. Ullman, *Semantics* (Oxford: Blackwell, 1962).

R. Wodak, *Disorders of Discourse* (London: Longman, 1996).

Index